Practical Ethics in Counselling and Psychotherapy

Linda Finlay

Practical Ethics *in* Counselling *and* Psychotherapy

⑤SAGE

Los Angeles | London | New Delhi
Singapore | Washington DC | Melbourne

SAGE

Los Angeles | London | New Delhi
Singapore | Washington DC | Melbourne

SAGE Publications Ltd
1 Oliver's Yard
55 City Road
London EC1Y 1SP

SAGE Publications Inc.
2455 Teller Road
Thousand Oaks, California 91320

SAGE Publications India Pvt Ltd
B 1/I 1 Mohan Cooperative Industrial Area
Mathura Road
New Delhi 110 044

SAGE Publications Asia-Pacific Pte Ltd
3 Church Street
#10-04 Samsung Hub
Singapore 049483

Editor: Susannah Trefgarne
Editorial assistant: Talulah Hall
Production editor: Rachel Burrows
Copyeditor: Sarah Bury
Proofreader: Bryan Campbell
Marketing manager: Samantha Glorioso
Cover design: Wendy Scott
Typeset by: C&M Digitals (P) Ltd, Chennai, India

Library of Congress Control Number: 2018954011

British Library Cataloguing in Publication data

A catalogue record for this book is available from the British Library

ISBN 978-1-5264-5928-2
ISBN 978-1-5264-5929-9 (pbk)

Contents

About the Author

Dr Linda Finlay is an existentially-orientated integrative psychotherapist and supervisor (UKCP registered) currently in private practice in the UK, although she has worked in various institutions in the mental health field since 1978. In her role as an academic consultant, she teaches and mentors psychotherapy students and supervises doctoral research work in training institutes across Europe. She also teaches psychology, counselling and research methodology at the Open University, UK, and she coordinates the Research Ethics Panel for the 'Investigating Psychology' course. She has published widely – see www.lindafinlay.co.uk. Her most recent books are *Relational Integrative Psychotherapy* and *Phenomenology for Therapists*, both published by Wiley. Her particular research interests include exploring relational dynamics and applying relational-reflexive approaches to investigate the lived experience of disability and trauma. She is currently Editor of the *European Journal for Qualitative Research in Psychotherapy*.

Preface

When SAGE first approached me about writing a book about ethics, my response was hardly positive. 'What do I know?' I asked myself, shame kicking in. 'I don't have any expertise to offer!' Another voice inside my head joined in: 'Ethics – ouch, that sounds dry and boring!' Once I began thinking the idea over more calmly, however, I realised I might in fact have something to say. I've always been interested in the everyday ethical questions and dilemmas that confront us as practitioners in the immediacy of every relationship and moment of practice. My passion for the project of writing about *Practical Ethics* started to grow. I began to see the topic as thought-provoking, compelling and dynamic, and as encompassing all areas of life, not just therapy.

I've been involved in the mental health field since the 1970s. Over the years, I've engaged in hundreds of dialogues about ethical and relational dilemmas with friends, colleagues and in supervision. I've also sat on formal ethics committees (particularly those related to research), which continue to raise challenging conundrums. While top-down guidelines offered by books on ethics and professional codes can be helpful at times, all too often the sheer messiness, ambiguity, uncertainty and complexity of practice defies easy, clear-cut answers. As practitioners we're left with trying to exercise our professional judgement as best we can in the given relational-social context.

Ethical dilemmas tend to arise when there is a clash of rules, values and/or needs. Our task as therapists is to unravel the strands. The central argument of this book is that *relational concerns* should drive professional action and that there is room for individual judgement, intuition and creativity. This is the message I wanted to bring to the fore. I may not be an ethics 'expert', but it seems I can engage with the topic as a knowledgeable and reflexive relational practitioner.

This is not a traditional ethics book concerned with professional rules, codes and standards. It does not concern itself much with ethical violations, disciplinary action and liability claims, nor does it offer a theoretical examination of ethics in terms of principles or philosophy. My aim is to explore how our values (personal/cultural) and our professional guidelines play out in the immediacy of our emotionally intense, moment-to-moment therapy encounters.

A key aim of this book is to encourage discussion and debate within our profession. Throughout I offer my own perspective, particularly on the many examples drawn from everyday practice dilemmas. But at every stage the door is left open for you, the reader, to take your own position: one that arises from your values and practice. While at times you may find your ideas or assumptions being challenged, perhaps in uncomfortable or disconcerting ways, I hope you will also find some of the examples and stories affirming, and even inspiring.

I invite you to dwell with the many different examples and dilemmas and to recognise the lively debates in progress. I hope you will be stimulated by the questions raised and challenged as you encounter other practitioners, some of whom may take positions different from your own or have different perspectives on what is 'right' or 'wrong'. The main thing, as I see it, is to think and talk about the ethical issues that arise in our world, and to consider how ideas and practices change over time and vary according to context. There are rarely easy answers, particularly if we let the relational-social context drive our approach and decision-making.

The chapters in **Part I** explore the context of practical ethics, taking a relational approach – what I call 'relational ethics'. I begin by laying out what constitutes relational ethics (Chapter 1) and thinking about how we might use professional codes and legal frameworks relationally (Chapter 2). Chapters 3 and 4 consider the ways we 'care' as professionals and how we might enact our ethics more broadly outside the therapy room. **Part II** explores relational ethics in terms of how we engage therapeutic relationships ethically through boundarying, holding and containing processes. Specific guidance is also given on the processes of starting and ending therapy, practices which are laden with extra ethical considerations. **Part III** includes five case illustrations (stories) designed to show relational ethics in the action of everyday practice.

Throughout the book I use case illustrations to consider ethics across diverse settings, theoretical approaches, cultures and countries. The aim is to show the sheer range and depth of the counselling and psychotherapy field. Most examples have been taken from published sources or are constructed fictionalised accounts. Some are based loosely on my experience, but with these I've changed some details to ensure anonymity. A few excerpts have come directly from clients who have generously given their specific consent to reproduce their words.

My use of terms needs special comment, as language itself carries relational-ethical implications around respect and care.

- I use the words 'therapist' or 'therapy' to encompass the range of practice across the spectrum of counselling, coaching and psychotherapy, and to bypass debate about the meanings and convergences of these terms. Sometimes I will use a specific term where it relates to particular situations under discussion.
- Mindful of the diverse theoretical frameworks we can draw on, I've tried to keep theoretical language and concepts to the minimum. As far as possible, I've briefly explained specialist jargon the first time it is used.

- I deliberately use the 'singular they' instead of clumsy versions of 'she' or 'he'. This is my attempt to be gender-neutral. Mostly with the case studies, I've put client and therapist as different genders. While sometimes this is done to highlight gender issues, for the most part it is designed to enhance clarity and readability.
- I use the term 'we' throughout to encompass therapy practitioners. Writing the book often felt as if I were talking to other therapists, so the 'we' seemed natural. That said, I appreciate that sometimes you may not want to be included in the position I'm claiming for 'us'. If my use of 'we' grates, I apologise in advance: it is not my intention to speak for you.
- I use the term 'client' rather than 'patient' or 'analysand' as that's the common parlance in my field. However, 'the client' can sound rather objectifying. To counteract this, most of the clients in my examples have been given names. The aim is to help us see each of them better as a 'person'. I'm afraid I don't show as much respect to 'the therapist', who mostly remains an anonymous object!

The process of writing this book has proved a real journey. I've learned a lot along the way. I now feel clearer about, and more comfortable with, the topic of ethics and its impact on my practice. My growing edge has been to find my integrity and establish clearer, cleaner boundaries when faced with the morass of relational messes that occur routinely in practice.

At every stage, writing this book has been a challenge. How to capture the charged complexity, tensions, pains and delights of the therapy process? At times I've been dogged by discomfort and uncertainty, particularly when I've become aware that my practice has been less than 'perfect' and not as knowledgeable, ethical or relational as it could (should?) be. I take comfort from knowing that I've cared, tried to follow professional guidelines, and I've thought deeply about my practice. We all make mistakes and there is value in simply striving to be a 'good enough' therapist.

As someone who prizes dialogue, I contest the notion that any single view is 'correct' – and that includes my own. I want to be open to different arguments and to respect those clinical choices which come out of a person's own training, values and contexts. This is not simply about being 'non-judgemental'. It's also about *actively respecting* others' positions and developing awareness of diverse cultural perspectives. I prefer to be *reflexive* rather than knowingly certain. I would rather not assert or impose professional expert directives. This is the relational-ethical stance I hope to convey throughout this book.

Linda Finlay, 2018

Acknowledgements

Many people have helped with the evolution of this book. I could not possibly have written it without regularly consulting others for their affirmations and different perspectives. I am especially grateful to Vivian Finlay, Steven Wells and the anonymous reviewers, who critically read drafts and offered invaluable advice, and also to Susan Ram for her expert transformational editing. In addition to drawing on many nourishing conversations with supervisors, colleagues, friends and clients, Ann Marie Clarke, Anne Gilbert, Rich Hycner, Sarah Greening, Jo McMahon, Lydia Noor, Barbara Payman, Anne Pettit, Amanda Phillips-Wieloch and Rob Tyson have all offered their wise counsel. I also couldn't have written this book without the continuing challenge and support offered throughout the process from Mel Wilder – my emotional rock and ethical touchstone.

Finally, in terms of the publication process, I need to acknowledge the publishers Wiley and Sage. Chunks of the material in Chapters 5–9 have been drawn from Finlay, L (2016a) *Relational Integrative Psychotherapy: Processes and Theory in Practice* and have been reproduced with the kind permission of Wiley-Blackwell Publishers. For this current book, special thanks need to be extended to Susannah Trefgarne (commissioning editor) for inspiring me to engage with this project, to Talulah Hall (assistant editor), who helped me navigate the permissions process and successive drafts, and also to Sarah Bury (copyeditor), Vanessa Harwood (production editor), along with the rest of the publishing team for seeing the manuscript through to publication. Of course, any misunderstandings and mistakes within this book are mine alone.

PART I

THE CONTEXT OF 'RELATIONAL ETHICS'

Preamble

> Relational ethics requires [therapists] … to act from our hearts and minds, acknowledge our interpersonal bonds to others, and take responsibility for actions and their consequences. (Ellis, 2007, p. 3)

Ethics are not just remote, detached, philosophical principles enshrined in professional codes. Ethics are all about us, intricately worked into the personal and professional values which shape our work and give it meaning. They permeate *every* moment of our counselling and psychotherapy practice.

'Relational ethics' sees ethics in terms of relationship rather than directives. What's in the client's interests and risks of harm depend on the meanings in the situation. A therapist who asks lots of questions could be seen as invasive or genuinely interested. If a therapist encourages a client to do more self-care, it might be viewed as caring or critically blaming. The holding of a time boundary may feel safe or harsh. A therapeutic challenge issued to a client could be in their interests *and* feel uncomfortable simultaneously; one client might feel stimulated by it, another threatened. There are few hard and fast rules. It all depends.

Rather than simply respecting clients and prioritising their interests, relational ethics demands that we recognise the interconnection between therapist, client and our wider communities (Faris and van Ooijen, 2012). Professional guidelines have practical implications; they require us to be mindful about these wider relationships, critically appraising the impact of an imbalance of power and the use of unthinking or instrumental ways of relating.

The four chapters in Part I introduce the foundational ideas of relational ethics. They consider how our professional codes are applied practically within therapy and in our wider social world. You're invited to marry externally-derived professional standards and internally-derived personal values in thoughtful, reflexive ways which attend to the specific relationship involved.

1

A Relational Approach to Ethics

A relational approach to ethics intertwines relational sensitivity with containing ethical frameworks. Our focus here is on ethics that embrace a relational attitude and acknowledge how moral and ethical horizons are ever-present in our therapeutic relationships (Gabriel and Casemore, 2009). Ethical guidelines, although useful, can never prepare us sufficiently for situations arising in practice which make our heads spin and hearts ache (Ellis, 2007; Finlay, 2012). Ethical judgements need to be made in context and it's complicated. We can aspire to certain standards of practice but may not always meet these. The question is how to be a *good enough*, ethically responsive therapist.

This chapter adopts a relational approach to ethics in practice – 'relational ethics' for short. To illustrate this, eight **situations from practice** are sketched and the relational-ethical challenges involved in each are highlighted. The next section highlights the **values** which underpin relational ethics. The concluding reflections section begins a pattern of concluding each chapter with personal thoughts and an implicit invitation for us to dialogue – you and me.

Relational ethics in practice

Virtually every ethical issue and dilemma we encounter can be answered with the phrase 'it depends'. Professional standards, personal values, legal requirements, agency policy, cultural **context** *and* relational considerations all complicate the field. At times our relational concerns may clash uncomfortably with wider professional, legal or institutional requirements. We face the unending professional challenge of marrying our personal values and wider professional and social contexts in ethically thoughtful and reflexive (critically self-aware) ways rather than rigidly following rules or defensive practices. In addition, relational ethics drive us towards collaborative, responsive, respectful, compassionate and authentic relationships as opposed to exploitative, instrumental or habitual ones. Beyond the bounds of written codes, there is an important place for professional experience and intuition. And, there is room to get it 'wrong' sometimes. When our behaviour falls short of the values we aspire to, we can still be a 'good enough' therapist.

The following eight vignettes illustrate typical ethical dilemmas, all of them potentially problematic. I invite you to dwell with your own responses to each before moving on to the ensuing discussion. Have you ever been in similar situations? Are there some situations where you have a clear and instant response and others where, while less sure of your ground, you have an intuitive sense of what feels right for you? Notice your reactions and what that tells you.

As you think about the eight specific situations presented here, you may well find professional standards, legal requirements and your own personal moral code conflict, pulling you down contradictory paths. All this before considering the extra complications of specific interpersonal and cultural contexts and your own professional intuitions! (These strands are set in bold below to show the way the issues are intertwined.)

Following each vignette, I indicate the issues at stake, then express my personal response (in italics) and invite you to dialogue with me. If you disagree with my ethical position, why is that? Do our personal values differ? Do we come from different theoretical perspectives? Or is it to do with the fact that we practise in different contexts and/or cultures?

1.   A client texts a long message to you between sessions. He has experienced a melt-down following a traumatic meeting at work and requests a brief phone conversation as he's 'desperate'. Do you oblige?

Discussion

The primary ethical dilemma here concerns the need to hold a **professional** boundary and safe frame on the one hand, while the client's desperate and acute need for support demands compassion and empathy. Overlaying this is our own desire (need?) to help. Professional and **personal** values may collide here, and institutional and **legal**/contractual structures also need thought. For example, some therapists may agree a 'no text rule' in advance or even prohibit between-session contact.

I know therapists who routinely offer text support between sessions to offer 'holding'. However, personally, I would avoid offering therapy support out-of-session. Here, the well-meaning but unwary therapist could fall into the trap of communicating out of hours. (I've been there myself and learned the hard way when the therapy went pear-shaped.)

From a private practice perspective (it could be different in other settings), I would argue that providing extra contact between sessions is likely to prove counterproductive, for in these uncontracted times the normal safe relational frame is not available, and contact may be unduly rushed. Outside the formal therapy frame, too, we are likely to be tired, distracted, poorly grounded and unfocused. In addition, it could be that our client is replaying (in or out of awareness) a history of creating situations where they are not properly seen, thereby ensuring their needs cannot be met (Finlay, 2016a). For these reasons, I would simply acknowledge the text and offer (if I could) an extra formal session to talk through the trauma. Had I felt pulled to 'rescue', I would want to explore that in supervision.

2. A client is filling out an application form for a job and admits she is tempted to lie about her history of mental health problems. Do you condone this?

Discussion

This situation taps directly into our **personal** morality regarding the importance of truth-telling and honesty. But there are also professional, legal and relational considerations.

Many **professional** codes explicitly state the need to deal with others truthfully, with integrity and in straightforward manner. The professional standard implicated concerns our professional integrity and the need to work ethically and consider the law. In practice, of course, this can get muddied.

It would be worth exploring the nature of this client's history some more. Did she become ill and hospitalised, and receive a diagnosis? There may be some associated trauma and stigma here which could be useful to explore (see Chapter 5 which discusses the issue of diagnosis some more). Otherwise, if her 'history' is simply having therapy, maybe this can be normalised. She may need reassurance that she is not 'mad' or 'ill' and that many people have therapy to handle life stresses or issues.

Legally speaking, both employment law and professional duty of care (ours and the employer's) are relevant. All employment is based on some sort of contract, and material non-disclosure is relevant. If the undisclosed fact could have had a bearing on the decision to employ, then this could be breach of contract. From the employer's perspective, they have a duty to act with care. If they are aware that an employee has a history of mental health issues, they need to treat that employee appropriately and not, for example, put them under inappropriate levels of stress. In this sense, it may be helpful for everyone if the employer is aware of the client's history.

The relationship of trust between client and therapist is also at stake. **Relationally** speaking, when do we impose our own standards on clients rather than encourage autonomous choice? Also, if we're too critical, the client may be reluctant to tell us things out of fear of negative evaluation.

(Continued)

(Continued)

My personal starting point would be to acknowledge the harsh reality of public ignorance regarding mental health problems and the social stigma surrounding it. I would feel sympathy for this client, who might suffer at work if they disclosed their full history. I might also raise the possibility of the potential employer being sympathetically unconcerned about her previous history or ready to benefit from some psychoeducation (my political agenda). I would note (for later consideration) that relational work related to self-acceptance of her history might be useful for this client.

While I might be tempted to condone lying on an official (legal) form, I know this would be wrong, and would say so. Nor in my professional role could I encourage deceit. However, I would want to try to express myself in sympathetic and protective terms rather than critical or judgemental ones. Discussion with my client about disclosure could be helpful to her and prove a useful lesson for the future in terms of when it's OK to disclose or keep things private.

3. Your client often makes racist and anti-immigrant comments with which you strongly disagree. Do you share your own views?

Discussion

This situation highlights the role of **personal values** (and beliefs/attitudes) together with wider issues concerning **social responsibilities**. Some therapists consider it as good modelling to own and express a social or political position, while others are reluctant to introduce personal views. The **professional** standard at stake concerns the obligation not to condone, collude with or facilitate any prejudice, discrimination or oppressive behaviour.

How and when we might challenge prejudicial behaviour is the tricky bit. Some therapists might accept (in their mind) that this is the client's way of talking and not jump on it; others wouldn't let it pass. Some might tacitly agree with some prejudicial stereotyping.

Whether or not we disclose our own views is a personal and professional boundary issue about which opinions and practice diverge considerably. Some of us routinely express our views; others do not. **Relationally**, compassion and respect are relevant touchstones, but we must also consider the possible impact of our views on the client. Might they feel criticised or disparaged by us if we express opposing positions? Might this damage our therapeutic relationship? If we withhold our views but they emerge later, perhaps through a third party, might that undermine therapeutic progress?

It is also worth considering what we embody in terms of our ethnicity and the impact that has on others unconsciously and transferentially. Might there be some unspoken dynamics here? For example, a client who is black/Asian may well feel some subtle, unspoken, prejudice coming from a white therapist. And it would be important to note possible projections around this, i.e. where one unconsciously attributes characteristics that feel unacceptable in oneself on to others.

I hope that I would not ignore racist slurs and would challenge them immediately, at least discussing my discomfort with 'stereotyping'. And I know that I've let racist comments slide in the past. Ideally, I would want to encourage exploration of what my client means and believes, and perhaps why. This requires a tricky balancing act, because by being critical of a client's views we may drive them underground and contaminate therapeutic progress. This is where intuition and artful practice come in.

I know therapists who are open (even outspoken) about their political views and who openly own their cultural background and ethnicity. I am more reticent. Is my political position relevant? Might it offer some useful modelling? Sometimes I might own my own stance as part of being authentic and transparent – provided I thought this would deepen the therapeutic alliance and/or model respect for difference.

4. At the end of an emotional session, your client asks for a hug. Do you give it?

Discussion

This question goes to the heart of **personal** and **professional** boundaries. The answer depends on many things, including the specific relationship involved, the wider context and what the hug might mean to both parties. Would the hug be therapeutic for the client and in their long-term interests? If the hug was perceived as invasive or sexually suggestive (for either person) or confusingly ambiguous in intent, it would violate important **ethical** and **relational** boundaries. (See the theoretical debates around touch in Chapter 6.)

In my (humanistic) practice, yes, I probably would consider giving the hug (though I wouldn't normally hug clients unless the client invited it, or I had first checked their consent). While I've sometimes given a hug because it seems to be 'expected', my growing edge is to be less adaptive and not just go along with hugs particularly when they feel uncomfortable, automatic, dissociated or ambiguous. I would want to explore the client's possible needs and what the hug might represent. It's not my job to supply a client's apparent emotional needs through reflex action. In fact, deliberately withholding a requested hug (not easy to do) could prove more therapeutic if it encouraged the client to find self-soothing resources. While the hug may be good to give and receive, I don't believe it necessarily healing in itself. The relationship is the guide, and here I'd follow my intuition.

5. You have a client who is a counsellor himself. It emerges that you both want to go to the same special experiential professional-development 'masterclass' workshop. You had put your name down for this event a month ago but now your client reveals he would like to go too. How do you proceed?

Discussion

This is both a professional and a relational issue. At a **personal** and **professional** level, some therapists would argue that as both professionals involved have the right to attend, fairness dictates that the one who put their name first should go. However, ethical codes advise us to avoid dual/multiple relationships with clients and to make every effort to avoid relationships that risk confusing an existing relationship, with adverse implications for your client. Intimate, experiential workshop situations that take place in small groups are highly likely to disturb current and future boundaries too much for client and therapist to attend together, even as practising therapists (a formal lecture might be different but the presence of the therapist/client – or even supervisor/ supervisee – could still be distracting).

It is in the careful and protective management of these boundaries that **relational** aspects come in. If dual relationships prove unavoidable – for instance, if you both live in a small community and meetings outside therapy are expected – then you need to clarify and mutually manage boundaries and ensure the confidentiality of your therapeutic relationship (Gabriel, 2005). An Australian code of ethics, for instance, explains this professional-relational intertwining in strong terms, recommending that decisions be made in the best interests of the client:

> 1c. Practitioners 'avoid situations where the care of a client may conflict with their own interests, such as personal, financial or professional interests. They make decisions in the best interests of clients, not for personal motives'. (Psychotherapy and Counselling Federation of Australia, 2017, p. 8)

Our **professional** responsibility would lead us to explore the awkward possibilities of dual relationship raising awareness of likely encounters in professional and maybe social contexts. Ideally, this would have been aired thoroughly during the initial contracting phase, where a strategy would have been mutually agreed and regularly reviewed. Some therapists would favour having an open discussion with the client about going to the workshop.

If a therapist is reluctant to step down, is there a 'whiff' of feeling competitive with the client? Or if the therapist has a sense of 'it's not fair', where might that come from? Asserting one's own needs while giving the client an autonomous choice to go could be seen as being congruent and relational, and as offering good modelling. But it might also set up a later relational rupture if the client decides to go and it ends up being uncomfortable/confusing. These issues should all be explored in supervision/therapy.

I would try to prioritise the therapeutic relationship and what would be in the client's best interest. My application may have come first but if I knew my client wanted to attend, I would quietly step aside (informing my client of my 'sacrifice' would feel manipulative). If I've already disclosed my intentions to go and then found out the client has signed up, I'd feel somewhat invaded and I'd take it to supervision to explore what's going on in the process.

However, it all depends on the event involved. A public lecture might be possible for us both to attend; an intimate experiential masterclass is a different matter. I've had the situation a few times where I've attended a public lecture and met a client or ex-client. In those circumstances, I just tried to be unobtrusive and used our next therapy session to explore the mutual impact and any uncomfortable feelings arising.

6. A new client with profound and chronic shame issues discloses that she was sexually abused by her father between the ages of 8 and 11. She has few memories of her childhood, can't remember details, and her father has long since passed away. How do you handle this?

Discussion

Any disclosure of sexual abuse – particularly of a minor – raises huge **professional** (ethical and legal) challenges, to say nothing of the relational dimension of how harrowing it can be for the client to talk about it and for you to hear the details. That the father in this instance is no longer alive takes out the need for official 'safeguarding' action, although some consideration needs to be given to who else may have been involved and possible implications for current relationships. Our legally mandated 'duty of care' requires us to create a safe environment for vulnerable people, to ensure they're safeguarded and protected from harm. When an adult reports historical abuse and there is no indication of present abuse, it is best to facilitate the adult to consider taking the matter further rather than for the therapist to take action. Beyond this duty of care, the guiding professional ethic is to serve the client's best interest, where we are required to carry out our work with reasonable skill and professional competence. There is also a 'consent' issue regarding the focus and type of therapy engaged in. Given that wider **legal** ramifications may be involved, it may be important to check current, formal professional guidance on disclosures of child sexual abuse: for example, the British Psychological Society (2016) *Guidance Document on the Management of Disclosures of Non-recent (Historic) Child Sexual Abuse.*

At a **relational** level, it is vital to demonstrate how seriously we take the disclosure, which may itself be a new and significant healing experience for the client. Plus, we must reassure the client that total responsibility for child sexual abuse lies with the adult perpetrator.

In this situation, much would depend on my relationship with the client and whether we were engaged in short-term or long-term work.

For brief therapy I would not want to open up material we could not work through adequately and would recommend a deeper, more long-term exploration if this was something the client wanted to work on. My second concern would be to work slowly and carefully to ensure my client didn't get re-traumatised. Does she have the resources and support (both internal and external) to do necessary trauma work? If not, we might jointly agree to avoid old trauma work until the time felt right and she was ready.

I would see the initial priority as working gently together, focusing on issues of trust and shame. I would also try to respect and honour what might be her current coping strategy of not remembering. It would be wrong to try to force memories,

(Continued)

(Continued)

especially given the danger of suggesting or imagining events (akin to 'implanting' false memories). Additionally, I would want to ensure I was well equipped to do the necessary trauma work and that I myself was supported, probably through supervision. I see therapist self-care as an ethical imperative for such work (see Box 3.3).

7. A 14-year-old girl admits to smoking with a 17-year-old boy at school and generally 'fooling around'. She asks you to keep this a secret from her parents (who are paying for her sessions). Do you?

Discussion

It is necessary to find out more about the nature and extent of the 'fooling around' to assess the young person's safety and to weigh up the risks. The ethics at stake involve a **personal** and **professional** judgement call (and intuition?) about when/if something is dangerous or constitutes self-harm (where it becomes a 'safeguarding' issue). In extreme cases, as with evidence of drug dealing, legal sanctions may apply.

The extra ethical challenges posed by working with children and young people explains why such work is increasingly seen to require further training. 'The psychotherapist commits to recognise the boundaries and limitations of their expertise and techniques and to take the necessary steps to maintain their ability to practice competently' (United Kingdom Council for Psychotherapy (UKCP), 2009). Therapists who don't have the required training or experience need to ensure they have the appropriate specialist support (see, for example, the British Association for Counselling and Psychotherapy (BACP) guide: *Core Competences for Work with Children and Young People* (2018b)). Beyond professional competencies, the answer to any question around working with children and young people depends on the child, their age, your relationship, and relationships with their parents/guardians. It also depends on the institutional and cultural context, where particular rules and laws may apply. If working in organisations such as the National Health Service or schools/colleges, therapists have a responsibility to formally consult the designated safeguarding person in that setting.

Awareness of the **law** is essential. For instance, in many American states a teenager must be 16 in order to engage in sexual activity with someone who is 4 years, or more, older. Otherwise such activity is legally considered 'statutory rape' or 'sexual molestation' and, as such, must be reported to child protection services or the police. In other contexts, confidentiality is mandated by both professional ethical guidelines and the law (exact details vary throughout the world). A client's legal entitlement to confidentiality exists in the context of a therapist's duty of care and a specific therapy contract. However, public interest may take precedence over those agreements (Bond and Mitchels, 2015). Interestingly, in surveys of British and American psychologists and therapists regarding their experiences of ethical dilemmas, by far the most common concern (and uncertainty) relates to confidentiality (Welfel, 2013).

If she is being seen in family therapy but the confidential information came out in additional one-to-one work, I would share the information (or better, encourage the young person to do so), having previously established a 'no secrets policy' in the family therapy. However, if she were my client – even if the parents were paying – I would probably try to hold the confidence as our initial contract (signed by all parties) would have included a clear confidentiality clause. The situation would be trickier if the risk of harm was more acute: for example, if the young person was taking drugs or having sex. Although these limits to confidentiality would be stated in our initial contract, that doesn't make the decision about when to break confidentiality any easier. And, I'm aware of some discomfort as I write all this as I know I sometimes let some disclosures slide.

8.   You are newly diagnosed with a serious, but manageable, chronic illness. You are mindful that you tire easily and so you plan to pace yourself by seeing only three clients a day. You are concerned, however, that you may need to occasionally cancel sessions at short notice. Should you inform your clients about your condition?

Discussion

This is a complex issue that needs lots of thought, and discussion in supervision. This question came up on one of the 'This month's dilemmas' pages of the BACP magazine *Therapy Today* (April 2018) and generated a range of responses highlighting that there are no easy answers. The ethics at stake involve **personal** and **professional** judgements around assessing potential harm to both clients and your self. Three ethical issues are particularly implicated in the dilemma above: self-care, self-disclosure and contracting.

With regard to self-care, we have a responsibility to put into place appropriate self-care to help us maintain our mental and physical health. By pacing your contact with clients, you're engaging in good self-care. Supervision would also be essential to help you monitor your ability to be available and responsive to clients.

Whether, and the extent to which, you disclose your condition will need to be negotiated on a case-by-case basis. Many therapists would argue that it is inappropriate for clients to know the full details of a therapist's health issues, not least because clients could get pulled into doing some care-taking of you and cross a boundary. There is a balance to be struck where we might be able to own (and model?) our humanness and vulnerability without necessarily threatening the client's trust in our ability to maintain a safe holding environment.

In terms of the contracting, it may not be necessary to inform everyone about your health status, particularly if they are unlikely to be affected. However, clients who might be impacted by cancellations or your own limitations need some opportunity to discuss implications, so they have a choice about whether to continue with you. This might be something to explore when negotiating (or reviewing) the therapy

(Continued)

(Continued)

contract. The contract also needs to make explicit what might happen if you are unable to work for a period. For instance, it might be possible to arrange for a locum therapist to act in your place or to consider referring on to other services. The UKCP (2018a) offers some relevant directives for worst case scenarios:

> 37. Ensure that you do not work with clients if you are not able to do so for physical or mental health reasons, or when impaired by the effects of drugs, alcohol or medication. 38. Make considered and timely arrangements for the termination of a therapeutic relationship, or if you are unable to continue to practise, ensuring that clients are informed and alternative practitioners are identified where possible. 39. Have arrangements in place for informing clients and, where appropriate, providing them with support, in the event of your illness or death. (UKCP, 2018a, pp. 11–12)

Once others are involved, there is an additional **legal** obligation to attend to issues around confidentiality and data protection (see Box 2.1).

I find it hard to answer this hypothetical question as it would depend on my condition and on the specific relationship with each client. In terms of self-disclosure, thinking relationally, I would probably choose to give some information about my health status if it was going to impact on the therapy, but without details. Working as I do with longer-term clients, I would see this as 'grist for the mill' and, anyway, I suspect they would probably sense that something was amiss in the transference, so why not be open? Thinking about the contracting process and the impact of my personal values, I am uncomfortable with the power imbalance in private practice where therapists are able to cancel sessions without penalty while clients are charged. I might consider offering a free session if I did not give adequate notice of cancellation though I know many practitioners would make other choices.

Challenging values?

Underpinning relational ethics are our **values**. Values are a shorthand way of describing what's important to us, individually and/or collectively. For instance, we might embrace values like respect, compassion, honesty, dialogue and openness, and turn away from values to do with greed, cynicism, intolerance or excessive materialism (Somers and Stephenson, 2013). And value systems are complicated; they sometimes clash and can evolve.

Life socialises us into acquiring values (deemed acceptable in our culture) about the kind of person we 'should' be. They are learned from childhood and soaked up from our parents, teachers and society at large. For instance, a colleague once told me of her history of being the daughter of an Indian draper and how she had introjected a fierce message from her father that they would 'not have goods made from sweated labour in this shop'. She took this message in – it was as though she *had* to if she was going to truly belong to, and be accepted by, this family. To this day, this therapist tries to buy fair trade goods, acutely aware of who might have been exploited in its production.

As we mature, we often take our values for granted but we can also choose to acquire other values and challenge what we've been taught. For example, if a therapist has grown up in a large family where 'gossip' is the norm, the confidentiality required professionally may be challenging to learn. Having an awareness of the need to *question* and *update* values helps.

In the therapy context, our values are ever-present and are revealed in myriad subtle ways as something we aspire to, both in the things we say and in what we 'give off' (perhaps unconsciously). This is a point that Peter Lomas (*psychoanalytic* psychotherapist) makes in an interview with Windy Dryden when he highlights the role of **morals** (beliefs about right/wrong):

> The way the therapist behaves and the expectations he has of the patient show... his [sic] moral stance in life, and in society. Whether, for instance he believes that people are equal; ... what his attitude is to intimacy; to what extent he feels people should be open and close with each other or not; what he believes about money. The way he dresses is as revealing as is the way he speaks to the client. Does he for example believe in gentleness or roughness? Is he a permissive kind of person who is going to give a lot of space to the patient or is he someone who will go in for a lot of confrontation and challenge? (Dryden, 1985, p. 99)

Lomas continues to make the point that our cultural values are partly derived from our **professional socialisation** and theoretical commitments. Gillian Proctor (2018), for instance, discusses the challenges of working in forensic settings with violent clients as a *person-centred* therapist and how clashes of values can be found both with clients and with the service. At a personal level, it can be hard not to feel disgusted, horrified and angry at what clients have done. As a person-centred therapist, however, she aims to try to understand her clients without judgement, focusing more on the reasons why they have committed the offences they have. Supervision becomes vital when her values and experiences seem to get in the way of getting closer to clients' perspectives.

At an institutional level, Proctor points out how the moral base of person-centred work is at odds with the general culture of forensic services in the UK, where it is the job of the 'expert' professionals to protect the public from 'dangerous criminals'. She argues instead that it is the job of mental health professionals to reduce clients' distress and leave policing, control and public protection to the criminal justice system.

Petruska Clarkson (1999) also highlights how our personal and professional values can clash. In the following quotation she discusses the intentional use of values in *gestalt* counselling:

> Gestalt practitioners, on the whole, do not profess neutrality towards client issues about which they have strong values. ... A Gestalt practitioner I know has refused to take on a man who came wanting help with a weight problem while pursuing a spare-time practice of hounding and beating up Pakistani children on the estate where he lived. In another instance a man, complaining of severe depression while maintaining an incestuous relationship with his fourteen-year-old daughter, refused to see any link between these two aspects of his life, and adamantly maintained

that it was not harming her and that he would not stop. The counsellor refused him treatment and referred him to another agency. (Clarkson, 1999, p. 73)

What's your position? Could you work with violent people, including rapists, murderers and paedophiles? How do your personal values and theoretical perspectives influence your choices? Professional guidelines emphasise respect for our clients, and working in their interests, but we also need to be aware of our limitations and degrees of choice. It's about being aware of implications when our conscience demands us to take a different line.

Negotiating values relationally

The challenge of working with our values and morals is that they carry different meanings for different people and they may clash. In the following passage, Lomas highlights the dilemma of how far you let a client go their own way when you don't approve of it. The classic conundrum here is whether we allow a client 'freedom' of choice to harm themselves:

> I believe even if one takes a neutral stand it could at times be immoral to sit back and let someone do something very destructive. The ultimate example would be suicide. If one really thought a patient would commit suicide and was going to do so for stupid reasons, sick reasons, it would seem to me that I would want to do something or say something to stop him. (Dryden, 1985, p. 99)

Attuning relationally to our clients' needs/situation means also recognising their values and morals, how these mesh with ours. To give a specific example, consider the interlinking values of *respect* and *autonomy*.

   Respect is a much-used term when it comes to ethics and it's worth probing it more deeply. Respect concerns how we listen to and relate with clients (in curiosity and compassion), and take into account *their* meanings, situation and uniqueness. Can we respect their 'difference'? The client deserves to be seen as a *person* – one who has worth and value. In addition, clients may bring us their vulnerable parts, but do we see beyond appreciating their strengths and competences in their wider lives? Do we respect them enough to go into partnership with them, ensuring consent for each step of therapy? Can we honour the client's life choices, respecting them to make decisions that are best for them as well as to be respectful of the way they've creatively adjusted to life's tensions? In this sense, respect and acceptance are twinned values.

   Roger Casemore (2009) discusses the importance for him of the ethic of 'autonomy' as involving respect of the inherent dignity of others and their freedom of choice. He challenges some therapists' tendency to help others excessively (enabling?), albeit out of altruistic motives. He suggests we should work towards holding an 'ethically mindful position in which we look after ourselves and take the risk of allowing others to struggle and to do things for themselves' (2009, p. 29). Here, he points to the need to respect the other's own capacity and to help them be more resourceful themselves rather than directing them or doing things for them which fosters more dependence and risks dumping our values on to them. Such values apply both to work with clients and to wider relationships.

Proctor (2018) extends this argument, suggesting that *person-centred* therapists value and respect the autonomy of the client as opposed to the approach adopted by some others which draws more on 'beneficence' (making judgements about what might be best for them). The autonomy she promotes comes from ensuring clients' informed consent and taking an approach which is non-judgemental and honest.

> The more I respect the autonomy of a client and try and understand their experience, often, the more they are able to work out for themselves why they do the things they have done and take steps to be responsible and stop hurting others. (Proctor, 2018, p. 113)

Yet, the value about promoting the client's autonomy is more complicated if we consider the cultural and relational contexts. Thinking **culturally**, it's worth recognising that respecting that the autonomy of individuals tends to be a Western construct. In many African and South/Far East cultures, primacy tends to be given to the well-being of family or communities (Welfel, 2013). This warns us to attend carefully to the context and be cautious about assuming uniformity across cultures.

Thinking **relationally**, consider the situation where a client has a dilemma facing two courses of action; one is a duty response, the other is what they want to do. A therapist who values 'autonomy' may well encourage the client to work out their priorities and choices. But what happens if the client asks 'What would you advise? Can you give me some perspective?'. How would you respond and why? One answer might be a straightforward one, emphasising that it's the client's choice and not to reveal any views. Other therapists would argue for giving honest answers to clients' direct questions – this prioritises 'honesty' and 'authenticity' values over autonomy.

Relationally-speaking, some clients may need to hear that the therapist is engaged with their problem and cares enough to respond to the expressed need. Might there be a role here for the therapist to at least enlarge the picture rather than simply batting it back non-committedly? I'm reminded of one of my clients who recently said, 'you say things my mother never said, and I needed her to'. The problem perhaps at the heart of this conundrum is how to ensure we do not undermine clients and take away their choices and control by imposing our own values. If we can self-disclose without overly influencing clients' choices, it may be helpful. For instance, it might help to own one's own values (perhaps explaining some reluctance to do so) but also highlight different possibilities for the client.

Concluding reflections

In this chapter I've highlighted the way that professional codes intermix with our cultural and personal values. When we add the relational dimension into this 'soup', the complex dilemmas and diversity in our practice are revealed. We negotiate micro-ethical decisions all the time and these contribute to the uncertainty and challenge of our practice.

Often these dilemmas are not just about 'right' and 'wrong'; instead, we find ourselves in situations where we're forced to decide between conflicting values and needs. It then comes down to how *reflexive* (critically self-aware) we are, respectfully considering the individual, relational *and* social **context** – it's that stance which, I believe, goes to the heart of being ethical.

From my discussions with colleagues about ethical conundrums like the ones above, I am aware of the shame and anxiety they may evoke. Partly, this shame may be related to recognising one's imperfections or to tensions caused by going against (betraying?) socialised values. Partly, it's about exposure. I feel this vulnerability as I expose my own personal and professional responses in writing. It is hard to disclose publicly what action (or lack of) we have taken. Then, when we're confronted by ethical uncertainty, how easy is it to admit our own confusion and discomfort? It's natural to worry about the negative judgements of others. And, in an increasingly litigious environment, our anxieties about being 'reported' inevitably fuel anxiety, perhaps nudging us into avoidant or defensive practice. It is important for us all to acknowledge how the private, confidential and intimate nature of our work behind closed doors generates potential for secrets and shame.

Only through experience and extensive processing of relational-ethical concerns and uncertainties in supervision and other professional forums is it possible to build confidence in our own clinical judgement and intuition. Given that we routinely operate in ambiguous, murky, risky waters, we all make mistakes and misjudgements; we don't always follow the values we espouse or aspire to. It is vital that we discuss these issues regularly, both with each other and formally in supervision.

Discussion questions

1. Take one ethical dilemma that has arisen in your practice and critically discuss the *personal* and *professional* values involved, while noting the professional and *legal* implications at stake.
2. Can/should therapists be neutral facilitators of clients' development?
3. Examine three core values that shape your practice. Do these pose you any dilemmas in practice?

Summary

Relational ethics intertwines relational sensitivity with containing ethical frameworks. Ethics permeate practice, professional codes, legal frameworks as well as personal and cultural values and morals. While codes and guidelines equip us with useful maps and anchors as we navigate these turbulent waters, they rarely offer definitive, clear-cut rules. They cannot replace active, relationally-attentive, ethical decision-making where we marry our personal and professional values and standards in thoughtful, reflexive (critically self-aware) ways. Such practice stands in contrast to the rigid pursuit of rules as part of some protocol or defensive reflex. Ethical judgements need to be made in context and it's complicated.

2

Professional Codes and Legal Frameworks: Thinking Relationally

Ethical dilemmas like those discussed in Chapter 1 must be understood in the context of law, professional standards and the (inter-)personal and cultural values enshrined in *Professional Ethical Codes*, which seek to set out ways to care for both client and therapist.

Do you know the codes of your professional body? Are you familiar with their requirements and concerns? Many practitioners admit to merely skimming through them, rating them 'dry' and not particularly relevant to the specific, complicated challenges of everyday practice. Space doesn't permit discussion of the many possible codes and guides here, but I offer a taste of their style and spirit.

This chapter sketches some of the key ideas enshrined in professional **codes**, drawing on examples from across the world. The next two sections discuss the **relational implications** of both codes and legal frameworks. I spotlight the layers of complexity by looking more specifically at two topics: 'diversity' and 'record-keeping'. The chapter ends with concluding reflections.

Professional ethical codes

Most, if not all, professional ethical codes of practice explicitly or implicitly agree that:

> the therapist is responsible for acting in a competent, respectful, boundaried way, with integrity, and in the best interest of their client.

It sounds simple but once you start probing what this all means for different people in different contexts, it gets complicated.

Professional ethical codes have a dual function: (1) to offer an ethical framework; and (2) to specify expected conduct and behaviour. **Frameworks** are a general outline of various 'principles', 'values' and 'standards'. They serve as aspirational mission statements. When faced with ethical dilemmas, what is articulated in the code can help guide professional behaviour and decision-making. They also protect clients and safeguard the reputation of the profession.

Codes of conduct are more directive, offering specific 'rules', actions and behaviours that are legally and professionally required or prohibited. They might, for example, forbid sexual harassment, racial intimidation or the use of drugs and alcohol prior to or during work.

In the UK, where I work, the British Association for Counselling and Psychotherapy (BACP) provides detailed guidelines, together with numerous additional resources, videos and legal practice guides. Their 'Good practice in action' resources offers valuable information on many aspects of practice including confidentiality, contracting, record-keeping and choosing a supervisor. Their foundational document, *Ethical Framework for the Counselling Professions* (BACP, 2018a), aims to foster an ethical resourcefulness that is responsive to diverse contexts. It starts with a section on 'our commitment to clients' and then lists how we should put clients first, work to professional standards, show respect, build appropriate relationships, maintain integrity, and demonstrate accountability and candour. Attention is paid to values, principles and the moral qualities we strive to uphold, including care, diligence, empathy and humility. The final section on good practice offers more detailed guidelines, together with information relevant to supervision, training/ education, research and self-care.

This Framework has evolved through extensive consultation and revision. (It's important to remember that codes evolve – ideas about what is 'right' change.) It aims to be responsive to new ways of working (digitally, for example) and to acknowledge the changing landscapes of practice (including coaching and counselling/psychotherapy under the inclusive bracket of 'Counselling Professions'). Tim Bond, the main architect of the new Framework, has influenced the development of ethical thinking in counselling and psychotherapy in the UK for over 30 years. (For a deeper understanding of the context and process of this Framework, and the controversies surrounding it, see Jenkins, 2015.)

Of particular interest to me in this document is the recognition that *ethics-in-practice* are not clear-cut: practitioners practise differently and sometimes principles and values clash, for instance, personal and professional interests can conflict with 'putting clients first'. Our obligation is to take as much care as possible, discuss issues in supervision, and be appropriately accountable for any decisions we make. Put another way, an action doesn't become unethical if it is controversial and goes against some principle.

Some ethical frameworks explicitly distinguish between ethical *'principles'* (the ideals to which the profession aspires), *'values/morals'* (what matters personally or culturally) and *'standards of behaviour'* (legal obligations where sanctions can be imposed).

The Canadian Counselling and Psychotherapy Association (2007, p. 2) presents the fundamental **principles** succinctly:

a. Beneficence – being proactive in promoting the client's best interests and well-being
b. Fidelity – honouring commitments to clients and maintaining integrity in counselling relationship
c. Non-maleficence – not wilfully harming clients and refraining from actions that risk harm
d. Autonomy – respecting the rights of clients to self-determination
e. Justice – respecting the dignity and just treatment of all persons
f. Societal Interest – respecting the need to be responsible to society.

Other codes list similar principles and values. The British Psychological Society (BPS) (2018) offers its own version, which focuses on four ethical principles: respect, competence, responsibility and integrity. Integrity here, for instance, involves being honest, accurate and consistent in actions while setting aside self-interest, being objective and being open to professional challenge.

Closely linked to such philosophical principles are **moral values**. For example, the BACP (2018a) itemises these as the personal qualities one aspires to achieve (even if we don't always meet them): candour, care, courage, diligence, empathy, fairness, humility, identity, integrity, resilience, respect, sincerity, wisdom.

It's worthwhile taking time to reflect on each of these in relation to practice. *'Resilience'*, for example, seems to me to be an interesting personal quality. We commonly promote it in our clients but how often do we consider it in terms of ourselves and our practice? Resilience links to an imperative for us to actively engage with our own self-care as part of *care* and to ensure we don't burn out ourselves. It is akin to the airline safety instruction we receive to pull on our own oxygen mask before putting one on a child.

Standards of behaviour are usually more specific and directive. Take the following examples from the code of the American Psychological Association (APA) (2017):

3.02 Psychologists do not engage in sexual harassment. Sexual harassment is sexual solicitation, physical advances, or verbal or nonverbal conduct that is sexual in nature, that occurs in connection with the psychologist's activities..., and that either (1) is unwelcome, is offensive, or creates a hostile workplace or educational environment ... or (2) is sufficiently severe or intense to be abusive to a reasonable person in the context...

3.04 (b) Psychologists do not participate in, facilitate, assist, or otherwise engage in torture, defined as any act by which severe pain or suffering, whether physical or mental, is intentionally inflicted on a person, or in any other cruel, inhuman, or degrading behavior that violates 3.04(a).

3.05 (a) ...A psychologist refrains from entering into a multiple relationship if the multiple relationship could reasonably be expected to impair the psychologist's objectivity, competence, or effectiveness in performing his or her functions as a psychologist, or otherwise risks exploitation or harm to the person with whom the professional relationship exists.

6.02 (c) Psychologists make plans in advance to facilitate the appropriate transfer and to protect the confidentiality of records and data in the event of psychologists' withdrawal from positions or practice.

What is your reaction to these four directives? Perhaps the first two seem 'obvious'. However, a minority of therapists do make sexual advances towards clients/supervisees and others are employed to help perfect torture techniques. Does this indicate narcissism, ignorance or something more sinister? (See the section on the 'shadow side' in Chapter 3). Beyond not being abusers ourselves, we also have a professional and legal duty to safeguard 'adults at risk' of significant harm (be it from self-neglect, abuse, exploitation and modern slavery) – see, for instance, the Adult and Care Act 2014.

Clause 3.05 of the APA Code appears to offer a straightforward highlighting of issues around boundaries, our competence and our duty to avoid harming clients. But 'harm' can only be assessed by carefully considering each individual and each relationship. Therapists' underlying intent and client sensitivities all need to be factored in. Then it's a judgement call about what would be the appropriate or proportionate action.

I find the last item a salutary reminder about the need to ensure my record-keeping systems are comprehensively managed. In the long term, nothing can be ruled out, including the possibility of one's own death. I confess to not always having been so mindfully conscious of this requirement. It's not simply a question of following a rule. I need to factor in the *care* required if, for whatever reason, I was suddenly not there.

From this brief exercise of looking at the directives, we can see that there are masses of issues to discuss. Things become even more complicated – overwhelmingly confusing even – when we consider the *relational* implications of the advice in the codes. What becomes clear is that 'right' or 'wrong' is more fluid and less clear-cut; it's about weighing up competing personal values and professional judgements and considering the particular context.

Relational implications of professional codes

Bland lists of principles and directives can spring to life with the aid of examples from everyday practice. This section takes a more explicit look at the relational implications of such documents, with the spotlight on 'diversity' as a key topic, in a bid to shed light on the complex challenges we face daily.

It is immediately important to recognise that practice law and guidance vary according to time and place. Yesterday's correct practice, or that gleaned from overseas sources, may be inappropriate to our specific situation or culture. In this book, I focus primarily on the codes relevant to practice in the UK, the context with which I am most familiar. However, the codes/guidelines operating in your own culture and modality may be different. Even within the

UK, material differences exist between codes for psychoanalytic, humanistic, cognitive-behavioural and systemically-orientated practitioners.

The generic principles laid down by the United Kingdom Council for Psychotherapy (2009) recognise that practice decisions are challenging and that guidelines may clash with personal values. One therapist, for example, might break *confidentiality* to inform a psychiatrist that a client is suicidal (*duty of care*, non-maleficence), while another would respect the client's right to choose to take their own life (*respect*, right of *autonomy*). One therapist might value *humility*, arguing that it is important to know our limits and to listen to clients rather than assume a more knowing position. Another might argue that clients gain hope and confidence from our assured *power* and expertise and that to deny knowledge is unduly self-deprecating, even inauthentic. Is there a way to 'engage in collaboration and negotiation from a position of expertise' (UKCP, 2018a, p. 5)?

The introduction to the UKCP (2009) Code includes the statement: 'The psychotherapist commits to engage with the challenge of striving for ethical practice and conduct, even when doing so involves making difficult decisions or acting courageously' (p. 2). I'm struck by the appreciation shown for the difficult work we do that involves both challenge and risk. (NB: This statement has been omitted from the 2018 draft version, which is a loss, I think.)

Example of 'diversity'

Every therapeutic relationship involves specific relational-ethical challenges. It's therefore helpful to hold individual clients in mind when considering the practical application of professional guidelines. Consider, for example, the value in most codes about 'respecting diversity', such as that from the UKCP Code (2009):

> 2.1 The psychotherapist undertakes to actively consider issues of diversity and equalities as these affect all aspects of their work. The psychotherapist accepts no one is immune from the experience of prejudice and acknowledges the need for a continuing process of self-enquiry and professional development...
>
> 2.3 The psychotherapist undertakes not to engage in any behaviour that is abusive or detrimental to any client or colleague based on the above factors.

There is much of relevance to working *relationally* in just these two selected items. First, the Code highlights the importance of diversity and equality while drawing attention to the continuing spectre of prejudice in our society. Second, it affirms that we are required not to act in any harmful way. Third, it asks us regularly and actively to self-reflect, and to consider how these issues might arise in our practice as part of our professional development.

Are you aware of any lurking prejudice you might have about a client's sex, age, colour, appearance, ethnicity, disability, sexuality, social/economic/ immigrationstatus, lifestyle, religious or cultural beliefs? Most of us have some judgements lurking. The challenge is to recognise how these may adversely affect our relationship with clients, and vice versa. It's also worth being aware of when we might silently condone prejudicial behaviour. When do we take a stand against oppression, perhaps challenging those who make prejudiced comments? When we fail to do this, what lingering relational elements might be stopping us?

I know of an experienced senior therapist who owned, with some shame, that she was prejudiced against obese people. From many hours of processing this in therapy and supervision, she learned she could lose a degree of compassion and inadvertently be critical of her larger-bodied clients. This was something she always needed to contain mindfully in practice.

Another therapist I know was approached by a client who had undergone a sex change. He found it hard to relate to his client and felt both out of his depth and reluctant to discuss details of her sexuality. After the initial session, and through supervision, he concluded that he was not the best therapist for this client. He discussed this openly with his client, offering to refund the fee charged for the first session. The client, appreciating the therapist's honesty, decided to stay. They eventually developed a strong, trusting relationship in which the therapist learned to see his client more as a person and less as a label. The therapist's understanding and interest grew as he learned more about 'transgender', 'transvestite', 'transsexual', 'gender fluidity' and 'LGBTQI+' categories and how his client preferred to be seen as 'trans-historied' (her birth certificate details had been changed and she was no longer a member of the trans-population).

As part of your continuing professional development it is useful to keep reflecting on whether you work better with some types of clients rather than others. Perhaps you feel more comfortable with clients who have a similar background to your own? A good question to explore in supervision is *why* certain clients appeal more to you or challenge you. Also, it's worth examining your growing edges and how you might promote practice that actively combats oppression and prejudice.

Relational implications of legal frameworks

Occasionally, we need to look beyond professional concerns and seek legal guidance. In addition to 'laws of the land', the law is relevant in our professional standards associated with contracts, duty of care/negligence, confidentiality and record-keeping, and so on. Legal requirements laid down by professional indemnity insurance bodies are also important.

The law is just another framework – a relatively neutral one that involves subtle, sometimes conflicting, interpretations and judgements. When it comes to the protection of the public and detection of serious crime (such as murder, rape, treason, child sexual abuse), the law is clearer but still grey. What constitutes 'sexual abuse', for example? If a client fantasises about murdering someone (which is not illegal), how do we judge intention and risk? Another example is how laws concerning 'negligence' apply where appropriate professional standards are breached, resulting in damage. Again, the field is grey as professional standards involve judgements. Plus, courts require proof of damage, which can be hard to establish, measure or redress. For this reason, therapy complaints are usually processed through professional bodies or settled out of court (Mitchels and Bond, 2010).

To make it more confusing, the law varies across countries – including across the four nations of the UK. I find the differences in law between the UK and the US interesting. British therapists often have more leeway to exercise professional judgements. For example, in the US, therapists have a duty to warn or protect third parties if there is a risk that a client may be dangerous to them (see details of the 'Tarasoff law' and controversies surrounding it www.psychologytoday.com/blog/media-spotlight/201407/revisiting-tarasoff). In the UK, there is no legal duty to protect potential third-party victims, although the courts would probably accept breaches of confidentiality as being 'in the public's interest' (Bond and Mitchels, 2015). The point to note is that therapists should seek legal advice before breaching client confidentiality due to the complicated legal picture involved.

Even within the same country, different professional codes and legal frameworks can offer subtly different positions. I'm interested in how some guidelines come out explicitly against things like torture or 'conversion therapy' whereas others are silent. Try this for yourself: take an issue of personal interest and contrast what the different codes from across different professional groups say about it.

The law is often framed using terms like 'reasonable' or 'appropriate' or 'proportionate' or 'normally'. While ensuring necessary flexibility, these caveats muddy the waters. I can think of many situations where one therapist would say something is 'appropriate' while another coming from a different modality would argue the opposite. The professional debates around the use of touch are a case in point (see Chapter 6).

Sometimes laws work against the therapeutic relationship, intensifying the relational challenges of practice. For instance, the 'confidentiality' enshrined in ethical codes is not absolute; it may be necessary to breach it. Such action can compromise trust in the relationship. It's easy to follow laws and rules blindly, and this can be seen when we fall into defensive, protocol-driven practice with the spectre of official complaints (see Chapter 4) looming as a possibility. Might this make us less creative and courageous (to use the UKCP term) in our relational work?

Example of record-keeping

To give a concrete example of how the law impacts our relational work, consider the issue of record-keeping (something many of us fret over at times).

In *legal* terms, therapists are required to keep records which are confidential and kept secure. It is worth keeping in mind the laws of your particular state/country. Some do not have any laws concerning mental health professionals and records. Others have specific guidelines, for instance, that records need to be kept for seven years or until any minors turn 18 and become legal adults. At times, records may need to be produced in court. There may be a whole intricate set of laws about subpoenas for courts and whether they are for testimony or records or both, and if 'therapist privilege' is being asserted, and so on. At such moments, we need to be careful about which details are revealed, and how. That said, it's worth remembering that it is a rare event to have to produce records formally in court. Occasionally we might be asked to write a short summary giving basic information, such as dates and the number of sessions and their general focus. It's handy to have notes to refer to here.

Rather than thinking about the rare situation of having to produce notes in court, we should perhaps be more focused on the fact that clients may have a right to see their notes. It is therefore a professional ethical imperative to keep an accurate record, to write notes which are professionally appropriate and respectful (and, where relevant, anonymised), and to ensure they are stored in secure ways.

More specifically, from May 2018, the European Union's *General Data Protection Regulation* (GDPR) replaced the Data Protection Act 1998 (see Box 2.1). It is worth checking with your professional body for more specific details as to what is required by law in your country or by your professional indemnity insurance company. It is also important to keep updated, as policies and practice change over time in response to misunderstandings and legal loopholes.

Box 2.1   Data protection: Some implications for therapy

The European Union's General Data Protection Regulation (GDPR) changes the way we process (access, use, store, destroy) personal data and seeks to give people control over how organisations use their data; **personal data held on an individual belongs to that individual.** Only *data which is relevant/essential to our work should be kept.*

Clients/supervisees have the right to see *any* data we hold about them (that includes personal details, such as address, and other information on the contract, plus any clinical notes that might be written as an *aide-mémoire* relevant to the progression of the work). If clients find their data to be inaccurate, then they have the right to ask for it to be corrected. They have the right to know where and how we store their details; if they are concerned about the security of storage arrangements, then alternative action needs to be agreed. If they ask to see the notes, then we are required to respond within a month. Any breaches need to be disclosed within 72 hours.

It is our responsibility to keep personal data safe (password protected if online and/or in a locked cabinet). Personal data should not be given to third parties unless it is legally compelled or consented to in advance. The exceptions here are those covered in the initial 'contract' if there are concerns about risk to self/others, or when action needs to be taken in the event of our death or incapacity.

> On any professional websites we need to include some information about not copying, sharing or using any information without consent. Further, details about what information the webhosting company collects should be indicated, for example, 'This website is hosted by xxx which uses xxx to determine how many people are using the site and to maintain its function. None of this information identifies anyone personally. Disabling cookies on your internet browser will stop xxx from tracking any part of your visit.'

The *relational* context creates additional ethical challenges for note-writing. It can be difficult to 'hold' the client's story from week to week, particularly in the context of a busy practice or deep, complex work. Some therapists use notes as an *aide-mémoire* to remember the story or even particular details, such as a child's name.

Providing a contrary argument, I know one senior therapist practising in the UK who takes a stand *against* writing notes. She does not want to 'fix' the client by boxing them into words or categories. She prefers to stay relationally focused and work with whatever emerges in the here-and-now rather than being influenced by thinking based on previous sessions. In other words, she is exercising her professional judgement in going against guidelines *and relationally justifies the decision*. (Note: the UKCP *Draft Code of Ethics* (2018a) accepts 'deviations' from ethical practice standards if they're 'justifiable before peers, supervisors and clients').

Whether or not notes are written, relational ethics demands that we attend to our own processes and *counter-transferential* responses and writing notes can be invaluable here. However, it's unlikely we'd want all this material opened up to others as part of our 'formal notes'. If clients saw those writings, they might feel disrespected, objectified or even concerned about our professional solidity. These risks need factoring in.

If notes are cursory and too brief, they can compromise our therapeutic competence and self-care. On the other hand, overly detailed notes may compromise client confidentiality and our own right to privacy. In other words, notes are unfit for purpose if they are damaging if seen by the client or when outed into the public domain.

One way through this morass is to keep formal notes brief. The BACP (2018a) puts this nicely, recommending that we only keep notes that are 'adequate, relevant and limited to what is necessary for the type of service being provided'.

Some therapists favour using set formats, for instance, the SOAP or DAP formats. SOAP stands for Subjective (the issues from the client's point of view), Objective (observations about the content of the session), Assessment (professional impressions of what is going on with the client) and Plan (anything to be followed up in the next session, or actions the therapist needs to take). DAP stands for Data (the content of the session), Assessment and Plan.

Other therapists like to keep notes in the form of a line or two about the focus of the session and then keep separate, *anonymised* 'process' notes. Practitioners often go down this route of having different types of writing. In legal terms, this is tricky because, technically speaking, *all* documentation referring to the client *might* need to be produced. Case notes, the client's drawings/writings, texts/messages/emails, supervision notes, records of assessments and process notes could all be demanded by either the client or the courts (Bond and Mitchels, 2015).

Concluding reflections

In discussions with others, I am acutely aware, when reading anything about professional ethics and codes, how they are often perceived as 'dry and boring'. Underlying those reactions, they can also elicit discomfort. It helps to remember that, other than complying with the laws of the land, ethical frameworks offer guidelines and standards for us to *aspire* to. As therapists, we don't always behave with integrity or always respect others; we make mistakes, we get confused and uncertain; we're not perfect. It's unhelpful even to strive to be 'perfect' as surely making mistakes is part of the process? For me, the key point is finding the comfortable – if tricky – balance between following professional guidelines and being a *human being*.

I find the cultural differences in codes and practices instructive and interesting. The American Psychological Association's (APA) code, for example, is highly detailed and directive, with many 'do's, don'ts' and legal assertions (linked perhaps to the more litigious cultural context in the US compared to other countries?). These contrast sharply with the more explicitly relational UK codes, with their focus on general principles and values. The *Code of Ethics* from the Psychotherapy and Counselling Federation of Australia takes the relational focus even further, emphasising that it is 'in the attention given to all aspects of the client relationship, as well as relationship with colleagues, students, the profession and the broader community, that ethics is put into practice' (PACFA, 2017, p. 1). It seems that today's increasing interest in relational ethics is being mirrored in the evolution of our codes.

I support this development. Speaking as a relational therapist, I believe our professional actions depend on the relational context (and the socio-cultural one – see Chapter 4). I dislike dogma, particularly when an unexplained instruction comes from an authority that says I *must* do something a certain way. On the other hand, I respect professional codes and try to be attentive to them, so there is a tension here.

Being professional means taking responsibility for one's own clinical decisions. These decisions are always made in particular cultural, relational and individual contexts. The various professional codes mostly offer us a *direction* rather than directive. It's up to us to apply them sensitively and appropriately, having thought about them, ideally in dialogue with others. The danger is when, in our shame or discomfort and fearing censure, we take our practice 'underground'.

I know, for example, when I feel a little reluctant to take something to supervision, it is probably precisely what I should take!

I'm aware that my own response to dilemmas which arise in supervision (my own and those of my supervisees) is often 'I really don't know; it just feels right'. It's about trying to be a *'good enough therapist'*, rather than one who perfectly follows the rules. In fact, I can bristle in rebellious mode if I'm told I 'have to' do something 'because it's a rule'. Beyond the formality of laws, codes and guidelines there is always space for professional experience, common sense and intuition. This is the artistry of therapy, the subtle process that dances in the mysterious 'between' of the therapy relationship. I hope to capture some of this in the chapters that follow.

Discussion questions

1. Take one of the standards or values in a relevant professional ethical code. Critically explain its implications for your work with clients.
2. Professional standards take precedence over personal values. Discuss the arguments for and against this statement.
3. To what extent do professional ethical frameworks hinder, rather than support, the therapeutic relationship?

Summary

Professional guidelines for ethical practice tend to emphasise key principles: namely, that through our duty of care, clients should be respected and protected; informed consent should be regularly and formally obtained; data protection and confidentiality should be maintained; and more. These guidelines sound straightforward but, in practice, every therapy encounter exposes ethical uncertainties and relational challenges that are context-specific (concerning both the immediate relationship and its wider cultural context). Relational ethics involves seeing ethics in terms of *relationship* rather than codes and directives. We need to find ways to interweave our personal values and professional standards in reflexive, relational ways rather than rigidly following rules.

3

Care as a Relational Ethic and its 'Shadow'

Underpinning our work as therapists is the care we strive to offer and enact. This goes beyond technique and professional principles like 'duty of care'. Although there are parallels with the caring we might offer in our lives more generally (for example, when we're being nurturing parents or a supportive friend), in several important respects *therapeutic care is distinct and different*.

This chapter explores how we do our caring as part of relational ethics. It begins with a discussion of what is meant by **therapeutic care** before moving on to explore the **shadow side of care**: situations when care is oppressive or when therapists become burnt-out through having given too much. In this second section I also consider the complexities of our professional power and how it can be abused. The third section touches briefly on the spectre of **complaints** in response to breaches in care. The penultimate section, before the concluding reflections, focuses on therapist *self*-**care**.

Therapeutic care

In the following quotation, a client describes her experience of being cared for in a letter to her therapist:

> Words can't express how much you mean to me. When I first came to you I wanted you
> to take away my anxiety. I hoped you'd do it in a couple of sessions. In the end we took

two years. I'm glad now that we had that time. That was the time I needed to learn how to help myself and care for – rather than harm – myself. If you had just taken away my anxiety, I would have been dependent on you. Instead, you were just always there for me, supporting me, caring for me, teaching me.

I have some special memories of our tears, our laughter, your TLC, your understanding. Our time together was precious. I will remember it forever. Looking back it's like looking at jewels in a jewelry box. You taught me that I was worthy of being kept safe. You never judged and you allowed me to be Me. This was a Me I had never let myself know. And now I can say that I like Me! I can handle things now when things go pear-shaped in the future. This was the magical gift you gave me – another precious jewel which I will carry with me always.

With love and heartfelt gratitude always,

Maruna

(Finlay, 2016a, p. 146)

Research (for example, Levitt et al., 2016) shows that therapists' care allows clients to feel safe enough in sessions to put aside defences and be vulnerable as they engage in self-exploration. Self-acceptance and self-care come by internalising the therapist's caring and validation. In this, there is a place for the transformational impact of **love** – namely, a boundaried, ethical, compassionate, responsively attuned *Agape*-type love (Charura and Paul, 2015; DeYoung, 2015b). Research also shows that therapy is compromised when clients perceive caring to be insincere, infantalising or overly involved. It is thus relationally and ethically important to consider how best to care.

Most (if not all) professional codes highlight the importance of our duty of care: that is, working with the client's best interests to the fore and to an appropriate standard (that is, making them our primary concern and providing an appropriate standard of service; BACP, 2018a). This duty requires therapists to take reasonable steps to ensure clients are not harmed, whether physically or psychologically, during therapy. In terms of ethical principles, this involves the practice of *beneficence* and *non-maleficence*, along with integrity, competence, equality, and so forth. However, such practice is complicated. How do we reconcile the requirement to 'do no harm' with the need to allow harmful feelings to be felt and expressed? Clients will some-times leave therapy sessions feeling worse. While we can say this is a necessary part of the 'process', there are delicate judgements here as to what is in their interests.

We show our care by unconditional acts of kindness, gentleness, warm-heartedness and appreciation – what Miller Mair calls 'compassionate atten-tion' (Mair, 1989, p. 229). We're attentive to the other's needs, sensitive to responses, and alert to how much care is beneficial and what clients can use-fully take in. It's about attending, by listening to their needs and grumbles, and responding positively without losing ourselves or retaliating defensively when our own wounds are touched. Where possible, the caring takes place in a context where there is a 'glow of respect for what matters in particular lives' (Mair, 1989, p. 74). Mair describes this special **attunement** thus:

> It takes ... persistence and the patience of the birdwatcher and the hunter to sense the tiny movements in the grass that tell clear tales to those who know what they are involved in coming still to know. (1989, p. 229)

The attunement needed is also one where therapists attune to what's important to the client. Trautmann (2003) discusses this in relation to seeking a therapist who can be attentive spiritually and attune to her own soul's stirring:

> I specifically needed to know about the nature of our therapeutic relationship and whether the therapist would be available for 'soul work' ... I had to know that I could bring all aspects of myself to the relationship and that my soul yearnings would not only be accepted, but would be valued and care-fully explored. (2003, p. 33)

Similarly, Patricia DeYoung (2015b) has highlighted the role of **relationally validating connections** based in 'right-brain-to-right-brain' communication when working with clients who experience chronic shame. She draws on Daniel Hughes' clever acronym 'PACE', which stands for 'playfulness', 'acceptance', 'curiosity' and 'empathy' (see Box 5.1 and www.danielhughes.org/p.a.c.e..html). These relational elements intertwine in practice. For instance, DeYoung points out that neither curiosity nor empathy works particularly well alone:

> Curiosity without empathy can feel intrusive, at worst like a kind of voyeurism. ... Empathy alone can be the end of a conversation; with interested curiosity, empathy opens up into new conversations. (2015b, p. 84)

There's a distinction to be made between 'caring-about' clients and 'caring-for' them in the sense of providing them with a service (something with the potential to be paternalistic). With *relational* ethics to the fore, I would also like to advance the additional notion of 'caring-with'. If paternalism is equated with a 'masculine' version of care, **caring-with** is a 'feminine' version of ethics rooted in the relationship, receptivity, responsiveness, reciprocity and relatedness (Noddings, 2013). Here, our humanness (regardless of being male/female) is to the fore: 'We may have to forsake our professionalism and take up our common humanity in extended caring relations' (2013, p. 184). Mandić (2016), working from an existential orientation, offers a resonant description of a psychotherapy encounter where he highlights the attuned, caring-with human disposition involved (see Box 3.1).

Box 3.1 A phenomenological description of 'caring-with'

We sit and meet each other in our gazes ... I sense that she is a little shy and unsure of herself. Neither one of us is very sure about what might happen next. I feel a twinge of sadness mingled with familiarity – this is how I experience many moments like this – and I give a reassuring smile, as if to acknowledge her unease. Her eyes manage to hold my smile, before then looking down and away. Her gentleness almost overwhelms me, and a film of wetness starts to feel itself form over my eyes.

As I hear her tell me about a difficulty in her relationship, I am immersed in what I'm hearing, how she is choosing those words, how she expresses herself in her tentativeness, the tone and timbre of her voice, her subtle mannerisms and gestures, her pauses, her rhythms, and her cadences. How she stops and starts all bring me to her and yet this tells me that I am never her, and that I can never be her breath. I am humbled: this is her life that she is unfolding and showing me. Being curious, attentive, and present, things that I already understand about myself when I am with a client, do not capture the aliveness of being with her. Every moment has a valency, a charge, an intensity of its own. I have no props, I can only be, rather than do, anything, and a wish to understand her, to be some-*one* for her. I have no desire to absorb her to be me, or to take her over, but to simply meet her as herself...

As I now come to a point where I hear her concerns ... I want to provide an earth that can bear her weight. I want to be the planter of seeds of possibility for her, long after she has finished seeing me. Her life is not broken, not bad, or wrong, it just needs the nutrients to make that seed take root. And I sense it all only through being a human being, just like her. (Mandić, 2016, pp. 111–112)

The care described in this section goes beyond simply fulfilling ethical requirements. It arises from our compassion and dedication. And sometimes we slip in our caring – we're human after all. We get preoccupied, tired, bored, irritated, impatient, thoughtless and we can lose our focus or inadvertently hurt or confuse a client. In our professionalism, we mostly hold in check these micro-moments, where caring temporarily recedes.

The 'shadow side'

While acknowledging the delicately attuned, dedicated ways in which we enact care, it's important not to romanticise this process or ignore its vulnerability to corruption. At times, therapy can go seriously off-track, creating opportunities for care to morph into something altogether different. Care can become subverted or even become an abuse of power.

Subverted care

In our day-to-day practice there will inevitably be times when we find ourselves less disposed to care. Life challenges and personal history, together with pressures and events, can get in the way, creating moments when we ourselves become care-less, vulnerably needy, overly aggressive or no longer appropriately available for our clients. Even the most grounded and best-intentioned therapist can get ground down, sucked dry, exhausted, distressed and vicariously traumatised. During such experiences of burn-out we cut ourselves off from our clients' pain and lose our empathy, compassion and care. Page (1999, p. 56) pinpoints the problem:

> It would not be particularly atypical in one week for a full-time counsellor to see five people who were seriously abused or damaged as children, two who are deeply depressed, one who is in danger of starving to death as a consequence of eating disorders, three who have been bereaved and another two whose partnerships or marriages are disintegrating.

As Page notes, it takes great reserves of patience to sit with clients who are stuck in abusive situations or endlessly repeating self-destructive patterns or who disintegrate in front of our eyes. In the face of frustration and helplessness, we may find ourselves succumbing to our 'shadow' side: the Jungian notion of the often unknown, unconscious dark aspects of self which we seek to repress.

> Shadow aspects of self are dark and dank. They reside in the mouldy basement of our unconscious where ill wishes and self harm fester and breed. Like a ... viscous [sic] dog foaming at the mouth, our shadow aspects are just waiting to be cruel, and that ferocity is as easily directed inwards as it is outwards. (Green, 2012a)

In this dark side of caring, therapists' needs and power may be unhealthily acted out, turning care into harm. Clients can be harmed when boundaries are too tight or too loose. Their prospects for progress can be undermined by excessive smothering (as when a therapist does too much holding) or by a therapist who is too distant and *with*holding. Client safety may be threatened when their therapist doesn't contain – or when so much containing is done, out of awareness, that therapy becomes 'rescuing' or oppressive. If an exhausted, pressurised therapist starts to resent the care they are required to give, lurking anger can be acted out (unconsciously) in bullying, manipulative, seductive or persecuting ways.

There is a *relational* dimension that needs to be factored in. For example, in situations when therapists feel overwhelmed, they may project their own dependence and neediness onto clients, perhaps infantilising them in the process. In turn, clients may become overly dependent on their therapist or idealise them excessively. Through its ability to meet a therapist's needs in some way, this process can feed their narcissistic grandiosity. Alternatively, we might be working with a client who 'expects' to be criticised or even humiliated by their therapist. Somehow, through projective identification, we find ourselves caught in persecutory relational dynamics. Or a client might unconsciously be seductive, setting up the stage for a replay of past abuse.

Training is another context ripe for the emergence of the shadow side. Wilkinson (2018) explores the ways in which relational dynamics can serve to bolster a trainer's potency. For example, a 'needy' student who asks to be fed information and supported/contained may trigger a process by which the trainer is pulled into a 'rescuer' response (as in 'I'll find a placement for you' or 'Here's a good passage to quote'). This may result in the trainer inadvertently patronising the student by spoon-feeding.

Power

With subverted care, the relational-ethical issue at stake is therapists' power (Proctor, 2002; Finlay, 2004). The essentially unequal, non-reciprocal nature of the therapist–client relationship is exposed through the authority and 'expert' knowledge we possess in our **role** as therapists. After all, we set the rules and norms of therapy; we can ask probing, intrusive, private questions while not disclosing ourselves; we direct; we contain; we have the power to diagnose and offer authoritative interpretations; we can label a client's protests as 'resistance', and so on.

Existential therapist Ernesto Spinelli (1994) cites his own experience, during training, where the therapist in a weekly two-hour therapy group imposed an arrogant, dogmatic interpretation. In addition to being offensive, it was *anti-therapeutic* as an opportunity to explore his actual relationship with his parents was lost:

> About four weeks into the group process, the male trainer strongly urged the group to begin to address him and his colleague as 'Daddy' or 'Mum' in order to expose long-term conflicts which, he declared, each of us held in our unconscious. This request struck me, as well as several other trainees, as being somewhat ludicrous and I voiced my distain of what I saw as the heavy-handed attempt to impose a 'transferential relationship' on us. ... Cutting my argument short, the male trainer intoned: 'Mr Spinelli, it is understandable that you have such a reaction to my suggestion since you are, of course, an orphan.' When I responded ... that both my parents happened to be alive and in good health, his reply to me was: ... 'It doesn't matter whether your parents are actually alive or not, the issue is that you are a *psychic* orphan!' (Spinelli, 1994, pp. 97–98)

Yet, *power in therapy is complicated and layered.* It's **relational** and enacted between people in particular contexts; it needs to be seen in the context of an ongoing, mutual, interactive relationship where individuals exert degrees of agency, choice and control. In other words, power is not a 'thing' that is possessed by one person over another.

In a therapy context, therapists mostly exercise power in **benign** ways, *geared to the client's interests.* This is the case where therapists seeking to 'empower' clients claim the authority to somehow grant that power; or where they assert their 'potency' as someone who can hold the client's process and inspire confidence; or where a therapist might choose to relinquish authority in the face of a client's assertions.

Importantly, therapists must manage intense relationships over time, a process which involves deeper dynamics of mutual dependence, power and powerlessness. Here the **personal histories** of both therapist and client need to be factored in. Both will have had times of feeling power-full and power-less.

Sometimes, when people are abusive, they are attempting to re-assert power and may feel powerless. The important question is how this is enacted in the therapy room. We don't want therapy to repeat patterns from people's histories of violence, manipulation and/or powerlessness. Sometimes unconscious transferences or the therapist's narcissistic needs get in the way. The practice of therapist power can in certain circumstances become manipulative and malignant, especially when expressed through financial exploitation, coercion and psychological, physical and/or sexual abuse.

Therapist power also needs to be seen in a **cultural-historical context**. In the past, big names in psychotherapy, from Carl Jung to Fritz Perls, reportedly engaged in sexual relations with clients – apparently with therapeutic intent. Today this is considered totally unacceptable, blatantly abusive and open to legal sanction.

As the *#MeToo* movement has emphasised, power differentials often result in victims failing to lodge complaints in a timely way. While a victim may be hesitant to complain on the basis of a single act, they may feel emboldened by an accumulation of complaints from fellow victims. New organisations are arising which seek to combat sexual assaults by supporting victims. An example here is how the organisation *Callisto* enables 'victims' to input the identity of perpetrators and be supported to follow through if a match is found with previous complaints.

Power also arises in the context of broader **institutional practices** and **social divisions**. Clients under medical care may find it hard to refuse medication. Students may feel they lack power to influence how their syllabus is delivered. A supervisee might find it hard to go against a supervisor's advice. Older colleagues may patronise younger ones. A lone black student may feel marginalised in workshops where everyone else is white and issues of colour are airbrushed away...

Similarly, professional power is cross-cut by societal structures of gender, race, ethnicity, age, disability, sexuality, and so on. The term *'intersectionality'* is used to highlight how we experience different levels of power/powerlessness and privilege in different relational contexts. People don't fit into neat categories. Intersectionality captures the complex ways in which the effects of different forms of discrimination interconnect. White, male clients can threaten black, female therapists; a straight, macho Latino client may put down a transsexual Asian one; a middle-class Indian client who is a Hindu may inadvertently show prejudice against a working-class Bangladeshi therapist who is a Muslim, and so on. As one client reveals, the exercise of power is far from being a one-way street:

> You shrinks seem to think you are these powerful beings. Your literature paints images of clients as helpless, vulnerable, pliable, weak creatures at the mercy of you omnipotent people. ... Well, let me tell you something about power ... I am better educated than you, which gives me more power than you have with your Ph.D. As far as I can tell, I am much wealthier than you, which gives me another form of power over you. ... Additionally, I am an attractive woman, which gives me the undeniable power that sexy women have over men. Finally, I can destroy your career with one call to your licensing board. So much for your illusion of your power. (Zur, 2009, p. 161)

In this quotation, the client challenges the therapist's omnipotent 'role power' and turns the tables. The power being described relates to Starhawk's (1987, cited in Proctor, 2002) distinction of '**power-over**' versus 'power-from-within' and 'power-with'. Power-over is domination; power backed by authority, force and control. Power-from-within is linked to empowerment and is an inner strength that comes from being connected with others and the environment. Power-with occurs in collectives, with groups of equals and involves the power to suggest and be listened to.

Applied to therapy, therapists commonly aim to minimise power-over and encourage **power-from-within** for *both themselves and the client*. In other words, we don't 'give away' our power to clients, we hold our own power while encouraging clients to find theirs. While holding our own, we can also be vulnerable and allow ourselves to be human. I appreciate Proctor's (2002) argument that the ethical position we take regarding professional power is linked to responsibility. She quotes Larner (1999, p. 48), who is highlighting the notion of 'true dialogue of unequals':

> The conscious movement of the therapist towards the other as an ethical stance allows a true dialogue of unequals, in which both therapist and client are powerful *and* non-powerful. ... The ethical challenge in psychotherapy is to minimise the therapist's potential to violate the other through therapy ... this is the potential violence of theory, authority, expertise and technology to override the client's contribution to their life narrative. (Proctor, 2002, p. 60)

Complaints about failures in care

The above quotation from the power-over client evokes the spectre of 'complaints' – a subject that tends to make us all feel uncomfortable. Space doesn't permit an adequate examination of this topic and I recommend you check out Welfel (2013, pp. 316–337) for a broad account of professional responsibility and complaints in the US. See also the BACP website for recent Professional Conduct notices, where complaints have been upheld, and Rogers (2013) for insight into the experience of complaints processes in the UK.

Procedures for filing ethics complaints vary considerably according to organisation, culture and the seriousness of the *misconduct* (involving mistakes and errors in judgement) versus *malpractice* (involving abuse and/or exploitation) (Box 3.2 uses two fictional case studies to demonstrate the difference between the two categories). Many professional codes recommend informal interventions as a first step: for example, dialogue between the complainant and the person who has been lax in their care and/or has potentially violated an ethical standard. Maybe just an apology is needed? Mediation or extra training may be advised. If the situation cannot be resolved, then more formal complaints or grievance procedures will be set in motion, perhaps with local or national ethics committees, or Professional Licensing or Registration Boards will be brought in.

See the following guidelines from the *Code of Ethics* of the International Integrative Psychotherapy Association (IIPA, 2018) which emphasises a relational, reconciliation approach:

Section 2: Whenever possible, matters related to ethics and ethical standards will be dealt with directly between the two or more parties involved in the perceived offense. Initially, a resolution of the conflict is encouraged at this relational level. If this attempt proves impossible, the ethical concern will be further addressed by the Ethics Committee.

Section 3: At the outset, the Ethics committee shall discern whether an ethical violation has occurred by the gathering of all possible information. As part of this process, they will consult with the aggrieved person/persons and the member against whom the allegations are made. Both parties shall have the benefit of a committee member being their mentor as part of a rehabilitative and healing process. Resolution at the level of conversation and interaction will be the preliminary goal. Members are encouraged to take the initiative in an informal consultation with the Ethics Committee for support and guidance when actions are pending or in process against them concerning alleged legal or ethical infractions.

Section 4: In the event that any member of the Association is formally accused of an ethical infraction, moving the dialogue from a consultation into an official complaint, such member shall be notified directly in person and in writing of the formal allegation. Such member shall be given the opportunity to respond to the allegations or charges and to meet with the committee. The object of the interactions shall be rehabilitative and reconciling, not primarily punitive. (IIPA, 2018)

Box 3.2 'Misconduct' versus 'malpractice'

1. **A case of misconduct** – A trainee therapist who has completed her studies and is now just gaining required client hours to become registered is developing a professional website and asks her supervisor for feedback. The supervisor notes with concern that on the website the supervisee claims to be a 'psychotherapeutic counsellor' with special 'expertise' in many issues, including substance misuse and marital problems. Although the supervisee claims to be qualified in certain techniques, such as mindfulness and CBT, in reality she has only attended an introductory weekend course and has no official qualification or credentials. The supervisor gently challenges what the trainee is proposing, pointing out that she has focused on marketing while forgetting her *duty of care* – an understandable, if thoughtless, mistake. He explains that the trainee is breaching the professional code by 'misrepresenting' herself as both qualified and expert, neither of which is the case. In claiming competence that she does not yet have, she risks, at best, misleading clients; at worst, harming and exploiting them. The supervisor draws her attention to the training institute's Code of Practice, which explicitly advises students to use the terms 'counsellor in advanced training', and also to their professional code of ethics, which warns against

misrepresentation and highlights integrity and competence. He encourages her to reflect on the limits of her current competence while acknowledging her strengths. Horrified at the potential impact of her actions (set in motion by her thoughtless copying of existing websites), the student immediately edits her website. She feels grateful to her supervisor for his timely intervention. No further action is needed; a case of malpractice has been avoided.

2. **A case of malpractice** – A client goes to her therapist's professional body with a complaint that she has been 'confused, hurt and damaged' by having both a friendship *and* a therapeutic relationship with her therapist. The client alleges the existence of a dual relationship where the therapist blurred therapeutic and social boundaries. The professional body investigates, hearing evidence from both parties. The therapist admits to extending therapy sessions beyond contracted times, sending personal emails and gifts, giving her client lifts home and sharing personal details of her life. The professional body then upholds the complaint, finding that the therapist's actions amount to professional malpractice with the service provided falling below reasonable standards of care and not being in the client's interests. A sanction is applied: the therapist must evidence her learning by producing two documents: (i) a reflection on what she had learned about the issues related to the allegations; and (ii) a reflection on power differentials in relationships and the need for clear contracting and boundaries.

In more serious cases of failures of care, wider **institutional structures** are activated. In malpractice cases of 'negligence' or 'incompetence', the therapist is vulnerable to having a complaint taken out against them. This may result in their being disciplined by their professional or organisational body. A formal 'grievance' can be brought if there is a possible breach of contract, and therapists may even face legal action. While civil suits against therapists for practising outside their competence are relatively rare, the thought of being 'sued' probably scares most professionals.

Welfel (2013) helpfully points out the distinction between making ordinary mistakes (something we all do) and 'negligence', for which one can be held liable. Referring to the law in the US, she states four criteria for a court to rule in favour of the plaintiff in negligence lawsuits: (1) the professional's duty to the client must be established; (2) the professional must have breached their duty of care; (3) an injury or damage to the client must be established; and (4) harm must be caused by the therapist's mistake. The reassurance for therapists here is that the standard for liability is rigorous, with frivolous lawsuits unlikely to be successful.

Therapist *self*-care

To protect our clients and ourselves from the 'dark side' of care (and pre-empt complaints or legal action), the practice of self-care becomes an *ethical imperative.* Our self-care must be constantly monitored as our circumstances and needs evolve. We should be alert to personal warning signs that indicate a need for more self-care and back this up with supervision to help identify these points and how to respond to them. Typical warning signs include: feeling anger, resenting the client, feeling bored or day-dreaming in a session, watching the clock, ending sessions early or cancelling them too often. In addition, there are the tell-tale signs that point to mental health issues: sleep problems, low motivation, anxiety, poor diet, substance misuse, and so on.

Many professional codes contain explicit directives about the requirement for therapists to attend to their health, for example, this one is from the Federation of European Psychodrama Training Organisations:

> 1.8 In order to be fit to practice, Psychodramatists should maintain an adequate balance of emotional and physical health … as a model for other colleagues and trainees. They should not knowingly practice if their mental or physical poor health is liable to have a detrimental effect on their clients. This includes the misuse of substances… (www.fepto.com/about-fepto/constitution/code-of-ethics-and-practice)

For a quick assessment of your current level of personal care, take a look at the self-care assessment questions in Box 3.3, suggested by Kramen-Kahn (2002). Look on this as a *risk assessment* we do on ourselves. As Amis (2017) notes, risk assessments should not be seen as one-way tests performed only on clients. Such self-monitoring also needs to be an ongoing process. 'We are never done with self-care' (Barnett, 2014).

Once aware that we have a problem, we can take steps to contain the 'shadow' and activate relevant support systems. Here **supervision** is particularly important (and can be reinforced by other sources of professional support) in order to share information about our clients and ourselves, gain perspective and explore the challenges of a given case or situation. In this safe place we can off-load and be held in ways that *parallel* aspects of the therapist–client relationship in that the supervisor is experienced as relationally safe, compassionate, congruent, holding and attuned (Gilbert and Evans, 2000; Hobman, 2018). Then, together with our supervisor, we may be ready to look at different ways of handling our reactions. As Amis (2017, p. 157) reminds us:

> Exploring options, reflecting on practice, re-framing and sharing decision-making processes is not a sign of weakness or inability to cope, but a sign of professional responsibility and personal strength.

If we are struggling with an ethical dilemma, other formal supports are also available. For example, we might contact helplines offered by professional bodies or professional indemnity insurance providers. Such resources also help us adhere to professional codes which normally require us to keep abreast of developments relating to our professional responsibilities.

Beyond formal structures, we need to mirror our approach to clients, viewing ourselves holistically and with compassionate care. Writing a journal or engaging in therapeutic writing, socialising, exercising, practising mindfulness, and enjoying hobbies or leisure activities can all help us to retain perspective and meet our own internal needs (Amis, 2017).

Box 3.3   Self-care assessment

Do you:

- appear competent and professional?
- appear warm, caring and accepting?
- regularly seek case consultation with another professional while protecting confidentiality?
- at the end of a stressful day, frequently utilize self-talk to put aside thoughts of clients?
- maintain a balance between work, family and play?
- nurture a strong support network of family and friends?
- use healthy leisure activities as a way of helping yourself relax from work? If work is your whole world, watch out! You do not have a balanced life.
- often feel renewed and energized by working with clients?
- develop new interests in your professional work?
- perceive clients' problems as interesting and look forward to working with clients?
- maintain objectivity regarding clients' problems?
- maintain good boundaries with clients, allowing them to take full responsibility for their actions while providing support for change?
- use personal psychotherapy as a means of maintaining and/or improving your functioning as a psychotherapist?
- maintain a sense of humor? You can laugh with your clients.
- act in accordance with legal and ethical standards? (Kramen-Kahn, 2002, p. 12, cited in Barnett, 2014)

Concluding reflections

For Mann (2010, p. 241), the most important 'field condition' of the therapeutic relationship

> is not our ability to adhere to the rulebook, it is our attitude, our honest care for the wellbeing of our clients and our profession. We might make mistakes but in our bones we know right from wrong – what is more, I believe that our clients know that we do too.

Like Mann, I feel touched by the wonderful and extraordinary compassionate care I see many therapists offering. I'm in awe of those charged moments in therapy when therapists open themselves, in unknowingness and vulnerability, to deep transformative relational contact.

I love the concept of 'caring-with', understood as the state of being rooted in receptivity, responsiveness and reciprocity (though I appreciate that in practice such relatedness is not always possible or realistic). Similarly, I really appreciate DeYoung's work on being 'relationally validating' and having a playful, accepting, curious, empathic (PACE) connection. I also love the notion of nurturing 'power-from-within' for *both* therapists and clients. These enthusiasms of mine, I can own, stem from my humanistic, feminist stance – how we enact care depends very much on context, to which our theoretical biases contribute. The important thing is to find your own level of appropriate 'caring' for the type of work you do and to be reflexive of how you might use and abuse power.

I am saddened when I hear therapists so fear complaints that they engage in rigid rule-following, defensive practice and forget to be human/humane; and I feel compassionate when therapists' care falls short due to their own dissociation and defences. Perhaps the most important thing an effective therapist learns is the importance of *self-care*, including giving oneself time to reflect and be both supported and challenged in supervision.

We all make mistakes and misjudge things out of ignorance or thoughtlessness; the more so when we are caught up in knotty relational dynamics. However, I'm less forgiving when therapists fail to reflect on their potential to oppress and impose their own interests or needs onto another; when they claim to *know* what a client is experiencing or needs. I agree with Rowe (1989, cited in Proctor, 2002, p. 12) when she says: 'The most dangerous people in the world are those who believe they know what is best for others.'

Discussion questions

1. How do you show care to clients?
2. How do you show care to yourself?
3. What 'shadow' lurks in your process and practice?

Summary

Therapeutic care, with relational ethics to the fore, involves being human and being responsive, respectful and receptive to the other. Despite our best intentions, life challenges and pressures can grind us down, leaving us less responsive to our clients or even traumatised and burnt-out. We can also play out unhealthy relational dynamics which can result in care being subverted and turning in abusive directions. If we are not to lose our empathy, compassion, care and perspective, it becomes an ethical imperative to take our self-care seriously.

4

Living Ethics within a Social World: 'Walking the Talk'

This chapter argues for living our ethical values and principles as part of our everyday way-of-being in life rather than following 'rules' that are applicable only to therapy (Casemore, 2009). The central premise is integrity and humanity in relationships with self and others, inside and outside the therapy room. This involves more than simple concern for other individuals. It's about our wider social relations and the extent to which we care about, and collectively fight for, our wider communities and the world. It's about speaking out against inequality and injustice, engaging in anti-oppressive practice and promoting health and well-being in others.

In this chapter we move from a focus on the caring therapy relationship to thinking about the socio-cultural dimension that embeds every therapy moment. Here, the relational ethical therapist will respect clients' values and heritage – and acknowledge their own – recognising the relevance of the relational mix between therapists' and clients' social location (regarding their gender, ethnicity/race, class, religion, sexual orientation, age, disability, and so on).

This chapter starts by hearing from four therapists about how they live their ethics in the wider world. I call this '**walking the talk**'. The next two sections focus, respectively, on the linked topics of **cultural sensitivity** and **anti-oppressive practice**. The penultimate section explores the possibility of being an **agent of socio-political change**. I end with my personal take, emphasising how, in life, we can fall short of lofty ethical ideals but we can still care.

'Walking the talk'

It seems to me that our highest ethics involve a *way of being* rather than what we do. Sometimes the most ethical action is to wait, watch, hold and not do anything. It's about a disposition or orientation where we strive to promote and enact certain values (personal and socio-cultural): integrity, respect for others, humility, wisdom, justice, kindness, inclusion/diversity, and so on. It's also about trying to build compassionate, responsive relationships and communities. And, of course, we don't always fully reach these values in our everyday living.

Our values apply to our relations with the wider world, as much as to our work with clients. After all, it makes little sense to follow certain principles at work while ignoring them in daily life. Indeed, many therapeutic approaches also build in lessons for life. Carl Rogers (1980) talked of his *person-centred* approach as being a life-affirming way of being and not just a therapeutic technique (Proctor et al., 2006). He advocated treating others humanely, relating with them on a person-to-person basis, being committed to their growth and self-enhancement, and listening deeply and empathically:

> I have often noticed that the more deeply I hear the meanings of this person, the more there is that happens. Almost always, when a person realizes he has been deeply heard, his eyes moisten. ... It is as though he were saying, 'Thank God, somebody heard me.' ... He is released from his loneliness, he has become a human being again. (Rogers, 1980, p. 10)

It is not surprising to me that many relational therapists have concerns about social, political and/or environmental issues in their wider lives. Seeking to 'make a difference' and contribute to society, some live their ethics by being vegetarian or using organic products; some do charity or community work; some offer counselling to disadvantaged groups; some are politically active, engaging in protests and joining campaigns and demonstrations; some teach and encourage the next generation to think and promote ethics; some choose a spiritual path. They are all, in their own chosen ways, living their ethics by taking responsibility for their role and impact in the social and natural world.

Below, four therapists explain their ethical living:

> I used to be something of an activist for what I believed. I marched, protested, was part of groups which agitated and, for five years, volunteered for an anti-poverty non-governmental organisation. It was an exciting and challenging time. It was good to be part of what felt like a movement for change. On the other hand, my idealism did come up against harsh realities which I found difficult to cope with. I discovered I had little control in front of some very powerful and self-interested forces.

> This lack of control in the face of power mirrored situations in my childhood which had led to me being abused. I sunk into a profound depression. Healing has been a long and hard journey.

> These days I am faced with a dilemma. I still have my ethics, yet I know the interests which keep society as it is are strong. The choice I have made is to recognise what

I can do and leave the rest. For instance, irresponsibility, wilful ignorance and the primacy of profit has meant that people – whether in government, in business or as individuals – are threatening the health of our planet with the over-use of plastic. I live by the sea. On my daily walks I see how human discards are choking the environment and the wildlife. I am profoundly saddened and angered. My protest is small but meaningful to me. I organise and take part in beach cleans.

Sometimes the bigger picture is too complex, too tough, too immovable to make a dent in. We can all, however, search for an ethical way of being within our own limits within our own communities. Knowing our limits and those of our communities is also useful in the therapeutic environment. It is the art of the possible within an imperfect frame.

(Kate Evans, psychotherapeutic counsellor, UK)

I am a 'healer'; my childhood dream was to be a medical doctor; I became a psychotherapist. I had my own practice in rural Alaska for over 30 years, working with families, couples, individuals and groups. I also volunteered with Hospice groups as a trainer, teaching new volunteers how to work with their patients dealing with grief and bereavement issues. I worked with another not-for-profit agency as a volunteer to train teachers and school nurses how to provide support groups for children who had emotional or peer group challenges. I joined a local Rotary club because I wanted to make a difference in the world. Rotary is a group of business and professional people who unite to promote world understanding and peace, through service projects locally and globally. As a Rotary volunteer, I travel widely, including to Myanmar/Burma, to participate in a health care project providing preventive health information to hundreds of local villagers in the poorest part of the country, Rahkine State, and prosthetic arms to dozens of people in Yangon/Rangoon who had waited lifetimes for help. I also spent months in Russia, immediately after the Communist era, and I helped Russian Rotarians to increase their understanding of the concept of volunteer service. I visited many Russian Rotary projects, including orphanages, assisting where possible. As a systemically-oriented therapist, I know that individual efforts can positively affect families and communities.

(Vivian Finlay, licensed marriage and family therapist, US)

Throughout my 30 years of psychotherapy practice, my personal development and my mission to help others with theirs has been my highest priority. I believe in the value of doing the personal work such that we can 'be the change we wish to see in the world' (Gandhi). I have come to know myself as a woman of faith, deeply committed to living a spiritual life. My journey, like everyone's wishing to develop their higher potential, has been difficult and challenging, and wonderful and inspiring. I am rooted in my Jewish history ... honouring all that this means to me ... knowing in my core how atrociously dark 'man's inhumanity to man' can become. For me, 'ethical practice' takes on an all-important dimension seen through this lens. It becomes critical that we adhere to sound and humane values and actions, and confront our shadow: To honour, respect and value all others (human and animal) is my guiding principle ... aspiring to show kindness, understanding and compassion whenever I can.

In 2010, I learnt of a spiritual training for 'men and women deeply committed to serving people of all Faiths and no Faith' ... I felt called ... a two-year journey of challenge, difficulty, awe and joy led to my ordination in 2012 as an interfaith minister. Since then I have become a Buddhist, a mindfulness practitioner and teacher, and most recently a vegan, while continuing as a psychotherapist. I am a trustee of a charity promoting reconciliation and peace.

Veganism, for me, encapsulates my respect and valuing of all life, my passionate love of animals – and well illustrates the need to *daily renew our commitment to act from our 'highest aspirations'*. Whatever our values or ethics, 'temptation to stray' is all around us. ... On a recent holiday to a prime culinary area for fresh fish (my past favourite) ... a fierce internal battle ensued ... 'to eat or not to eat fish'. I didn't eat. But I had to work at it.

(Barbara Payman, psychotherapist, UK)

I am a woman of colour and bi-sexual. I have always fought for the rights of any minority groups. My values place acceptance and respect of diversity highly. People should feel free to become who they are or want to be. This is the value that I take into my psychotherapy practice.

I have signed petitions, gone on marches and spoken out at various conferences and events over the last 20 years in favour of same-sex marriages and, more recently, against conversion therapy, which I see as both pseudo-scientific and institutionalized child abuse. I am proud to be an Ontarian and that our state finally banned conversion therapy in 2015. That 37 out of 53 countries in the Commonwealth still criminalize homosexuality shows us there is still work to be done.

I admire the current LBGTQI movement. If I were younger I would probably come out and call myself 'queer' to flag up gender identity and politics beyond sexuality. I am ashamed to admit that I haven't the courage to do this now at my ripe old age and given my ethnicity. I have disclosed my sexuality to clients on two occasions (mostly I wouldn't) when I knew they were struggling with their own identity and they asked me about mine. Times are changing. Younger professionals seem more open now and they have different political fights to put their energies into.

(Name withheld, clinical psychologist, Canada)

Over to you: What do you 'care about'? In what direction does your **moral compass** point? What values, motivations, concerns, priorities and principles provide you with ongoing guidance in your life generally? To what extent have you been aware of these? Have they morphed over time?

Being culturally sensitive and engaging in anti-oppressive practice

In common with many professional codes, the American Psychological Association (APA) lists 'social justice, diversity, and inclusion' as a subset of the Association's core values. Similarly, APA journals try to support inclusion, promote diversity and be broadly representative by publishing a range of contributions. How successful they have been is beyond the scope of this chapter; I simply want to highlight the values promoted. The starting point is cultural sensitivity, which can be extended to embrace anti-oppressive practice.

Cultural sensitivity

Cultural sensitivity is expressed through therapists showing openness to other ideas and refraining from imposing their own **cultural values** on clients (Johannes and Erwin, 2004). It involves showing awareness of the importance of people's (sub-)cultural and intergenerational backgrounds and respecting diversity through culturally-adapted or responsive interventions. There is a 'strength in owning one's ignorance and naiveté about other cultures' and showing a willingness to learn (Alleyne, 2011).

A culturally sensitive therapist working with a client from another culture needs an extensive range of working competences. They may make a point of learning something of the client's beliefs, social practices and language. They may strive for a better understanding of cultural differences, for example, different notions of wellness/illness and help-seeking behaviour. It's about educating oneself and having an intention to try to understand. And they will also seek to explore their own biases and predilections. They also may need to be able to work with interpreters or to tap into the knowledge of cultural informants. A culturally sensitive and competent therapist is also reflexive about their own limitations and about the impact of wider social-cultural aspects on the therapy relationship (Lago, 2011). More than this, there is an embracing of humanity, and an instinctive humility in the face of other traditions and practices.

In the following case example of couples' work, the therapist [Golnar Bayat] brings cultural assumptions to the fore as she tries to open up space for her clients (Marwan and Mary) to talk about their cultural values. The focus of the work was to help them recognise their clashing beliefs, assumptions and expectations about the meanings of, for example, 'togetherness' and 'closeness', and how they demonstrated their love in different ways:

> There were facets of what Marwan described particularly to do with notions of honouring his family, duty towards his mother, obligation towards his unmarried sisters and commitment to economically supporting his siblings, that puzzled and infuriated Mary. ... Those were moments when my cultural familiarity with Marwan's elevation of interdependence between his small family of Mary and himself and his greater family back at home, and my familiarity with Mary's elevation of the needs of her small family unit above all others, allowed me to hold the frame so that Mary and Marwan's differing definitions of what constituted 'family' could emerge into the forefront of their dialogue with each other. Similarly, Marwan could explore what he meant by the 'coldness' that he experienced in his relationship with Mary and her family. Mary had heard this as an accusation and felt scolded by it but when explored it became clear that Marwan was referring to the absence of the close physical contact he had been socialized into ... which in turn Mary experienced as 'too close and intrusive'. (Nanda and Bayat, 2013, pp. 224–225)

Similarly, consider the following dialogue involving an unqualified translator, which also shows how meanings can get lost in translation and have important clinical implications. (Of course, such miscommunications can equally occur when we're speaking in the same language!).

Clinician to Chinese-speaking client: What has your mood been like?

Interpreter to client (in Chinese): How have you been feeling?

Client (in Chinese): I don't have any more pain, my stomach is fine now, and I can eat much better since taking the medication.

Interpreter to clinician: She says she feels fine, no problems. (adapted from Marcos, 1979, p. 173)

[For further information on working with interpreters, see the excellent online resource from Victoria Transcultural Mental Health (2017).]

For a different example, consider the *evidence-based practice movement*. Kousteni (2018) presents a critique of the current research evidence base, arguing that it pays insufficient attention to wider social factors related to diversity and, as a result, compromises treatments for minority populations. This 'context of discrimination', she argues, is dominated by an individualistic perspective of mental health which regards symptoms as the result of biological and/or personal dysfunction. And as most research is conducted with white, educated, middle-class participants, questions need to be raised about the extent to which findings can be generalised to ethnic minorities and wider world communities. She calls for a different framework of evidence-based psychotherapy which includes contextual factors (societal and relational) that influence both the client and therapy process. Do you agree with her?

I value being culturally aware and sensitive. However, there are tensions here that complicate the process. When acknowledging cultural differences, it's easy to fall into the trap of making gross **stereotypical assumptions**. Are we showing prejudice when we ask someone who has a different colour or accent 'Where are you from?' or if they 'eat Western food'? These could be respectful questions; they might also be experienced as racism. Is a hearing person showing prejudice by assuming the deaf person who signs would choose to join the hearing world after a cochlear implant? Is it wrong to assume that a white, middle-class male holds power and authority? Not every white, middle-class male feels powerful. Yet maybe some would. At times it can feel hard to get it 'right'.

Things get even more complicated when there is a **clash of values** arising from different sub-cultures. Consider how some religious groups are against homosexuality and end up supporting the oppression of gay people. Or what about those who are 'pro-life' who vilify women who choose to have an abortion? The point is that we *live among tensions* that are often impossible to resolve. The best we can hope to achieve is a position of being curious and open to others and remaining relatively unknowing about their cultural heritage.

Anti-oppressive practice

Anti-oppressive theory and practice focuses on **social justice** and the need to challenge socio-economic oppression in all its forms. Therapists who engage in anti-oppressive practice aim to be inclusive, to respect diversity and to challenge power imbalances at every level, whether those inherent in the therapy relationship or in the client's wider social context. These therapists acknowledge the political domain more explicitly both within and outside the therapy relationship. As you read on, you'll have to decide where you stand and whether anti-oppressive practice fits your value system.

Aileen Alleyne (2011) argues that **prejudice** and discrimination are so pervasive that none of us is immune from them. Presented below are some examples she provides of the subtle racism and hidden racial prejudice that can manifest in therapy. It's important to remember that similar problems arise in relation to other prejudices: for example, against people with particular religious beliefs, or alternative gender identity, or those with a disability.

1. Pre-judging and holding negative thoughts about clients based simply on foreign-sounding names.
2. Ignoring or not checking out how to pronounce foreign names.
3. Failing to notice or avoid the client's race (i.e. being 'colour blind'), thereby ignoring both human diversity and the individual.
4. Showing indifference to a client's specific cultural and racial experiences.
5. Assessing black minorities as not having the capacity to introspect or relate to symbolism.
6. Assessing the clients as resistant or avoidant because they focus more on family rather than on 'I' (which would be the more typically Western focus).
7. Assuming all members of a racial group will adhere to similar cultural norms.
8. Assuming every black person is scarred by oppression.
9. Fixing the other as 'different', as in 'I don't expect you to know much about rural England'.

As Alleyne argues, these subtle forms of racism can be both culturally oppressive and infantilising. She gives the following case example of an incident that was explored during her own experience of receiving therapy:

> I recalled being asked by my white therapist how I was feeling about a very painful and challenging situation I had recently negotiated in a psychotherapy training experiential group. It involved me, the only black student ... being the recipient of a white student's racist projection. ... My white colleague brought to the ... group session, a dream she declared she couldn't make sense of. She described her terror at being attacked by a big black gorilla. ... All eyes were turned towards me, some darting, others lingering in an embarrassed and accusatory way...

> The incident triggered and re-opened other painful experiences of being subtly targeted because of my race and it was as if I had been re-wounded in the same place...

> In responding to my therapist's question of how I was feeling about the difficult experiential group situation, I shared with her that although I was deeply affected by the unpleasant event, I had remained strong. I communicated that I was pleased with myself for being able to challenge the facilitator for his lack of intervention and

not utilizing the situation to deal head on with real underlying conflicts of race and culture differences in the group. I described to her a personal technique employed when faced with adversity – a tip from my dear mother, which is to call upon our ancestors to wrap their arms around you in times of need. ... I let my therapist know about a family script that had helped me to remember that I was truly loved as a human being...

I felt I had built up a safe relationship in the nine months of working with my therapist, and was looking – at least initially – for a warm, empathetic and supportive reaction to my traumatic experiences in the training group. Instead, I received a bald and cold response which was, 'you clearly utilized a lot of mechanisms to shore yourself up ... are we in danger of being a bit holier than thou?' (Alleyne, 2011, pp. 120–121)

Alleyne felt smacked in the face by her therapist. It made her reluctant to share other personal pains and achievements. Of course, as therapists, we can all make 'mistakes' or get caught up in a process, resulting in our intervention striking the wrong note. What we don't hear from Alleyne is whether she and her therapist ever repaired the rupture – and if the therapist owned and reviewed her ungenerous approach.

Therapists concerned with anti-oppressive practice will aim to monitor any stray thoughts which move towards subtle racism and/or being dehumanising. It's about asking questions and not making assumptions. At its most political, it's about actively challenging oppression when it is witnessed. Would you agree with Alleyne when she says that not challenging racism perpetuates it; we become part of the problem and not the solution?

I personally do agree. This is not a matter of 'political correctness' (a politically-loaded term often deployed to deny the reality of discrimination and oppression). Rather, it's about teasing out and challenging lurking pernicious beliefs while finding the balance between challenge and respect for others' positions. It's about interrogating one's use of language, which may subtly perpetuate prejudice or oppression. It's also about handling other people's bigoted projections and defensive responses (for instance, the way people can be 'colour blind' or avoid discussions about diversity) while nudging them to a deeper critical consciousness. I like Mark McConville's message:

My advice to myself: the work is not, paradoxically, to make myself a paragon of racial blindness; the work is to discover how I participate, and how I have participated, in the racist culture that blinds me. (2005, p. 15)

In a broad research study investigating how to teach multicultural sensitivity and diversity (see Box 4.1), a female Asian faculty member takes up these points:

Despite challenges and frustrations, it is also extremely rewarding witnessing the powerful transformation in students as they move from confusion, resistance, anger, and negativity, to courage and risk taking in challenging themselves, classmates, family members, and friends. I see my role as that of a cultural guide. Through difficult dialogues, I create opportunities for students to develop an antiracist perspective, assisting them in understanding the source of their hostility, shame, guilt, resistance, and fear. This requires me to exercise patience, support, and encouragement while simultaneously being the 'devil's advocate'—constantly challenging them and enhancing their awareness and sensitivity about race and culture so they evolve to be proactive in speaking out against racism in their personal and professional lives. (Chung et al., 2018, p. 223)

Research such as that cited in Box 4.1 reminds us how we get socialised into anti-oppressive practice. There is a role here for training institutions and professional bodies, both to set standards and to monitor practices. However, while arguing for the promotion and monitoring of anti-oppressive practice by professional bodies, Gilbert and Orlans (2011) also see it as a *moral issue* – as something individual practitioners might tussle with. In other words, we need to work out *where we stand as individual therapists*, and how to apply our stance in specific personal-relational-cultural contexts.

Box 4.1   Promoting dialogue about race

Chung RC-Y, Bemak F, Talleyrand RM and Williams JM (2018) Challenges in promoting race dialogues in psychology training: Race and gender perspectives. *The Counseling Psychologist 46*(2): 213–240.

Recognising the currently unstable racial climate in the US, four ethnically diverse faculty members engaged in a qualitative 'self-study' of their multicultural teaching practices. By critically analysing their narratives and group discussions, they explored the challenges inherent in participating in what they call 'authentic race dialogues' and suggest how to promote these dialogues in psychology training. While each faculty member had unique experiences, their common experience included how they all needed to:

1. establish credibility with students early on – 'Our narratives suggest that sharing our personal experiences of race and racism with students while demonstrating a critical consciousness and understanding of issues of privilege, power, biases, oppression, and discrimination, promotes faculty credibility.' (p.231)
2. process emotional reactions (including monitoring triggers and countertransference of self and students) – 'It is essential for us to be aware of, and acknowledge, our own race dialogue triggers by constantly monitoring our own emotions throughout the race dialogue process.' (p.232)
3. create safe brave spaces when facilitating race dialogues in the classroom – 'Given that race dialogues can become highly emotional and evolve into feelings of anger, fear, frustration, resistance, annoyance, or guilt…, it is important to generate a safe and trusting space where students are comfortable expressing feelings and viewpoints, sharing their stories, and challenging each other in a respectful, open, and honest manner.' (p.232)

Being agents of socio-political change

As I write (in 2018), certain global socio-political trends are apparent. Disenchanted electorates are being seduced by authoritarianism (often involving a strong, centralised state), anti-immigrant nativism (prioritising the interests of the 'native-born') and resurgent populism (the view that there are two groups in society: the people and the corrupt elite). Democracy and good governance are being undermined by the widening gap between rich and poor, the self-interested actions of powerful elites and the placing of corrosive greed and profit before people and social good. Aided by the internet, the media is becoming weaponised and corrupted as purveyors of news and information manipulate, incite hatred and support naked hyper-partisanship which plays on people's fears and prejudices. In addition, the use of social media is turning in increasingly narcissistic directions. On top of everything, the ravaging of the global environment continues apace, beneath the looming spectre of global warning. Just two decades into the twenty-first century, our world seems riven by segregation, exclusion, division, discrimination, prejudice, racism, xenophobia, mass immigration, terrorism, modern slavery and war.

What can we, as therapists, do to counteract this daunting state of affairs? Should we even try? The new *UKCP Draft Code of Ethics* (2018a) advises therapists to: 'Uphold human rights, promote equality and respect diversity, practise self-enquiry, and challenge prejudice or improper discrimination in yourself or others.' Applying this in practice isn't always straightforward, however. As Proctor et al. (2006) note, the connections between *person-centred* approaches and politics is complicated, particularly when approaches of non-judgemental, unconditional respect of individuals obscures structural inequalities which need challenging.

Over several decades, *gestaltist* Philip Lichtenberg has argued against divisive forces and in favour of promoting egalitarian goals. He has highlighted the importance of having open, curious *I–Thou* dialogue in everyday life as something that can change society, for example, by challenging bigotry based on projections. Similarly, other relational therapists focus on the power of relationship to build bridges and heal division. Lynne Gabriel, in an interview with Brown (2017) argues that 'counsellors are perfectly placed to be "change agents"', at both the micro and macro levels From their frontline position, she says, counsellors are well placed to challenge such notions as 'there is no such thing as society' and work to better our communities. Would you agree? Do you think we have a role to 'mend the world' and offer some 'social healing' (Melnick and Nevis, 2009)?

In his Presidential Address for Counseling Psychologists (February 20, 2018), Martin Heesacker, Professor of Psychology at the University of Florida, opted to present an explicit political critique of the policies of the serving US President, Donald Trump:

> The Trump administration's anti-Muslim and anti-immigrant rhetoric, its failure to support the rights of transgender people, its approval of the Dakota Access and Keystone oil pipelines in native and environmentally sensitive lands, and its emphasis

on law and order and celebrating police brutality a couple of weeks ago over Black Lives Matter, all represent threats to member diversity and to our diverse members, so we must respectfully but effectively overcome and counteract these sentiments and actions. (Heesacker, 2018, p. 82)

The group *Psychologists for Social Change* (www.psychchange.org/) has recently highlighted key aspects of the impact of 'austerity' measures in the UK on public mental health in their 'briefing paper' compiled by McGrath et al. (n.d.). Noting that the top thousand richest people in UK have as much wealth as the poorest 40% combined, they argue that 'equality is the best therapy', and that power and privilege can no longer be ignored.

It is imperative to take into account the psychological costs of austerity for individuals and communities. ... There is clear and robust research linking recent austerity policies with damaging psychological outcomes. ... Mental health problems are associated with markers of low income and social economic status in all the developed nations. ... Since the financial crisis, suicides have increased in European countries that have adopted austerity policies (UK, Greece, Spain and Portugal), but not in those who have protected their welfare state (Iceland and Germany). (McGrath et al., n.d.)

If you're interested in such work in support of social change, check out forums like this and also journals such as *Psychotherapy and Politics International* or *The Journal of Critical Psychology* or *Politics and Psychology*. The *Free Psychotherapy Network* also points to many relevant resources and discussions: https://freepsychotherapynetwork.com/.

Another example of social action by a therapist is provided by Erene Hadjiioannou, a psychotherapist and integrative *psychodynamic* counsellor. When interviewed by the UKCP about her work with Support After Rape and Sexual Violence Leeds (SARSVL), she explained how these roles had allowed her to align herself in a more explicitly political way, enabling her to become a therapist and activist working in the service of her clients beyond the therapy room:

We live with complexity in our everyday lives, so we need to really engage with it as much as we can in service of our clients, particularly around sexual violence. There is so much focus on the micro aggression that women face and dispelling the myths around rape and sexual violence, I think that's a responsibility we have outside of the therapy room as well as inside. This is especially important as women will internalise these myths, and these manifest as the blame, shame, and guilt that are seen in a particular way when working with sexual violence. (Hadjiioannou, quoted in UKCP, 2018b)

In this example, Hadjiioannou is engaging explicitly with politics and power in her passionate fight against women's oppression. Do you value her stance? Or do you think therapists seeking a more accepting, tolerant, non-judgemental stance should stay politically neutral and non-partisan?

Or perhaps you're simply not interested in politics? Back in the 1990s, I taught a foundation degree course on social science which included politics.

Students' responses varied. Some admitted they shut down when it came to politics; it was 'boring', they said, mentioning their greater interest in individual psychology. Since then I've met therapists who have said similar things. This challenges my own values. At one level, I want to *respect* their preferences; I don't want to imply they are 'wrong' in some way. However, I do believe that it is 'better' to be socially aware and politically informed. It's not just about *Politics* (big P) to do with governments; *politics* (small P) concerns issues around power.

I certainly think it is vital for the development of ourselves as practitioners (and as a profession) to at least think about wider social aspects and to talk with others about how these impact on our therapy (Proctor et al., 2006). And what is my remit as a therapist? Should I just concentrate on listening to my clients as individuals or should I be acknowledging the political domain? Should we celebrate diversity and work towards social justice? Regardless, we also have a role to play in safeguarding the interests and welfare of our clients beyond the therapy room. *There may come a time when they need us to raise our voices in support.*

Concluding reflections

Caring, as therapists and as people, is broader than simply relating with a client. I like Levin's reminder of this broader landscape of care:

> The activity of psychotherapy is an invitation to sacred ground. A healer for our times is required to care for the environment and community by addressing a range of socioeconomic issues such as globalization as well as the transpersonal and spiritual interiority of people's souls. (Levin, 2010, p. 147)

In this time of rampantly polarised social conflict, environmental threat, war (both military and ideological), and some would say 'moral bankruptcy', it could be argued (and I do) that we need urgently to re-establish some ethical touchstones. This applies to us as individuals as well as to us as professionals and global citizens. More than ever, I think we need to remind ourselves to *care*, to reflect and question our assumptions, and to engage in social dialogue and debate. Perhaps we can use social media and professional forums as arenas in which we can become better informed, maybe as a prelude to action?

I am still working out how to live my ethics and 'walk my talk'. I know that I frequently fail: I inadvertently hurt others and I don't do enough in and for the world. I *want* to be human and humane in my interactions; to engage in the type of caring that is rooted in relationship, responsiveness and receptivity rather than enacted through duty or habit. My commitment to dialogue, openness and sharing is the base of my idea of being a reflexive, culturally sensitive – even transcultural – therapist. Given my own multi-heritage background, cultural diversity and respect of difference and alternative perspectives will always be a priority for me. I also want to make a difference, to contribute positively to my community and society. I can only try to do this one encounter at a time.

With my belief in anti-oppressive practice, I *try* to challenge discrimination, prejudice and oppression where I see them. I am no less passionate about political causes and want to fight pernicious social divisions and corrupt power structures. However, here I'm usually less vocal, so probably less effective. At the same time, I am cautious about imposing my own values and also wonder if there is a danger of being too explicitly political with, or in the presence of, clients as they could react negatively. I'm still working out the balance. Although in my small private practice I make a caring contribution to healing the ravages of abuse and trauma, I admire those who raise their voices more loudly and work at the frontline with oppressed groups, such as with refugees, modern slaves and victims of torture. In this chapter I have sought to promote dialogue and reflection on social justice by voicing some of these wider socio-political concerns.

Our lack of 'perfection' probably stares us in the face every day. Most of us will have come into the therapy field carrying emotional baggage, having left a trail of existential wreckage behind us. In life, we'll have taken numerous ethically dubious actions, in ignorance, thoughtlessness or sometimes choicefully. Perhaps we carry regrets about our younger selves: times when we manipulated or hurt others, in or out of awareness. Some of us will have committed various petty crimes or lied and cheated when younger or under the influence of (legal and illegal) substances. Perhaps now we're burdened by an awareness of the gulf between our earlier behaviour and our current values. I know this applies to my own life. I can only recognise that I'm work-in-progress and that my values are continually being re-worked and updated.

Ethics remains something to aspire to; all we can do is hope we don't trip up too much as we live our everyday lives. I take comfort from knowing it is our very humanity that allows us to be flawed (Casemore, 2009).

Discussion questions

1. What transcultural competences would be helpful for working in a diverse multi-cultural area?
2. How might lingering prejudices impact on your practice?
3. How do you 'walk your talk' and engage ethics in your life?

Summary

All therapy relationships are embedded in a given socio-cultural context, one which involves a web of wider social relations. Beyond showing sensitivity to people's cultural background, we confront the question of our relationship with our wider communities and the world. To what extent should we involve ourselves in action for change? Here we might consider taking a more active stance to promote health and well-being in others by speaking out against inequality and injustice and engaging anti-oppressive practice.

PART II

RELATIONAL ETHICS WITHIN THE THERAPEUTIC RELATIONSHIP

Preamble

> Ethics has to be the first philosophy when considering the therapeutic relation-
> ship. (Charura and Paul, 2014, p. xxi)

Therapists aim to provide an emotionally caring, protective, facilitating space which respects and holds the client safely while simultaneously ensuring emergent emotional and physical responses are contained in ethical, professional ways. For example, the client must trust their therapist to keep them safe while they express overwhelming and potentially explosive feelings or explore past behaviour they consider too shameful, painful or private to be shared with anyone. The holding-containing-boundarying process is more than technique and protocols; it is a co-created relational process in which the therapist attunes to client need and the context while remaining grounded and present as a therapist. Clients can be harmed when containing/holding boundaries become too loose (unduly permissive) or tight (oppressive).

The chapters in this section explore the complex ethical and clinical judgements demanded by the relational therapy process, from first contact to holding, containing, boundarying and then eventually to endings. The point emphasised throughout is the need to move beyond simple adherence to rules. Therapy needs to be shaped by the specific situation in all its complexity: individual, relational, theoretical and social.

5

'First Contact': Creating Ethical Therapeutic Spaces

The initial stage of therapy involves far more than just the application of assessment and contracting procedures. Meeting a client for the first time, establishing a rapport with them, and negotiating how therapy will proceed, involves a complicated process which goes to the heart of relational-ethical practice.

This chapter focuses on this early contact we have with clients and considers what we can do to ensure a safe, therapeutic space for both client and therapist. The first section looks at what happens in the **first meeting**, while the second explores the nature of the **therapeutic spaces** we create. The ethical dimensions of how we conduct **assessments and plan therapy** are then discussed. The penultimate section focuses on the legal and practical aspects of **contracting**. The chapter follows the pattern of ending with concluding reflections.

First meeting

Contact between therapist and client starts with the initial telephone call or email enquiry or referral. The ethical principle at stake is one of *integrity*: we have responsibility as therapists to represent ourselves and the service we offer professionally and accurately. The Australian Counselling Association (2015, p. 5) states it as:

3.1.a Counsellors have both a duty of care and a responsibility not to mislead, misguide or misdirect [either overtly by publication or covertly by omission] clients as to the counsellor's level of competence. To do so is considered to be a most serious ethical breech as it increases the risk of harm to the client and damages the credibility of the profession in the eyes of the general public.

Here is also our **duty of care** and commitment to promoting the client's well-being, or at least not making things worse. Does it sound as if the person will benefit from therapy and are they ready for it? Are we the right person for them? Most major codes of practice emphasise therapist *competence* and the imperative to recognise our limits. For instance, the BACP *Ethical Framework for the Counselling Professions* (2018a, p. 6) highlights the requirement to work to professional standards by:

a.   working within our competence
b.   keeping our skills and knowledge up to date
c.   collaborating with colleagues to improve the quality of what is being offered to clients
d.   ensuring that our wellbeing is sufficient to sustain the quality of the work
e.   keeping accurate and appropriate records

Then comes the process of inviting the prospective client into the therapy space. Here the therapist tries to be appropriately open, warm and welcoming: a gracious 'host' offering a special kind of spacious 'hospitality':

The guest of the client comes seeking sanctuary, a safe place of protection where wounds can be carefully cleansed and healed. But where is the sanctuary, if not fundamentally in the heart of the host or therapist who is willing to face this living encounter and courageously open to it? (Kapitan, 2003, p. 74)

When a client first walks into your therapy room, they bring with them uncertainty, confusion and all their defensive structures. Why should they trust us? Why should they take the risk of exposing themselves to a relative stranger? What might enable them to open up, face their inner demons, and join us in a process of exploration and discovery? What might stop them from committing to therapy?

If answers are to be found to all these questions, the primary need is to create a safe, boundaried, reassuring, permission-giving space which allows vulnerability. Moursund and Erskine (2004, p. 109) explain:

The client needs to know that his [sic] therapist is trustworthy and competent and has his best interests at heart; but beyond that he needs the visceral experience of having his physical and emotional vulnerabilities protected. He needs to know that he will be neither humiliated nor pathologized as he begins to reveal his most secret thoughts and feelings.

In this first meeting, therapist and client seek to establish whether they can work together. There is a lot to process in these early moments of contact. As the two parties exchange information, they size one another up, drawing on their own experience as well as intuition. Stern and colleagues (2003, p. 25) liken this process to an animal-like dance of mutual sniffing out through 'inter-subjective searching, improvising, and co-creating'.

There are many clues to attend to, coming from what the person is saying explicitly and/or from their body language. There are also those subtle clues that emerge more intuitively in the encounter at both the intersubjective and the transferential level. Meanwhile, the client is doing their own sensing. Very likely they are wondering if they can trust us to keep them safe and work effectively with them.

Even at this early stage, it may help the client to be given **hope** that some-thing can be done and/or that research shows therapy can be effective regard-ing their particular situation. At the very least we have the obligation to indicate the nature and limits of the therapy being offered.

As the client tells their story we are pulled in. We become alert to the issues and vulnerabilities which seem figural and might in time become the focus of therapy. In these first moments we are also invited into a relationship in which we touch, and are touched by, the other. Sometimes we can find ourselves reacting in unexpected ways. Perhaps we sense being invited to repeat the client's early script patterns (such as being pulled to be a critical parent). With the potential for such counter-transferences and projective identifications, the work of the therapy begins (Clarkson, 2003). It's about trusting the process and believing the therapy is going in the direction it needs to.

All this suggests that *our **relational-ethical** obligation is focused on the rela-tionship itself*, rather than on our efforts to attend to the client's presenting pathology. As I talk with a new client, it may be that their manner (for exam-ple, whether they seem shy, distant, adversarial, puffed-up or keen to share with me) is of greater interest to me than their emerging pathology. What does contact with this person feel like? Do I feel denigrated, pushed away, leaned on...? As I focus on the 'between', what strikes me as particularly significant? What is it like for me to be with this client, who is (perhaps) tense, scared, shy, embarrassed, angry, seductively charming, playful, silent...? Am I finding it difficult to concentrate? Is this particular response of mine being hooked in some way? Subsequent work will then home in on what is continuing to be enacted in the relationship. A key area to explore (both now and in future therapy) is the extent to which the client's *particular* way of being in relation-ship is replicated outside the therapy room.

Risk assessment

One pressing issue that therapists are alert to in these early stages relates to **risk**. Is the client in danger of harming themselves or others? Are they con-templating suicide? (The predictive link between self-harm and suicide is sig-nificant.) Is there a history of trauma and abuse? Is there a child protection issue at stake? What kind of self-care do they currently engage in? Some therapists will ask explicit questions about lifestyle (for instance, drug use, alcohol consumption and dietary patterns). Others will have specific risk assessment forms they are required to go through with the client, as in the case of those using the CORE (Clinical Outcomes for Routine Examination) system.

Alongside risk, we also assess degrees of **resilience**. What helps to mitigate the risk and help the person do well under adversity? Here we'd look for the person's values, strengths and internal supports as well as external supports in terms of people and community resources.

Whatever initial interview questions are asked – and these will vary according to the therapist's modality, the individuals involved and the institutional context – it is important the therapist feels able to ask direct questions. This sets the tone for future interaction by signalling the therapist's desire for honest **collaboration** that is as open as possible. For example, if I feel reluctant to ask whether someone is self-harming, that in itself is informative. My reluctance might encourage me to wonder about the client's level of shame, or the possibility that some avoidant pattern is being recreated. I might even bring that into the open: 'I'm aware that I'm feeling reluctant to probe too hard about how much self-harming you're doing; yet it's important for us to be able to talk about this. I'm wondering if this is something you find hard to talk about?'

Discussion can then take place about the *meanings* of the **self-harm**. Is it a way of expressing emotion and is self-soothing (i.e. a distorted self-care strategy to survive) or a result of feeling actively suicidal (a strategy for self-annihilation) or something in between? Some individuals self-harm simply to feel something, to feel alive, instead of dissociated, desensitised, cut-off. The point is to listen, rather than to assume we already know their reasons.

This search for meanings is the start of turning the 'therapy space' into a 'therapeutic' one.

Hospitable therapeutic spaces?

The therapy space we invite the client to enter as a 'guest' is both a professional and metaphorical space. It grounds and holds client *and* therapist safely via norms which differ from those 'outside'. It is a facilitating, contained, private, healing environment in which it is safe enough for clients to express themselves openly – in ways that might be too painful or shaming or even taboo elsewhere. Outside the therapy space lurk fear, struggle, difficulty and danger; within its inner sanctum, trust and care hopefully prevail. It is also a place of challenge, experimentation and learning. For some, the therapy space is the only place where they allow themselves to be honest, vulnerable, protected and supported. It can also be a place of pain, resistance, struggle and battle, be it with emotions or with the therapist. To help the client face their inner tensions and darkness, the therapist tries to create a space of hospitality – *a relational home* – where the client can feel held, accepted, supported, respected, resourced, empathised with and challenged to grow (Finlay, 2016a). Then we try to deepen the space so there is room for the client and their process to emerge.

In my own creation of therapeutic space, I think of **'SPACE'** to represent our relational way of being. This stands for: Supportiveness, Playfulness, Acceptance, Curiosity and Empathy (see Box 5.1). I've taken this from Daniel Hughes' original formulation of PACE, applied in his family-based approach to helping children to establish a secure attachment to caregivers (see www. danielhughes.org/p.a.c.e..html).

Box 5.1 Therapeutic 'SPACE'?

The acronym SPACE encompasses several creatively-enacted, interlinked elements:

Supportiveness stands for the sensitive, compassionate, caring way of being therapists embrace when offering an emotional scaffold for clients to help with their well-being, resilience and recovery.

Playfulness involves lightness; warm spontaneity, gentle smiles, teasing and humour can all offer an antidote to heavy intensity and shame.

Acceptance helps a client feel seen, validated and not criticised.

Curiosity shows the therapist cares and wants to understand the client better. Together, client and therapist go exploring to make sense of experience.

Empathy concerns being responsively attuned, where therapists sense and feel into their clients' worlds.

Over time, the nature, focus and feel of the therapy space can change. *Existential* psychotherapist Ernesto Spinelli (2015) describes three stages that occur: Stage 1 is where the therapist hears and sees the client as fully as possible; Stage 2 is where the client is accepted in the presence of another and thus experiences an 'I' (the self) which may be different from the 'I' outside; Stage 3 is where the client takes the experience of therapy space and relationship back out into the outside world. This gradual movement of the therapeutic focus away from clients telling their story and sharing inner experience towards consideration of how clients are relating in their life relationships is most evident in longer-term work. There is less space in brief therapy to explore the person's life story, with work usually limited to fostering resilience and coping resources for 'outside'.

As the **physical therapy space** is the client's first point of contact with their therapist, it's important to have a private, reasonably comfortable space protected from intrusions and external noise. However, therapists working in units or institutions often have little control over their physical environment. One client came to me saying they had to end their previous therapy as the venue had changed. Their new room had a large internal window which meant any passer-by could see what was happening in the therapy. Clearly, this felt exposing and insufficiently safe and confidential.

Therapists who have a private therapy room will often work diligently to ensure the space is welcoming and capable of setting a client at ease. Calming colours, cushions and soft throws can help create a cosseting atmosphere, while professionalism can be underlined by the presence of books and displays of certificates. Other therapists might opt for an open, uncluttered space that invites 'free-play' and creative self-expression. What is crucial is what this physical environment may be communicating. While a dingy, musty-smelling room may convey neglect, a space that is overly clean and clinical may strike the client as cold and difficult to relax in. (See Gale (2015), who provides numerous ideas for creating therapeutic spaces and actual photos of lovely therapy rooms.)

What happens when the client first enters the room? If the therapist wants to convey a sense of acceptance and client autonomy, they can let the client make the next decisions: where to sit or whether to remove their shoes. The seating itself is relevant, too. What does the chair/couch/floor cushion feel like to sit in and what does the seating communicate about the relationship?

Clients with a history of trauma may be more vigilant and wary when first entering the room. They may choose to sit near a door or need time to check out the environment. I remember one client who, when we changed our therapy venue, needed to take several minutes to touch everything in the room – a ritual to help her feel safe and grounded. Other clients may be fully focused on their inner turmoil or on the therapist, with little conscious awareness of their surroundings.

I once attended an experiential professional development workshop held at a hotel. The trainer was visiting from another country and most group members were strangers. It took the first day before participants began to feel safe enough to work together. The trainer accepted some responsibility, owning that she too had felt 'out of place', resulting in her doing more lecturing than the group needed. She lost sight of the group and did not hold the group process. By openly discussing this, the group came together, eventually becoming a supportive container itself.

We could also consider taking therapy beyond the confines of a room. The growing field of ecopsychology or **ecotherapy** promotes using natural environments therapeutically to improve quality of life. Often driven by values and ethics concerning the environment, the work deepens connections between human and non-human worlds. Research has shown how exposure to nature can have a positive effect on mental and spiritual health (see Boxes 5.2 and 5.3). Therapeutic activities include animal-assisted therapy, horticultural therapy, eco-dreamwork, green exercise, wilderness therapy, conservation activity, and so on. *Wild Therapy* (Totton, 2011) engages how therapy might contribute to changing our relationship with the ecosystem while seeking to reintroduce into therapy more wildlessness, boundlessness, spontaneity and passion. Alternatively, nature can be brought into the therapy room imaginally (for example, through nature-guided mindfulness) or via 'homework exercises' or through the presence of a pleasing garden view. With all these alternative possibilities, extra care needs to be taken to find ways to ensure confidentiality, safety and containment.

Box 5.2 Equine therapy: 'Amy'

'Amy' was a 16-year-old girl who had battled anorexia nervosa and depression for several years and was actively self-harming (cutting). She had been exposed to many therapies, but none had broken through sufficiently to enable her to sustain recovery. She was referred to an existential-integrative therapist who offered equine-facilitated therapy. The 'co-therapist' here was multiple: a field of horses, themselves scarred by having been brutally attacked by a man with a machete.

Amy arrived at the facility on a hot Virginia summer's day wearing a thick, long-sleeved top. As we walked into the paddock where the horses were grazing, I noticed her pulling at the ends of her sleeves. Her eyes were downcast and her breathing was shallow, but she fixed a smile on her face in answer to every question I asked. The horses were at the opposite end of the paddock, about a hundred feet away from where we stood, when she noticed their injuries. I told her what had happened the day before as she stood rooted to the spot, transfixed by their scars, but still continuing to pull her sleeves down over her hands.

VL: I notice how you're pulling your sleeves over your hands.

Amy: Yeah, it's a bad habit I have. I feel self-conscious of my scars.

Amy pauses and squints at the horses still grazing in the distance; I wait to see what meaning she is making from seeing their scars.

VL: What do you see?

Amy: They don't seem to care about their scars. They don't seem to be paying any attention to us either.

VL: No, they don't seem to. Would you like to get their attention?

Amy ponders for a moment before taking a couple of steps toward the horses and stops.

Amy: I don't want to force them to be friends with me, but I do want them to notice that I'm here.

VL: How would you like to get them to notice you?

Amy begins to roll her sleeves up and slowly extends her arms, palms facing upward, toward the horses. As she does this, the three injured horses raised their heads, stop grazing, and begin to move toward us. The rest of the herd remained at a distance and continued to graze. Amy stood still with her arms outreached, with her scars on display on her

(Continued)

(Continued)

forearms, as one by one the horses come toward her. They take it in turn to sniff her arms before moving over to make space for the next horse to do the same. When all three horses had greeted her, they remained standing around her, waiting attentively. Amy began to cry softly. As she cried, one of the horses stepped forward and rested her head on Amy's shoulder. Throwing her arms around the horse, Amy began to sob. As she cried, the horse leaned into her, and I encouraged Amy to lean in and feel the embodied sensation of the horse supporting her full weight. I paid attention to her breathing, and raised her awareness to it by encouraging her to breathe in synch with the horse. Throughout this encounter, the other two injured horses remained by her side...

The horses had accepted her without question and stayed with her in her pain. (Lac, 2016, pp. 306–307)

Box 5.3   Ecotherapy research

- Kamitsis and Simmonds (2017) explored the practices of counsellors who implement ecotherapy within their consulting rooms. Thirty participants from six countries completed questionnaires and eleven were interviewed. Data were analysed using Interpretive Phenomenological Analysis. Therapeutic activities engaged in included: assigning nature-based homework exercises, facilitating an experiential connection to nature, nature-guided mindfulness/meditation and the sophisticated use of nature metaphors.
- Using mixed methods, Adams and Morgan (2016) evaluated the impact of the 'Grow' project – a nature-based intervention for people with experiences of mental distress. The project included activities such as wild food foraging and guided nature walks. They measured the well-being of approximately 100 participants and 88% said their participation in Grow had resulted in great benefit and significant changes in well-being (related to self-esteem, sense of belonging and coping with stress). See their animated film documenting their findings at https://mediastream.brighton.ac.uk/Player/5442.

When the therapy space becomes anti-therapeutic

In practice, therapy space is *not* always experienced as 'therapeutic'. Therapy may get stuck or it might re-traumatise the client. Perhaps **unhealthy dynamics** are being re-created, in or out of the awareness of therapist and client. I recently spoke with a new client who had left her previous therapist because she felt bullied by him and that replayed her history. In particular, she experienced her therapist as being suspicious and not believing her disclosures about her past experiences. Fearing the therapist's critical judgement, the client felt silenced.

With ethical concerns to the fore, therapists need to be aware of how clients can be harmed by boundaries that are too tight or too loose. If a therapist fails to provide sufficient containment, this can make a client feel unsafe. Or a therapist may contain to such a degree that therapy becomes 'rescuing' or oppressive. When the therapist's needs are placed above those of the client so that the client becomes the caretaker, an ethical line has been crossed. In the darkest, most extreme manifestation of the shadow side, therapy is experienced as coercive, manipulative or downright abusive (see Chapter 3).

While we are talking about a small minority of grossly unethical practitioners here, we all have a role to play in guarding our professional standards and ensuring the well-being of others. Mann (2015) argues that while most therapists are not sexual perpetrators, many run the risk of being complicit in pernicious sexual boundary violations because they 'turn a blind eye'. Turning a blind eye has the benefit of protecting friends and colleagues, and of forestalling any disturbance of our world view. But it's important to recall our ethical responsibilities here and to discuss concerns in supervision. Professional guidelines often recommend therapists first try to tackle the perpetrator individually and try to clarify the situation. If that proves difficult, more formal complaint channels need to be engaged. Professional organisations will offer advice and/or there may be an 'ethics person' who can be consulted informally in the first instance.

It also helps to remind ourselves that what takes place in therapy usually mirrors wider cultural values and practices. As professionals, we have a part to play in addressing public well-being issues. According to the 2013 figures from the Ministry of Justice, Home Office and Office for National Statistics in England and Wales, sexual violence is widely under-reported. Even so, reported numbers are disturbingly high. For instance, over two-thirds of university students in England and Wales have experienced sexual harassment, with more than 90% of this targeted at women. At the time of writing, the '#MeToo' campaign to 'out' sexual violence has exploded in popular consciousness and will continue to have effects we are likely to encounter in our consulting rooms.

In a broader argument relating to changing the culture of therapy, Mann (1997) suggests it is time we acknowledged the presence of the erotic in our therapy room to enable a more open exploration. He argues that erotic feelings and fantasies experienced by both clients and therapists can be used to bring about positive transformation. As professionals, perhaps we need to feel easier about discussing issues around sexual harassment and other abuse. How else are clients going to tell us what they need us to know about the darker sexual side of their histories and experience? Going further, Luca (2014) argues we need to acknowledge the sexual attraction that can arise between therapist and client and so move beyond taboo with its associated moralistic positions and shame. Berry (2014, p. 47) suggests that the self-deception which allows therapists to justify sexual relationships with clients may not be dissimilar to the self-deception involved when we avoid talking about sexual attraction. Can't sexuality be explored authentically as simply another universal existential reality?

Assessment and planning therapy

In addition to hospitably welcoming the client, we make attentive evaluations of clients' needs and dovetail these with what we offer as therapists. How we categorise and view our clients have profound ethical implications. It's about how we formulate their presenting issues and if/whether we engage diagnosis. Once the issue to be focused on has been established, therapist and client can work together to formulate a plan for how to proceed.

Assessment

In private practice, assessment can often be relatively **informal**, with the focus on hearing the client's story. Clinical observations about the way clients present will contribute to therapists' formulation of therapy needs. Here we gather information through objective observation (for example, of tone of voice, gestures, posture) and through subjective, embodied, intuitive sensings. We pick up both what clients 'give' and 'give-off'. Does what they say match their non-verbals?

Sometimes, more formal assessments are undertaken. Depending on the treatment context, some units require the use of **standardised questionnaires** towards determining levels of mental health and well-being or the use of **psychometric tests** measuring cognitive ability, perceptual function, etc. The relational-ethical implication here is to perform the tests in positive ways which minimise rather than increase clients' anxiety. Delivering batteries of tests without clear purpose and awareness of how tests are received is professionally dubious. Careful explanation of the nature of the tests – and then any results – helps.

For instance, on being referred a child who is underperforming at school, a psychologist might want to perform something like the *Wechsler Intelligence Scale for Children – Fifth UK Edition* (WISC-V^UK). This would contribute to the assessment of whether it's the child's ability or something about the school/ home context which is the issue. WISC comes in a digital format where the test is performed on a tablet, providing instant feedback. The child may feel reassured by the familiarity of 'playing games' on a computer; parents may appreciate the professionalism of the process.

Many assessment tools can also be used to chart progress and measure outcomes. The myriad of **outcome measures** available (published and informal) form a continuum. This reaches from objective measures utilising set criteria and measurements of behavioural change at one end to subjective feedback focusing on emotional responses at the other. Some are completed by the therapist, others by the clients.

In the UK and North America, three widely used outcome measures are:

1. **CORE-OM** (see www.coreims.co.uk/download-pdfs) – This is a 34-item generic measure of psychological well-being and distress, encompassing: i. well-being (4 items); ii. symptoms (12 items); iii. functioning (12 items); and iv. risk (6 items).
2. **Outcome Rating Scale (ORS)** (Miller and Duncan, 2000) – This copyrighted and licensed tool plots changes in how the client is feeling in four respects: i. individually (personal well-being); ii. interpersonally (family, close relationships); iii. socially (work, school, friendships); and iv. overall (general sense of well-being).
3. **Session Rating Scale (SRS)** (Miller, Duncan and Johnson, 2002) – Also copyrighted and licensed, this four-item tool focuses on: i. relationship (feeling heard, understood and respected); ii. goals and topics (the extent to which work was done as planned); iii. approach or method (the therapist's approach and fit with client); and iv. overall (whether something was missing or felt right in the session).

In the UK, the **Hospital Anxiety and Depression Scale (HADS)** (Zigmond and Snaith, 1983) is used by doctors in the NHS to determine the level of anxiety and depression a patient is experiencing. It is simple to fill out: the 14-item scale, can then be used as an outcome measure of changes in mental state.

In the current climate of 'evidence-based practice', therapists are exhorted to demonstrate the effectiveness of their work and this has become a professional imperative. The challenge lies in doing this in ways that are ethical and involve clients' *informed consent*. I have concerns when clients are handed several standardised assessments to fill out to get a 'baseline' of their functioning and are then left alone. Sometimes the focus on the person is lost in the therapist's (or institution's) instrumental desire to collect outcome research data.

The extent to which collecting data from clients via standardised measures is helpful is currently a matter of lively debate. Many practitioners argue that outcomes research is the way forward and urge practitioners to use outcome measures routinely in their practice (see Miller, Duncan and Hubble, 2005). The evidence suggests that the use of easily filled out questionnaires like the SRS (a measure of therapeutic alliance) or the ORS (a measure of outcomes) improves outcomes and increases client satisfaction and retention. Such practices can demonstrate professionalism and offer the client respect, engaging with them as interested service users rather than passive recipients of health care. However, much depends on how the various assessments are administered. In terms of ethics, as with psychometric testing, it's important to ensure any assessments are administered in a caring, responsive and not overly bureaucratic way. Clients need to know they are seen as individuals, rather than simply as research numbers or service 'consumers'.

Beyond client responses, wider ethical implications can be at stake. This is particularly the case in situation where therapists appropriate (plagiarise?) or modify existing instruments without attention to copyright and without respect for the rights of professional colleagues. Such practices may also compromise the reliability and/or validity of test results, rendering any scores obtained meaningless. The way tests are represented and used is crucial (Welfel, 2013).

Further, when it comes to doing **research**, participants should also give informed consent. This isn't always easy to judge, particularly when it comes to qualitative research where often it's not clear what is going to be elicited, say in-depth interviews. There is an ethical imperative, then, to be reflexive (Finlay, 2017) and to seek 'process consent', that is, to keep checking out if they are OK with the ongoing research/dissemination process and negotiating how best to proceed – relationally (Finlay and Evans, 2009). The care needed is shown in the following reflexive dialogue between Kim Etherington and two co-researchers/participants who were her ex-clients:

Kim: The process of doing this may very well open up things again, and I wonder what that would be like for you and what you would do then.

Stephen: I feel like I'm ready for that, I think I could cope with that now – at a distance. I could deal with that now.

Kim: How about you Mike?

Mike: [Pause] Mmm. Yes, I think so. I think I've demonstrated by recent events [his separation from his wife] that I can mobilize support if I need to.

Kim: But here we are now, moving into a different relationship, when I'm not your counselor. What would that mean if anything did come up? What might be your expectations of me if you got very distressed about something that was happening as part of the research process? I suppose my concern is – that if you needed counseling – I don't think it would be appropriate for me to offer that.

Stephen: That would be OK.

Kim [to Stephen]: But I am also aware that you have financial limitations that would make it hard for you to get counseling elsewhere. I just wondered if you had thought about that. ... There are other agencies where you can go for low-fee or reduced-fee counseling. ... That's not to say that I didn't expect this to be therapeutic, or that I'm not going to be able to be supportive as a researcher. (Etherington, 2007, pp. 606–607)

Problem formulation

Problem formulation can be understood as the 'story' (Gilbert and Orlans, 2011) therapist and client co-create. It describes the client's current way of being, along with their relationships and challenges, and addresses the following questions:

- What is it the client is struggling with? What life issues are currently figural?
- What is the quality of the relationship that is emerging between therapist and client, and how does this reflect wider social relationships?
- What is the client's relational history (including relationships with significant others, attachment style, early socialisation experiences)?
- How are they presenting? Are there signs of trauma, depression or other mental health issues?
- How is their life embedded in wider social-cultural, economic, political realities?

A client might, for instance, have sought therapy because of a recent bereavement with which they are struggling to come to terms. In this case the focus of therapy would probably involve both expressing the grief and finding new meaning in life. Or perhaps the client has a history of abusive relationships and they would like to form more satisfying, meaningful ones. If there are issues related to trauma in the past, the problem formulation might include a hypothesis related to repetitive, self-destructive relational styles, problematic attachment patterns and/or how the trauma is held in the body. A person's ethnic and cultural background might have particular significance if they are an immigrant or have come from a war-torn country or have been subject to racist abuse. Therapy is likely to focus on managing the challenges arising from this personal–political interface.

Working within an ethical framework requires us to maintain an attitude of **humility**, **curiosity** and **openness** rather than rush into 'knowing' explanations or theorising. The primary focus of the initial meeting is the client's description of their current struggle and way of being in relationships. I often will explicitly ask clients to tell their 'story', to respond to the question 'What is it like to be you?' In *relational* terms, that process of simply describing – and being witnessed – can itself be powerful and is potentially transformational. We need to be aware of the dangers of not properly listening or assuming we already 'know' this kind of story. It's all too easy then to jump in with ready-made solutions. A more respectful, empathically-attuning approach is required.

Use of diagnosis?

One of the most contested ethical questions in therapeutic practice relates to the use of diagnosis. For many therapists, engaging 'diagnosis' is little short of anathema. Humanistic/integrative practitioners prefer to embrace more intuitive, phenomenological ways of seeing that avoid resorting to diagnosis, perhaps viewing it as reductionist, dehumanising and anti-therapeutic.

The medical model has come in for considerable criticism, along with the mechanical, uncritical use of official diagnostic category systems. Relational-centred therapists understand that, when diagnosis is to the fore, we tend to selectively attend to those aspects which confirm the 'problem formulation' and there is a danger that we ignore information which does not fit. Further, as Irving Yalom (2001) notes, focusing on someone as a 'borderline' personality, for example, may actually bring out those very traits in a self-fulfilling prophesy. Taking diagnostic systems too seriously may 'threaten the human, the spontaneous, the creative and uncertain nature of the therapeutic venture' (Yalom, 2001, p. 5).

The **DSM** (*Diagnostic and Statistical Manual of Mental Disorders*; the latest edition is DSM-5), published by the American Psychiatric Association (2013), and the newly online World Health Organisation's **ICD-11** *International Classification of Diseases* (2018) which offers a common language and standard criteria for the classification of mental disorders plus world-wide statistics on health. The latest version of the DSM-5, has been the subject of vociferous debate (see, for instance, the 2017/2018 Special Issues – volumes 57(6) and 58(1) – on diagnostic alternatives in the *Journal of Humanistic Psychology*). Among the many points of criticism, there is a concern that normal human responses (including grief responses) could be labelled pathological.

Debate about classification systems aside, there is a place for understanding the wider medical-psychiatric view, if only as part of working responsibly in a wider mental health team or recognising a client's history and previous treatment experiences. For therapists working with people with severe and enduring mental health problems, it may be necessary to know if they have a clinical diagnosis such as schizophrenia or bipolar disorder. Such a diagnosis can provide critical information about their need for medication or the likely course, prognosis and risks of their illness.

Shahar (2018), for instance, argues for a humanistically-orientated approach which entails use of diagnosis and standardised assessment. Shahar promotes 'descriptive psychopathology' rather than diagnostic labels, recognising that mental illness exists and there is a need to differentiate patients' experience:

> He or she might actually not have depression, which will most likely be revealed by the findings of the standardized tests, and if he or she does, the tests will enable me to gain an appreciation of 'the poetics of the person's depression,' that is, what are the principal depressive experiences, how severe they are, and how they might coexist with the patients' self-structure and interpersonal environment. (Shahar, 2018, p. 5)

A more problematic dimension regarding diagnosis attaches to categories such as 'personality disorder' or 'stress disorder'. That such categories are regularly being revised, and sometimes discarded, is a salutary reminder that we're not dealing with facts and certainty when it comes to social behaviour; our work addresses phenomena that are culturally/socially created. A case in point is how the ICD-11 offers a new category of *Complex Post-Traumatic Stress Disorder* (which is seen to occur after prolonged abuse and violence) which doesn't exist in previous versions or in the DSM-5. Also, ICD-11 offers a new category of 'gaming disorder' as an 'addictive behaviour disorder' but this has not yet been adopted by DSM-5. As Gilbert and Orlans (2011) argue, any diagnostic formulation needs to be seen cautiously as a tentative and provisional hypothesis, not a 'label for life'.

In countries where therapy is paid for through insurance companies, some diagnosing might be necessary to meet insurance criteria. Therapists may record a formal diagnosis on billing forms but, respecting the relationship, the therapist and client would discuss this, noting the risks and benefits of actually using a diagnosis. General headings such as 'Stress Reaction' or 'Adjustment Disorder' might be made, emphasising temporary reactions to life stresses rather than a permanent illness. If they were not needing any diagnosis for insurance, billing or legal matters, diagnosis may otherwise be avoided. The inappropriate use of diagnosis, or even misdiagnosis, to obtain financial re-imbursement is unethical and may constitute insurance fraud, and be subject to criminal penalties. Therapists need to take care to ensure diagnosing is done in professionally-informed, culturally-sensitive ways (Welfel, 2013).

Rather than viewing the client as having a medical diagnosis or disorder, therapists tend to focus on the person and how they function in their lives. *Cognitive therapists* look at client's behaviour and thought patterns, concentrating on how they function in the here-and-now, in contrast to *psychoanalytic* therapists, who will focus on relational, developmental and attachment processes arising out of the there-and-then. *Existential* work focuses on clients' way of being-with others where there is more concern to do 'justice to the way clients live their lives, rather than to eradicate specific problems or focus on particular symptoms' (Van Deurzen and Adams, 2011, p. 1). Similarly, in the *gestalt* tradition, the emphasis is on observing here-and-now experience, attending to the client's embodied presentation as a whole. For example, the therapist might note that the person is inclined to be 'avoidant and deflects feelings at the contact boundary' (Finlay, 2016a, p. 21).

Goal setting

A cooperative therapeutic alliance probably underpins all effective helping (Clarkson, 2003). This alliance involves three main components: therapist and client agreement over **goals**; a consensus on the **tasks** and processes of therapy; and a positive, affective **bond** or attachment (Bordin, 1979). In other words, it is necessary to have at least some mutual understanding about the nature of therapy and some common desire to nurture a relationship built on trust, communication and acceptance. Research findings (for example, Cooper, 2008) commonly stress the value of clear contracting, agreed goals/processes and key information-giving to ensure mutual responsibility for the therapy. The client needs to have a sense of what they are aiming for. A solid therapeutic alliance acts as a platform which enables therapist and client to continue working together, even at those more challenging moments of therapy when one or other might want to withdraw.

For an example of how therapy goals are negotiated, consider the following case illustration:

> Marco had come into therapy following a traumatic 18 months after being diagnosed with prostate cancer, undergoing both chemotherapy and surgery. Although ... his

prognosis was now moderately good, he was left feeling vulnerable and anxious about his health. He experienced regular nightmares where violent deaths figured prominently, and he would frequently wake through the night with palpitations and in a cold sweat.

Phase 1: Establishing a therapeutic alliance and treating the anxiety disorder

The therapist's first intervention was to offer compassion for Marco's traumatic journey and respect for how he had found a way to cope. She reassured him that it was not surprising his anxiety was coming out in this way now that the pressure was off. 'Normalising' Marco's responses enabled Marco to express his existential terrors and explore the impact of his recent traumatic experiences.

The therapist described some recent research findings about the effectiveness of CBT and, taking a psycho-educational approach, guided Marco through some basic relaxation techniques.

The therapist's gentle approach in this early stage of therapy was focused largely on developing trust – in the therapist and himself. But more than simply giving information, the therapist worked relationally, recognising Marco's difficulty in accepting the therapist's care. ... Once Marco accepted the therapist was an ally, they were ready to work explicitly on reducing the anxiety responses. Marco was well motivated to engage in short-term therapy with the goal of learning anxiety...

Phase 2: Healing deeper relational wounds

After eight sessions, Marco's sleep disturbance was largely under control and Marco was invited to consider whether he wished to carry on with longer term work looking more deeply into the roots of his anxiety. He appreciated their work would undergo a subtle shift from the teaching-learning approach focused on his behaviour to a more open exploration of his current and past relational experiences. It had taken until now to feel ready to let go into the exploration. (Finlay, 2016a, p. 33)

Contracting

Therapeutic boundaries are agreed, set and maintained through the therapy contract (written or verbal). When we begin seeing a client, we negotiate the terms of therapy as we try to engage them therapeutically. Fees, the range and limits of confidentiality, and general arrangements regarding the timing and cancelling of appointments, all need to be established, along with various implicit and explicit procedures relevant to the context (private practice, public health care or the voluntary sector). It's also important to agree on the provisional focus and envisaged length of therapy, since both will have a major influence on the type of work attempted. Contracts 'allow everyone involved to share aims, hopes and preferences' (Amis, 2017, p. 44).

In **legal** terms, contracts (written or verbal) are legally binding agreements for both parties. They're particularly relevant in private practice, where there is an exchange of money and services. They establish professional service terms and conditions, rights and responsibilities, and expectations of processes and outcomes, and they explicitly obtain the client's *informed consent*. Contracts have practical and ethical functions; they're a concrete symbol of the intention to contain the therapy process safely and professionally. At the same time, the client makes a formal commitment to therapy.

Different practitioners use different contracts – there is no set template. Some guidance is offered in Box 5.4 (see also British Association for Counselling and Psychotherapy, 2016, for a more detailed document).

Box 5.4   Information needed for written contracts

- **Personal information/contact details** (and details about how these are to be stored/used).
- **Nature of the work being contracted or the service being offered** – The client needs to be given enough information to decide if and how they want to work with the therapist. This might include clarifying any risks that therapy might result in the client feeling worse before they can feel better, or that instead of 'feeling better' they might just end up with 'better feeling'. The client needs information about the nature of therapy, the therapist's responsibility and their own rights: to privacy, for example, or to ending the therapy at any point. It might also be relevant to state other possibilities for treatment.
- **Statement about confidentiality and the limits to confidentiality** – Respect for confidentiality is emphasised, assuring the client that information/data will not be shared without their consent or without sound legal and ethical justification. (Similarly, supervisors will assure confidentiality – and any caveats – including that, when writing or teaching, the anonymity of the client is preserved or consent is sought.) Beyond more extreme circumstances for breaching confidentiality (for example, a serious risk is posed to self or others, or child abuse), clients need to know that the content of sessions may be discussed in supervision. The agreement should specify if the client's name will remain anonymous. Clients also need to understand the implications of non-payment of fees where legal action (or use of collection agencies) will also compromise confidentiality.
- **Details about the frequency and number of sessions planned and length of session** – For brief therapy, the contract might specify 'up to' six one-hour sessions to allow one or both to end if the sessions are not proving effective; for longer-term work, more open agreements are established. While once-weekly therapy is commonly (arbitrarily?) advocated, the client may need or request something different and that should be factored in respectfully. The key is to consider what is *most appropriate for each individual and the planned treatment*: Once a week/fortnight/month? Three times a week? An hour/hour and a half/two hours per session? Any planned absences/ holidays should also be stated in advance if possible. Whatever the contract, it is helpful to agree regular reviews of the work, with re-contracting possibilities.

(Continued)

(Continued)

- **Aim or focus of the work** – For example, to manage emotions, or to develop resources and resilience, or change behaviour, or gain greater self-awareness and understanding of psychological needs and processes. The limits of the work should also be recognised; for instance, some problems can be dealt with in brief therapy, whereas others need more time.
- **Details about payment and fees** – In private practice, the spectre of money in the form of what fees are charged looms large and possibly carries deeper values and meanings for both therapist and client. Care still needs to be taken to work out the contractual obligations, how payment and invoicing will occur and the consequences of non-payment and/or what happens when there is insufficient notice of cancellation.
- **Handling missed sessions** – The relational-ethical negotiation revolves around self-and-other respect. Some therapists require, say, 48 hours' notice if clients are not going to attend or they will charge for the missed session. Some contracts may specify that therapy will be terminated if clients do not attend without giving notice. Also, it is useful to agree what to do if clients miss sessions (for example, are follow-up reminders offered?).
- **Details of emergency contact or other concerns** – In an emergency or in the case of health concerns, the client's GP or referring agency may need to be informed. If it's a child protection issue, social services or other authorities may need contacting. In cases of a trainee's habitual non-attendance, a report should be given to the responsible training institution.
- **Information about data protection** – Information needs to be given about data protection issues and clients may need to sign a document to say they have received and understood it. Some therapists in institutional contexts might be required to give full written details about GDPR (see Box 2.1); others might prefer a lighter touch and would resist going into lengthy, distancing explanations and keep to the basic facts: for example, that the client has the right to see any data that are held and that data are securely stored.

Depending on the context, other 'rules' might be agreed. With family therapy, for instance, there may be a clear 'no secrets' policy. Here is an excerpt from a contract used by a therapist in the US:

> When I am working with a couple or family (the treatment unit) and need to meet with one person individually, I will use my best judgment as to whether, when, and to what extent I will make disclosures from the individual session to the other(s) in the treatment unit. ... If you feel it necessary to talk about matters that you absolutely want to be shared with no one, you might want to consult with an individual therapist.... (Couples and family therapist, private communication)

For clients with safety and **risk** issues, extra care is needed when contracting. Perhaps a *'bespoke'* contract is called for? For instance, a therapist might negotiate a contract with a self-harming or suicidal client that they agree not to attempt suicide for a specified duration; or clients with a problematic substance abuse habit may be informed that they need to be sober when they attend therapy or else the therapist reserves the right not to see them; or both therapist and client might need to work together to manage the risks of the client who is sexually attracted to children while stating that if fantasy becomes reality the therapist will have to formally report it.

Contacting the GP in cases of concerns about safety and risk can be seen as a 'solution' and the end-point of the 'problem', in the sense that it gets handed over. However, a relational-ethical position would be to follow through with both the GP and the client. Explanations need to be given to the client as to why the GP is needed and the client could find it useful to hear what may happen as a result. For this reason, it is important to follow up if and what intervention the GP makes.

Contracting relationally

The contract offers a way of ensuring a holding-containing-boundaried frame, as Clarkson (2003, p. 56) acknowledges:

> Punctuality, cooperation and variations in timing, changes in schedule, vacations, holidays and unavoidable absences need honest and appropriate explorations to ensure that the *vas* – the container of psychotherapy – is not leaking or damaged.

Therapists differ in their contracting practice, modifying practice to fit the context and individuals concerned. There are no blanket rules, although a relational-ethical sensibility is called for. Some therapists make use of written contracts which both parties sign, each keeping a copy; others keep matters at a verbal level. Some will specify a set number of sessions before a formal review to carry on perhaps; others are content to offer open-ended contracts. Some will charge for the initial contracting session; others will not. It is worth thinking through the justification for all your choices. For instance, the argument for charging a fee values the professional's time and shows that professionalism to the client. Alternatively, the first session, acting like an initial consultation or estimate, might be offered for free as it's an opportunity to assess clients' needs and ability to pay.

The contract should be drawn up in a clear, supportive manner (Amis, 2017). Negotiations need to be framed in terms of 'informed consent', 'safety' and 'mutual respect' rather than following automatic procedures or 'rules'. Also, contracts need to be negotiated, formalising *informed consent*, rather than being coercively imposed on the client. Sometimes this can get tricky. Consider the client who has violent fantasies or is sexually attracted to children. Normally contracts specify that it might be necessary to report dangerous behaviour, for example to the police or GP, but this could mean some clients either refusing to sign or, worse, keeping 'secrets'. Together, therapist and client need to negotiate the terms, for instance, that there is no need to report unless active offending is involved.

If a client is reluctant to sign a contract, there may be commitment issues requiring further time and attention. As therapists, we enact relational ethics by respecting the *autonomy* of clients and assuming they can take some responsibility for working around their choices. We also show *respect* for their rights to privacy: for instance, by only soliciting information from clients which is relevant to the therapeutic process.

The issue of paying **fees** raises specific relational-ethical issues beyond the point that therapists' fee practices need to fit the law and any agency or insurance billing requirements. Issues around fees go to the heart of feeling valued, or not, professionally. First, some people find the process of paying or being paid uncomfortable. This is particularly the case in the UK where health services are largely free at the point of delivery and practitioners may not be used to charging. I've had supervision conversations around the way payment is handled. For instance, one therapist said that she felt like a 'prostitute' as her client left money on the table as he walked out. Other supervisees talk of feeling 'bad' charging clients for missed sessions.

Second, consideration needs to be given to what is an appropriate, non-exploitative fee regarding the client's ability to pay, the location of the service *and* the costs therapists bear to remain in practice. Many professional codes (for instance, that of the American Counseling Association), encourage professionals to provide some *pro bono* (without fee) services as part of a commitment to public welfare (see Welfel, 2013). Commonly, therapists consider using sliding scales to enable people with lower incomes to access therapy.

Irrespective of how the contract is specified, it should be regularly revisited – not least because in the information overload of the first session, it's hard for clients to take in all the implications.

The value of seeing contracting as an **ongoing *co-created* process** means that clients are actively involved in their own therapy. They themselves specify what they would like to gain from the process. A fruitful discussion can take place in the first couple of sessions about the person's motivation for seeking therapy and what they are willing to commit to. Research supports the value of engaging clients actively and continually processing their consent. As Cooper's (2008) summary of essential research findings stresses: 'At the heart of most successful therapies, is a client who is willing and able to become involved in making changes to her or his life. ... The key predictor of outcomes remains the extent to which the client is willing and able to make use of whatever the therapist provides' (2008, p. 157).

Concluding reflections

The processes involved in the early stages of therapy can, with sensitive application, ensure a therapeutic frame which keeps both client and therapist safe. This is unlikely to be achieved through the mechanical application of assessment protocols and contracting. Even at this early stage, it's important for therapists to move beyond 'doing' to remember our 'being'.

I embrace the *therapist-as-host* metaphor, with its emphasis on 'hospitality'. For me, this captures the sense of **openness**, **respect** and **caring-honouring concern** and **attentiveness** characteristic of the best therapeutic work. One of my early lessons was learning how Freud fed a hungry patient (the so-called 'Rat-Man'). If a client comes in and is feeling weak from not having eaten all day, wouldn't the relational-ethical – *human* – thing to do is to offer, at least, a drink and biscuit? I know of one therapy service for refugees and asylum seekers which lays out a buffet of food each day in the waiting room for those who need food. Some therapists would challenge these acts as messing with norms of practice (boundaries designed to ensure client safety). What's your view?

With my private practice contracts, I always like to ask clients if they have something they want to specify on the contract. For instance, they may request that they be contacted only via their mobile phone and never at work. I also require just 24 hours' notice if clients are going to miss the session; without this they may have to pay the fee. The reverse also applies: if I make a scheduling mistake, then the next session is free. (A senior therapist I know disagrees with my strategy, arguing against 'pseudo-equivalence' – a reminder that we all practise differently.)

Regarding **diagnosis**, my own preference – at both professional and moral levels – is to avoid focusing on it in a reductionist way. I prefer not to psychopathologise my clients, positioning them as occupying a category when the whole focus of the therapy journey is going to be about change and their evolving 'self'/'selves'. Unlike some other therapists, I tend to avoid explaining the 'problem' in terms of maladaptive behaviour and/or fixed personality styles. As I see it, such formulations limit our capacity to see the person as a whole. Pathologising strikes me as running counter to the ethos of an empowering, holistic relationally-orientated therapy. I do not want to exert power by labelling someone, in the process diminishing the other via an objectivising, reductionist gaze.

That said, there are times when I find myself unable to bracket certain observations: for instance, that a client seems to be exhibiting a borderline behavioural pattern or schizoid personality style. Sometimes, I will have awareness of formal psychiatric differential diagnoses. Ideally, I will corral such observations and set them aside as 'hypotheses to be revised' as I try to open to a fuller range of the person's being. Sometimes, I'm unsuccessful and as guilty of labelling and stereotyping as the next person.

When it comes to initial **assessment** and **goal-setting** practices, I believe these are best done through dialogue and with the client's active participation. If the person is required to fill out forms or questionnaires, can this be done relationally? Similarly, the initial assessment shouldn't just be a series of questions asked and answered. It's about exploring together and setting a tone for a future commitment to achieving as ethical, open and transparent a **collaboration** as possible.

Perhaps the most important ingredient in relational work is for the therapist to be 'present as a person meeting the person of the other' (Yontef, 1993, p. 24). It takes particular grace, humility and hospitality – beyond knowledge, protocols and skill – to make contact at the threshold of human relating, and to be ready to receive the gift of the other (Hycner, 1991/1993).

Discussion questions

1. In what ways can we ensure our therapy space is *therapeutic* and hospitable?
2. How can we ensure our contracting is done in relational-ethical ways?
3. Critically evaluate the idea that diagnosis is dehumanising and anti-therapeutic.

Summary

The process of meeting with and engaging the client, planning the therapy and contracting needs to be done ethically, in ways that nurture an effective therapeutic relationship. The early stages of therapy must involve more than a mechanical or uncritical application of assessment and contracting. Instead, the therapist tries to create a safe space of hospitality where the client can feel held, accepted, supported, respected, resourced, empathised with and challenged to grow. Therapist humanity, integrity, duty of care, respect, dialogue and informed consent are the key foundational principles involved in this process.

6

Ethical Boundarying

Boundaries structure the therapeutic relationship, ensuring a reliable, predictable, trustworthy frame to hold-contain testing psychotherapeutic processes. They guard the relationship and respect the rights and responsibilities of both client *and* therapist, as well as the separateness between them. Boundaries also enable us to enact our ethical responsibilities and professional integrity. They help us manage the asymmetry of power within the therapist–client relationship by setting limits to the therapist's power and to the potential intimacy of the therapy encounter (Amis, 2017).

Our professional codes go some way to addressing the need to maintain respectful, confidential boundaries. However, they do not detail the everyday relational boundary dilemmas we constantly encounter. These form the focus of this chapter. After describing the different types of **boundarying in practice**, the chapter discusses three **challenging issues**: dual relationships, holding the time-frame and the use of therapist self-disclosure. The spotlight is then put on a specific contemporary challenge: **digital ethics**. The penultimate section considers when boundary **transgressions** can be therapeutic.

Boundarying in practice

A boundary, by definition, is something that marks a limit or line we do not cross. The ethical boundaries we hold in psychotherapy are layered and multiple. For example, we have:

- **legal** boundaries – refusing to break the law or practising to avoid official complaints and malpractice liability
- **moral** boundaries – refusing to betray personal moral values, standards and beliefs
- **emotional** boundaries – refusing to allow another to intrude or get overly close (physically or emotionally) when it is not wanted and/or containing emotions that threaten to leak out in harmful ways
- **relational** boundaries – respecting privacy and the boundary choices of another or maintaining the client–therapist relationship as a professional rather than personal one, thus minimising the confusion of *dual* relationships
- **professional** boundaries – recognising responsibilities and maintaining professional integrity. (Finlay, 2016a)

Negotiating and maintaining these boundaries in practice presents a range of ethically grey areas and dilemmas. As Lott (1999) notes,

> there are a host of situations where the delineation of a boundary is less clear, situations that fall outside the formal ethics codes and lie instead on the cusp of principles and technique.

Clients will often push at and test our boundaries and we must decide when – and how – to hold firm. There are numerous situations where the delineation of our professional boundaries is relationally problematic or hard to maintain. Consider the situations in Box 6.1. Think first about your response before reading my own responses below.

Box 6.1   Boundary dilemmas

1. You are invited by a friend to a jazz club night. You discover that the saxophonist is one of your clients. Should you still go? If not, should you explain there is a 'boundary issue'?
2. A friend has asked that you see her teenage son (who you don't know) for therapy because you're the 'only therapist' in the local area she trusts. What would you answer? How about the situation where your supervisee is seeing your friend's child?
3. You have been supporting Tomáš over the last two years while he's been at college. He is involved in a fatal car accident and his parents, knowing the important role you've played, ask you to attend the funeral – something you want to do.
4. Cassie is the mother of three children, all of whom have been taken into care. She now has a new baby and has been referred to a counsellor by social services for an evaluation and help in developing her parenting skills. Social services have agreed ten funded sessions. On the seventh session, Cassie tells her counsellor that they are the only person who understands her and asks for more sessions as she's not sure what she would do if they

---

ended. She knows the therapist runs a low-cost clinic and she wonders if she could attend that.

5. A client seems to be in a pattern of asking you if she can swap her therapy times, as if testing the therapy boundaries. At least once a month she misses her planned session, often without notice. Do you agree to swapping times around if you have that flexibility in your diary? How do you handle the missed sessions?

6. A client of yours died two years ago and now her husband has sought you out to be his therapist. Do you oblige?

My responses

1. **Is it OK to meet clients outside sessions?** – If this was my dilemma, decision-making would hinge on the context. Ideally, I'd want to avoid social contact with the client. However, if I decided to go, then I'd discuss the implications of this with them and take steps to keep my distance while at the event. I wouldn't reveal this boundary issue to my friend as that would go near to breaking confidentiality.

2. **Friend's teenage son needing therapy – Do you take it on?** – This situation is tricky as it might be hard to hold boundaries. The client might reveal private information about your friend and it may be hard to avoid being drawn into discussing family affairs. Also, a possible unseen impact on the friendship itself needs to be considered. It would be best to recommend another therapist. If none is available locally, the son might consider having therapy online (for example, via FaceTime). If the therapy needed was only brief therapy and focused on psychoeducation, it might be possible for you to see him as a client. However, in such a case, contracting relating to confidentiality and social boundaries would need to be absolutely explicit and transparent, clarifying that social contact with the client would be limited, even after the end of therapy.

    If my supervisee was seeing a friend of mine (or their family member), I would suggest they went elsewhere for their supervision about this client. The boundaries feel too close otherwise. I'm aware of feeling some discomfort that the supervisee will be forced to hold some extra boundaries where my personal life is in the mix. In this scenario, it would be less 'clammy' if the supervisee wasn't seeing my friends professionally.

3. **Should/can we attend funerals?** – If I could attend relatively anonymously, then this might be acceptable. For example, I might attend the service but slip out before the gathering after. Some boundaries would need to be put in place with Tomáš's parents about confidentiality and the limits of what I could offer. I know a few therapists

who have attended clients' funerals. However, most would draw a line at attending weddings or other social events.

4. **Should we offer more sessions if a client asks?** – There are a number of pertinent issues in this case: (1) Is there a child protection or suicide risk that needs to be attended to seriously? (2) What is Cassie's motivation to stay in relationship? Might there be some manipulation here? (3) Has the therapist sufficiently graded the interventions, bearing in mind the ten-session contract? Might the therapist, out of their awareness, have been encouraging some dependence? With three sessions left, some good nourishing work could focus on developing Cassie's resources to help her through an ending. Such work would enable the boundary to be held. However, if it's decided that further sessions are needed, then this needs to be negotiated with the referring agency.

5. **How flexible should we be about swapping of therapy times?** – With my private practice, I support the idea of being a little flexible when I can, and this would be discussed in initial contracting as working both ways. (Some therapists would not choose to be so flexible or the policy of the work context may not support this). However, I ask for at least 24 hours' notice, in the absence of which I charge for that session. It's important to enforce such a rule, although I might be a bit more accepting the first time it happens in case the client hadn't understood. With this particular client the situation is trickier. Working relationally, I would want to explore what is happening in the process. Is the client simply too busy and overloaded? Or do they struggle with self-care issues, including the need to prioritise their therapy? What is the client communicating through their behaviour? Are they perhaps signalling a relational issue? For example, perhaps they got 'scared' in the previous session and are acting out their avoidance. Are they sufficiently motivated and engaged in the therapy? If not, maybe it is time to issue a robust challenge or think about ending.

6. **Should we see a client's spouse for therapy?** – Some therapists might take this on, but I suspect most wouldn't. If a supervisee asked me this question, I'd probably advise against seeing the husband as the boundaries don't feel 'clean'. It comes down to the level of relationship you had with the ex-client, your sense of allegiance, and how well you can hold the work with your client. Have you been privy to confidences about their marriage? The husband might feel you already 'know' his story in some way. This could be helpful, although you may also carry some unhelpful, distorted preconceptions.

    If the relationship with the client had been brief and relatively superficial, or the client had died many years ago, it might prove less confusing. If the therapy had been long-term work, there may be a pull to see this husband as you may feel a special connection and perhaps you both share sadness from the loss. But I wonder whose – and which – needs would be served here?

Versions of this scenario pop up quite often, for instance, when parents ask a child therapist to see another of their children or when a friend of a client asks to see you as well. The decision depends on the relational context. With the first example of working with a second child, I could see myself agreeing if it fits a rubric of 'family work'. I'd be wary of seeing the friend, however, particularly if the client was still in therapy. Too many issues around 'sibling rivalry' and splitting dynamics could occur in addition to the challenge of holding appropriate confidentiality boundaries!

Complex boundarying issues

In the clinical context, boundaries prevent unhealthy levels of acting out and keep both client and therapist safe in what is often a charged, intimate encounter. They also acknowledge the **power** imbalance that is unavoidably part of the therapeutic relationship and set limits for the therapist's expression of power. 'To live with this inherent power is to enter the realm of ethics. The only way of surviving as a true professional is to ... live with the paradox: to behave ethically and exert power – simultaneously' (Kruger, 2007, p. 21).

However, as discussed in Chapter 4, it's too simplistic to frame the issue as 'therapists have power; clients are powerless'. Power and control are multi-directional and experienced in different ways. We hold numerous boundaries with both clients and colleagues which have implications for power and control. It gets complicated as each boundary can mean something different to different individuals. This can make the boundarying process challenging and sometimes stressful. I once supervised a black female counsellor who felt oppressed when her white male clients made personal comments which felt racist and transgressed her boundaries. Sometimes it's our clients who control, exerting power that challenges our boundary lines. At other times, we need to be aware how our boundary transgressions may constitute a misuse of power (for example, if we 'invade' by being excessively self-disclosing) or even an abuse of power (if we fall into the trap of being sexually seductive).

Therapists clearly have a moral, professional and legal **duty of care** to ensure the safety, both emotional and physical, of their clients. Boundaries ensure that safety. However, it can be challenging to hold boundaries when juggling different work pressures. Afolabi (2015) notes the difficulty of being ethically mindful in the context of, say, the intensity of clients' needs, or conflicts with external agencies, or the possibility of condemnation from professional co-workers about clinical decisions taken. 'These factors, if not properly considered, can overpower, drain, divert and lure professionals into ethical slumber' (Afolabi, 2015, p. 33).

In a meta-analysis of studies from several countries, *confidentiality* was found to be the most common boundary problem faced by counsellors, followed by blurred, conflicting relationships (Pettifor and Sawchuk, 2006). These issues are examined below focusing on: multiple relationships, holding the time boundary and the use of therapist self-disclosure.

Multiple relationships

One significant boundary frequently enshrined in **professional codes** is the recommendation to avoid multiple relationships where possible. These involve situations where therapist and client hold dual roles or multiple relationships (concurrently or consecutively), such as being both therapist and supervisor or having other professional dealings or being in business together or having personal and social contact. The UKCP *Ethical Principles and Code of Professional Conduct* (2009) offers the following guidance:

> 1.5 Psychotherapists are required to carefully consider [the] possible implications of entering into dual or multiple relationships and make every effort to avoid entering into relationships that risks confusing an existing relationship and may impact adversely on a client. ... When dual or multiple relationships are unavoidable, for example in small communities, psychotherapists take responsibility to clarify and manage boundaries and [the] confidentiality of the therapeutic relationship.

The presence of multiple relationships risks compromising therapist judgement. It can interfere with the therapeutic relationship and be emotionally taxing for both people. Take the situation where therapist and client are both members of a committee which occasionally meets socially. It might be difficult to maintain confidentiality boundaries; the chances of inadvertently revealing something are high. In addition, it can be confusing for the client to see their therapist outside the therapy space. For instance, the client may find it challenging to see the therapist having other relationships outside their 'special' one. I recall one client who came to me for therapy after seeing her previous therapist go from being a familiar nurturing 'father figure' to presenting as adversarial and manipulative at a conference. This had shaken her trust in him.

However, much depends on *why* the boundaries are being crossed and the nature of the relationships involved. What are the therapist's motives? Is it in the client's interests? For example, if a therapist offers to introduce a client to some associates to help the client grow their own business, that might be acceptable, even beneficial. If the therapist revealed to these associates that the client was in therapy with them, or gave other details, that would be troublingly unethical. As another example, consider the therapist who has academic research expertise and who is working with a client undertaking doctoral research. It might be OK for the client to occasionally and briefly consult, asking the therapist for specific advice. It would not be OK for the therapist to actively supervise or examine the thesis.

The situation becomes even more problematic where *power* imbalances bite. For example, a supervisee who is also a client may defer to their supervisor-therapist and be afraid to express alternative opinions. In more extreme cases, the risk of harm can intensify. A client may find it hard to say 'no' to personal invitations by a therapist, fearing emotional fall-out or abandonment.

A useful rule of thumb is to consider whether a dual relationship is likely to create tension or confusion. If the answer is affirmative, it's probably inadvisable.

And the greater the divergence of role expectation/obligation, the greater the risk of problems emerging (Welfel, 2013). For instance, it is a relatively simple matter for an ex-trainer to become a supervisor. However, given the emotional attachments and transferential complications involved, it's tricky (but not impossible) for an ex-therapist to become a trainer who marks assignments written by former clients. And while it might be OK for a therapist to see a client who works as a cleaner in the anonymous office building where she works, it would be unethical to employ the cleaner in her house: that would be both overly personal and potentially exploitative.

There are numerous situations where, at times, dual relationships cannot be helped or might even be helpful (Gabriel, 2005): for example, in small, inter-dependent communities such as villages or in specific contexts such as those of the deaf or LBGT community. Here, the availability of a range of therapists and/or supervisors may be non-existent. Additional pressures occur during some experiential training programmes where tutor-therapists demonstrate therapeutic work with student-clients. Dual relationship pressures also arise in institutions such as universities, occupational health departments and mili-tary bases, where colleagues may become clients; or in treatment units where the therapist may also facilitate other therapeutic groups and activities; or when there is an overlap in professional roles such as being both researcher and therapist or supervisor and co-researcher. The rising profile of social media, with the attendant possibilities for contact via 'friends', is providing ever more space for the spectre of multiple relationships (Amis, 2017).

Relationally speaking, boundaries may need to be flexible at times and dual relationships are not necessarily wrong – it depends on how the relation-ship is affected. The important thing is to carefully weigh up benefits and any possible negative ramifications (see Welfel, 2013). This forms part of our seek-ing to be clean and transparent with clients towards keeping clear boundaries in place. Any risks of multiple relationships should be fully discussed with the client and the motives for the various relationships examined. Many codes, including The Australia and New Zealand Association of Psychotherapists (ANZAP) (2014), highlight the point that therapists always remain responsible for the boundarying even when clients initiate boundary crossings.

Holding the time boundary

Challenges to our time boundaries come in different guises.

1. When clients seek to carry on a session beyond the appointment time

It can be tempting sometimes to let go of time boundaries and extend a session when a client is in full emotional flow or on the cusp of a critical insight. A frequently observed phenomenon is the *'door handle comment'*, where a client saves up something new, significant or shocking for the last few minutes of the session: for instance, 'I am about to be fired from my job...' However, nor-mally it would be wrong to extend the session at this point. Clients are usually aware of the time passing and it is probably no accident that they have brought up critical material at the last moment. Consciously or unconsciously, the client may well be relying on the time boundary to guard their psychological safety: in other words, to save themselves from going more deeply into emotionally-charged material. Common sense should apply, although sometimes a couple of extra minutes might prove invaluable and be the humane response. At the very least, the therapist needs to attentively note the unfinished discussion to be held over until the next session.

2. When clients seek out-of-session contact

Whether, and how, to respond to calls for extra contact between sessions involves careful judgement. Clearly, some situations are sufficiently urgent to justify an immediate holding-containing response. But often the more advisable therapeutic response is to hold-contain the client within set appointment times by briefly acknowledging the client's need to make a connection but delaying detailed discussion until the next meeting. 'What your client begins to realize is that the kind of being-with that she counts on and longs for is best available to her in session' (DeYoung, 2003, p. 47).

Gutheil and Gabbard (1993) note the particular challenge of working with clients who might be seen as having a 'borderline personality disorder'. Diagnosis aside, certainly boundary issues emerge when individuals lack the confidence or clarity to assert boundaries in daily life relationships. This might result from a history where the individual's boundaries were regularly violated, or the person might have rigidly controlled boundaries that leave no room for spontaneity. A person (be it client or therapist) with loose or non-existent boundaries, for instance, may have learned this way-of-being in childhood as a way of coping with abuse. Not having boundaries in childhood may have served to keep them safe, since resisting abuse could mean more hurt.

When working with individuals with these sorts of backgrounds, some therapists view out-of-hours phone calls as necessary and expected. The likely inability of such clients to evoke a holding, soothing introject can trigger catastrophic anxiety related to fear that the therapist will abandon them. Phone calls are then a way to re-establish contact with the therapist and be soothed out of ill-advised, self-destructive behaviour. (See also the discussion on 'virtual holding environments' in Chapter 7.) Other therapists view such calls as counter-therapeutic and promoting dependency; they hold a firmer boundary to emphasise that phone calls are reserved for emergency situations.

3. Different cultural expectations

Another problem we encounter when attempting to apply time boundaries is one of cultural differences in expectations. This can occur when our work carries us to other places (for example, statutory services) or to settings with looser time boundaries. In such environments, appointments may be routinely overrun or cut short, with people getting called away on emergencies (Read,

2014). Here, attention needs to be paid both to the context and to the background of the people involved. When I worked in the NHS, it was not uncommon for patients to be called out of their counselling sessions to see the doctor. This kind of institutionalised boundary violation can be hard to fight when there is a lack of (professional-to-professional) respect.

When working with clients, we may need to factor in their personal values and cultural background when it comes to issues such as punctuality and attendance. Meyer's (2014) research comparing corporate cultures across the world suggests there is considerable variation between cultures here. While people from Germany, Japan and Switzerland tend to follow the stereotype of being sticklers for punctuality, those from parts of Africa, India and the Middle East have more flexible ideas of time. If a client is overly casual about time boundaries, this may not mean they are being disrespectful or have bad manners. Its worth exploring what the time boundary means to them.

Therapist self-disclosure

Careful, artful, intuitive judgement is needed for decisions about when and how to self-disclose. Exploration of this thorny, controversial area requires us to begin by recognising the different types of disclosure at stake:

1. Disclosure as an intervention giving here-and-now personal responses to the therapy process, where the therapist offers their thoughts and feelings responding relationally to the client.
2. Disclosure of the therapist's personal details (for example, about family or social circumstances).
3. Disclosure of current issues (for example, revealing a recent family bereavement to explain an absence).
4. Disclosure of the therapist's past history of pain, trauma or relational stresses.
5. Disclosures about strategies to manage emotion and the use of resources (for example, 'Walking in nature helps me to feel grounded and relaxed. The important thing is to find what works for you.').
6. Inadvertent disclosure of the therapist's tastes, predilections and interests (for example, information gleaned from looking around the therapy room).

The value of therapist disclosure is that it reveals the therapist to be a 'real' person, an authentic, congruent and transparent human being, who is capable of showing empathy which deepens the relationship. Self-disclosure can also help normalise experience or offer alternative perspectives. The art lies in judging whether to self-disclose and *if* we want to interest, charm or delight the client with our sense of shared humanness, judging *how* and *when to* do it (Clarkson, 2003).

The argument against self-disclosure highlights the breached boundary involved when the focus of the session shifts from client to therapist. In addition, self-disclosure increases the therapist's vulnerability. For example, the exposure might feel shaming later and/or could open the therapist up to being manipulated or negatively judged (Amis, 2017). Self-disclosure is also contra-indicated where – perhaps owing to their life circumstances – clients have poor boundaries or where therapists are extra-vulnerable to potential boundary violations (Taylor et al., 2010).

In general, disclosures about *process responses* (thoughts and feelings about what is happening in the moment in the work) tend to be more helpful than those about *personal or past experience*, which can test boundaries. Egan (2013, pp. 185–186) advocates doing self-disclosure in a contained way:

- Make sure that your disclosures are appropriate.
- Make sure that disclosures are culturally appropriate.
- Be careful of your timing.
- Keep your disclosure selective and focused.
- Don't disclose too frequently.
- Do not burden the client.
- Remain flexible.

Therapist self-disclosure of immediate responses can offer a useful – sometimes risky – model of authenticity, presence and openness. It typically occurs in the context of humanistic, dialogic ways of working. For example, I might share with a client that I am not feeling emotion in my body and that this is leading me to wonder if I am manifesting the client's own dissociation. By doing this, I am implicitly inviting them to become aware of their embodied responses. More controversially, I once shared with a client that I felt 'used' by her in the same manner as a soothing medication – something she discarded until she needed it again. Exploring this further, we realised how she herself had felt used and then abandoned in all her significant relationships. It was the start of her deciding to relate in new, less instrumental ways.

Whether disclosures are beneficial or problematic depends on the nature of the disclosure, the specific relational-social context and the **theoretical framework** adopted. Disclosures offered with the aim of raising the client's self-awareness occur more commonly in *humanistic-integrative* modes of working. They occur less frequently in pure *psychoanalytic* contexts, where the therapist is more of a 'blank slate' on which the client can project, and in *cognitive brief therapy*, where disclosure would be irrelevant. Self-disclosure can be understood as showing one's own personhood (as in *humanistic* work) or it can be about explicitly communicating counter-transferential experience (as in *psychodynamic* approaches). O'Brien and Houston (2007, p. 160) provide an example of the latter:

> Therapist: I am feeling some rather uncomfortable pressure on me to please you in our sessions, with what I say and how I say it. It occurs to me that this might be because it is how you are feeling – that there is some pressure on you to be interesting to your colleagues in the office, and an interesting client to me, or we may not want you.

I have known a few therapists who routinely self-disclose, either in or out of their awareness. At times, I have seen this create relational ruptures: clients might sense that the focus of therapy is no longer on them sufficiently, or they might feel required to soothe or validate the therapist (perhaps replaying their own history of taking care of others). As Clarkson (2003, p. 17) notes, excessive self-disclosure is abusive and a form of acting out of the therapist's 'need for display, hostility or seductiveness'.

I would recommend that therapists reflect on *why* they are self-disclosing and *in whose interests* (Amis, 2017). Is it an attempt to show compassion and empathy? Is it to become better understood by the client or to model something for the client? Is it about the therapist's need and feeling compelled to share? What is the likely impact on the relationship of this disclosure, and does it have the potential to overstep personal–professional boundaries?

It is also worth probing the **relational** nature of the self-disclosure. Is the disclosure in the service of the relationship? How is the client responding? If they ignore it, then maybe they are not yet ready to hear it, or perhaps they have difficulty with the increased level of intimacy. Are they seeing the self-disclosure in more negative terms, perhaps as a sign of lack of interest or, worse, as a boundary breach with the therapist manipulating the client to care for the therapist? Even if the therapist does not mean to do this, might the client – because of their history – feel pulled into an unhealthy dynamic? Alternatively, does the client enjoy hearing about their therapist? In their curiosity, are they inviting the disclosure to illuminate something? Do they experience the disclosure as showing therapist attentiveness and understanding? (Audet and Everall, 2010).

Thinking relationally, I find it useful to draw on *transactional analysis*. Self-disclosures seem to work best in *Adult–Adult* transactions between therapist and client. They are more problematic if the therapist is coming from a needy Child place, or when therapist and client are working developmentally or reparatively with the client's Child.

Digital ethics

The pervasive changes that have come with the 'big data' digital revolution have profoundly impacted professional relationships. Social media and online working provide new opportunities for therapy, potentially facilitating freer interactions. Simultaneously, they pose significant boundary challenges. With more work taking place digitally, therapists are having to evolve new boundaries while perhaps loosening others. It is becoming an ethical imperative for all therapists to consider their digital ethics in terms of both the use of social media and when doing online therapy (see Bolton, 2017, for a review of key ethical issues). In the context of escalating social media use, we can no longer avoid the issue just because it seems an ethical minefield or because of our own 'technophobia'.

Given that we are still at the start of this revolution, it is not surprising that neither practice nor ethical frameworks have properly caught up (see

Boxes 6.2 and 7.2 for current research in this area). However, there is guidance on the use of **social media** laid down in pockets of practice. For instance, the British Psychological Society (BPS) (2012) has published guidance on *e-Professionalism*. This includes the following:

- Clinical psychologists should not transmit any service user identification information via social media without explicit permission...
- Clinical psychologists should ... always consider the appropriateness of material submitted to social media and are strongly advised to use (and monitor and update regularly) privacy settings...
- Interaction with current or former service users via social media in a personal/social capacity should only be undertaken with caution... (British Psychological Society, 2012)

Such guidelines seem relatively straightforward and fit other ethical standards relating to privacy, confidentiality, having clean boundaries, and so on. However, there are some grey areas concerning social media, specifically, whether it is acceptable to communicate personal opinions via Twitter or photos via Facebook. The BPS (2018) position is that there is an expectation that psychologists will conduct themselves with *integrity in the public arena*. When it comes to interacting with service users via social media, the BPS (2012) is clear that contact with current service users is an inappropriate breach of therapeutic boundaries. However, there is scope to communicate with former clients and service users providing they are not deemed 'vulnerable' and providing the professional relationship and position of trust are not exploited.

The guidelines specifically caution psychologists to communicate clearly the boundaries of social media communication. Consider the following situation:

> Dorothy met with her client Leanne for eight weekly sessions before Leanne mentioned in passing that on a number of occasions she had written about what they talked about on her Facebook page. Dorothy was taken aback as she felt that they had agreed on confidentiality during their contracting. ... Leanne talked openly about how important her friends' views were to her and saw her counselling sessions as being 'like visits to the doctor'. (Amis, 2017, p. 82)

For many therapists, confidentiality is only contracted as a *one-way* requirement and they would not share Dorothy's discomfort. If concerns about exposure are an issue, then maybe 'mutual respect of privacy' should be established in the contract. My concern with this story relates more to Leanne's own boundaries and degree of awareness of the risks attached to over-disclosure (which can raise self-protection issues).

Amis (2017) offers a list of thought-provoking questions to do with digital ethics and boundaries. These highlight some of the risks posed by problematic self-disclosure and multiple relationships. I lay them out here with my additional thoughts in brackets. I invite you to reflect on your own position as you read them:

1. Do you have a presence on Facebook or other social media platforms? [And do you ensure appropriate 'privacy' settings and regularly review these? Have you considered having a pseudonym?]
2. If a client does an online search for you, what will they find? [Are you comfortable about this? Might it be useful to leave space in the therapy room to process any potential 'elephants in the room'?]
3. Do you post accessible personal details such as family photos online? [I try to only post stuff which I would be prepared to self-disclose verbally: for instance, about the number of grandchildren rather than details of my activities. And I only post using a pseudonym.]
4. What would you do if a current client sent you a 'friend' request on Facebook? [The BPS (2012) guidelines state that this should be formally declined.]
5. What would you do if a former client sent you a 'friend' request on Facebook? [This is more blurry: I would possibly allow for 'Linked In' contact if it was in the client's interest, but I probably would not go as far as being a 'friend'.]
6. Have you ever been tempted to 'Google' clients? [Is this out of curiosity or a safety/trust issue? The legal position isn't always clear about how acceptable it is to do background searches; at the very least, we need to be mindful of client's rights to privacy and of what is in their interests.]
7. Do you integrate appropriate apps into your therapy? [Some mindfulness and CBT apps are particularly beneficial. My current favourite is one called 'Calm Harm'.]
8. If so, where are the boundaries of therapeutic responsibility and how is this communicated to your clients? [Do you make sure the apps are 'safe', properly validated ones before recommending them? Have you tried them yourself? Do you follow up and embrace their use as part of the therapy?]
9. Do you offer [online] ... sessions such as Skype and FaceTime and how is this covered within your contract in respect of confidentiality, storage [of information], privacy, as well as outside with any insurance providers, etc.? [Beyond ensuring privacy, do you also ensure a professional space is maintained and how do you do this? When working online, it can be tempting to lounge in bed or other private spaces and wear clothes you wouldn't normally wear, crossing the private–professional line. For me, this would be inappropriate; I would question whether the therapist was fully present as a professional. It's also worth considering what the video reveals about your private spaces.]
10. Are sessions recorded and saved anywhere? [This is a particular issue for trainees, who should be transparent about the security put in place when working with transcripts of their sessions.]
11. How can you guarantee the security and confidentiality of session content? [At the very least, this should be discussed. Some care needs to be taken here: we need to be aware which sites/programs are more secure.]

12. Does your storage arrangement adhere to the Data Protection law of the country you are practising in? [This applies to written notes as well as digital]. (Amis, 2017, p. 67)

Attending specifically to online therapy work, it is important that both therapist and client are comfortable with the alternative mode of working (including using video and other online therapies). Amis (2017, p. 132) offers a challenge to therapists who are wary of embracing these alternative modes of working: 'Are we embedded in traditional practice to the exclusion of potentially new and successful methodologies?' If we are going to work digitally, then it is our ethical responsibility, she argues, to feel confident and appropriately trained in any alternative methods of doing therapy.

Box 6.2   Research and the digital revolution

1. **Lehavot et al. (2010)** surveyed 302 graduate psychology and psychotherapy students in the US to evaluate the prevalence of social networking and how it might encroach on professional relationships. Eighty-one per cent of respondents reported using some social networking sites. While many used security measures to limit access to their information, a notable number did not. The authors discuss the controversy sparked by therapists posting personal information when using social media networking. They explore the consequences of clients accessing this information, noting the possibility of increased potential for harm to practitioners. While expressing discomfort about the idea of clients looking up their personal details, the authors acknowledge that they themselves at times look clients up.

2. Also in the US, **Taylor et al. (2010)** surveyed (by an online questionnaire) 695 licensed psychologists enrolled in doctoral-level training about their social networking website (SNW) use: 77% had a social networking page and 85% of these reported using privacy settings. One hundred individuals also provided qualitative information about the challenges they face. Many of these participants admitted to feeling taxed when they discovered shared mutual friends with clients; most removed their pages or ensured the highest security settings. The authors discuss how younger psychologists use SNWs the most, thereby confronting particularly challenging dilemmas at a time when they are still relatively inexperienced.

3. **Finn and Barack (2010)** examined the process, outcomes and ethics of providing therapy online. Ninety-three e-counsellors and psychotherapists with at least a Master's degree (including social work practitioners, coaches, and so on) were surveyed (80% were from the US; 20% from other countries). Most believed their practice (which usually included some face-to-face work) was effective. However, the absence of consensus about ethical obligations suggests a need for more formal training.

4. **Fang et al. (2017)** explored the use of online counselling via qualitative content analysis of transcripts from 385 email sessions and 85 chat exchanges between 22 Master's of Social Work student counsellors and 33 undergraduate clients in Canada. Their analysis identified benefits that included increased accessibility, flexibility and immediacy; greater room for reflections; and an increased sense of safety. However, there were also disadvantages, including having to deal with technical difficulties and a heavier work-load.

5. **Morina et al. (2015)** performed a meta-analysis of 14 clinical trials applying virtual reality exposure therapy (VRET) to specific phobias. They concluded VRET is effective and has similar outcomes to in-vivo exposure therapy.

Can boundary transgressions be therapeutic?

Therapists learn to hold many boundaries with clients and colleagues. By doing so, we help keep ourselves, our clients and our profession safe. But the process is rarely straightforward. The art of therapy is to intuit when a boundary can or should be nudged or loosened, if not breached. And we don't always get it right, as the example in Box 6.3 demonstrates.

Box 6.3   Trangressing boundaries?

Arlene is 49 and in training to become a therapist herself. ... She has been in therapy with Paul for three years. At the end of their first session, he asked if she wanted a hug. After that, the hug became a regular part of each session's closing. Arlene became very attached to this ritual: '... The hug means caring, acceptance, validation. I was raised to feel it was wrong or bad to have any needs of my own. The hug says that it's okay to give affection, it's okay to be vulnerable, I don't have to be ashamed.'

Arlene's parents divorced when she was two, and she saw her father only on weekends. Arlene felt that her mother took things away from her if Arlene wanted them too much or if they made her feel too special.

One afternoon, about a year and a half into Arlene's therapy, Paul was visibly upset when he came into the waiting room to get her for their session. She looked at him sympathetically, and he said, 'I think I need a hug.' Arlene was happy to oblige. ... The next session, when Paul came into the waiting room to get Arlene, she rose immediately and hugged him, institutionalizing the spontaneous gesture of the prior session. She interpreted his lacklustre response as tacit approval of this new ritual.

(Continued)

(Continued)

Two months after the initial breach, as Arlene rose from her chair and moved toward Paul to give him what had become their routine session-opening hug, he stopped her. 'I'm not going to do this anymore,' he said. 'You want something from me that I don't want to give.' Arlene felt the rebuff was 'a slap in the face.'

Paul later acknowledged that he never should have asked Arlene for a hug in the first place and should not have allowed the hugs to continue, but that now he had to put a stop to them in order to take care of himself. Arlene's hugs felt too 'greedy,' too 'grabby,' too 'possessive' and that made him uncomfortable.

Arlene felt so devastated by Paul's remarks that she did not raise the subject of the hug again for many months. Once again, as in childhood, something good, something that made her feel special, had been taken away from her because she had been too greedy and let her needs show.

Paul's initial boundary breach arose out of his own need: he spontaneously used his client to comfort himself and, in doing so, failed to put his client's interests above his own. (Lott, 1999)

The situation in Box 6.3 calls out to be regularly reviewed (and challenged) in supervision. Perhaps some of the discomfort and tension – for both Paul and Arlene – could have been prevented by directly processing, in a more mutual, relational way, the impact of what has occurred *at the time*.

However, not all boundary transgressions are problematic. Gutheil and Gabbard (1993) helpfully distinguish between harmful '**boundary violations**' and neutral, even beneficial, '**boundary crossings**'. The Australian and New Zealand Association of Psychotherapists define these terms:

A boundary crossing is a deviation from usual therapeutic activity that is essentially harmless, non-exploitative, and possibly supportive of the therapy itself, such as self-disclosures, non-sexual physical contact, contact outside of the normal therapy session or small gift giving. In contrast, a boundary violation is harmful or potentially harmful, to the client and the therapy. Boundary violations frequently constitute exploitative dual relationships. (ANZAP, 2014, p. 13)

While noting that the empirical evidence indicates that boundary violations frequently accompany or precede sexual misconduct, Gutheil and Gabbard (1993) argue that 'slippery slope' violations do not themselves necessarily constitute malpractice. From one theoretical perspective, a boundary violation may be standard professional practice; from another, it may not be recommended. The intense debates (discussed in Chapter 7) surrounding the acceptability of touch in therapy is a case in point.

There are also times when the favoured therapeutic (or supervisory) action involves transgressing boundaries (Hobman, 2018). Boundaries are not absolutes; they need to be understood and negotiated in specific contexts; they can get blurred and sometimes this can be helpful. Boundarying to contain the therapeutic process is a **negotiated** process, not the application of a fixed line. Sticking rigidly to rules or engaging in fear-based defensive practice can create problems. The relational challenge is to work out each boundary question, freshly thinking about what the relationship needs, including when to soften a line or bend a boundary and be more spontaneously boundless. Therapists need to think deeply and carefully about the implications and relational consequences of their actions in terms of both boundary setting and transgressions. *The more relational we are in practice, the more challenging the processes of holding boundaries; each relationship needs to find its own thresholds.*

While professional opinion varies, it seems that boundary crossings can enrich therapy and enhance the alliance. But they can also undermine therapy and cause harm to the client. So, it's important to ensure boundary crossings put ethical concerns at the fore. It means: considering the individual circumstances and relational context; critically and reflexively thinking through the issues; and staying abreast of evolving legislation and case law, ethical standards, research, theory and practice guidelines. If therapists recognise that certain boundary decisions have proven problematic, they need to take responsibility and respond appropriately (Pope and Keith-Spiegel, 2008).

To give an idea of how and when boundaries *might* be transgressed therapeutically, consider the different examples below:

1. Lamprecht (2013) recommends the spontaneous, contact-full writing of letters to clients, outside (paid, contracted) sessions. Here the letter may offer valuable feedback to clients that they are important and thought about outside sessions. They also offer a symbolic psychic/physical link to the therapist, which may prove powerful for those clients who are insecurely or ambivalently attached to the therapist. Such 'relationally responsive' letter-writing can provide a valuable therapeutic function, although it needs to be handled sensitively and selectively.

2. A client asks for some feedback from his more academically-minded therapist about an article he's written. The therapist recognises the request is loaded: the client needs informed feedback and she is a good person to give it. But could he cope with critical comments from her? They discuss the potential boundary confusion. In reply, the client shares his frustration that he has few colleagues he can dialogue with at an academic level – his academic side is still a part of who he is so why can't the therapist talk to that part? He emphasises that it is precisely his trust in the expertise and honesty of the therapist that reduces his sense of his shame and exposure. If he can't share it in therapy, how can he share it more widely? The therapist agrees, and they use part of their session to talk about the client's work and what it means to him. They set aside extra (unpaid) time to engage the feedback, separating it from the therapy.

3. A supervisee is struggling in her work; she seems burnt-out and low. Previously they had discussed self-care and it seems the therapist is

doing all the right things to no avail. The supervisor, concerned about the possible impact on clients, probes what is going on with the supervisee's life more generally. The therapist reveals she recently had a miscarriage, triggering traumatic memories of a previous abortion when she was 14. The supervisor is compassionate, and they spend the rest of the session processing the impact of the miscarriage – a challenging balance, to talk therapeutically without giving therapy as such. She tentatively suggests the therapist might return to therapy to do some deeper trauma work.

4. Carla had been in therapy for three years when she was diagnosed with terminal cancer. Her therapist, Suyin, was faced with several dilemmas and sought supervision to handle the resulting relational boundary challenges. Together, Suyin and her supervisor agreed that it would serve Carla's interests to continue the therapy at Carla's home when she was no longer able to get out to the clinic. Careful boundaries were put in place to ensure the space remained 'therapeutic' rather than 'social'. For instance, the time boundary of an hour-long session remained fixed and Suyin did not accept offered cups of coffee. After a few months, Carla's physical condition deteriorated and therapy could not be sustained. Carla and Suyin worked through an appropriate 'ending'. Thereafter, with the supervisor's agreement, Suyin briefly visited Carla in her hospice a few times, always making sure to go at times when other visitors had left. This was explicitly seen as showing care rather than doing therapy and Suyin did not charge for her time.

Concluding reflections

With 'boundarying', the challenge for therapists is the fact that lines are not clear and pre-set. Boundaries mean something different to each individual and at different times. A hug can be perceived as warm and compassionate or as a boundary violation. Similarly, therapist self-disclosure can be actively sought by the client or perceived as invasive. Therapists need to intuit *how interventions will be received*.

The answer to any boundary dilemma must be seen in the relational, cultural (including institutional) context, which includes the therapist's personal values and theoretical preferences. Negotiations can get sticky when different organisations and cultures have their own limits of what is acceptable or not. I recall that when I was first training formally as an integrative psychotherapist, I felt thoroughly confused when I kept hearing the phrase 'It's a boundary issue', following which people would go mysteriously quiet. My many years of working as a mental health practitioner in the NHS had accustomed me to different boundaries. Confidentiality, for instance, was always understood to be 'within the team' and the idea of carrying patients' 'secrets' would have been taboo. Personal gift giving/receiving was also thought to be taboo, but I learned it could be psychotherapeutically helpful.

In my own practice, the boundaries I maintain with each client/supervisee subtly varies. Where possible I will try to *mutually negotiate* what feels appropriate. When the boundarying hasn't worked (for whatever reason), then it's an intervention opportunity: a chance to explore clients' process and relational needs (and my own).

In common with some clients, therapists also have boundary issues. We all make mistakes, whether in the form of feeling compelled to engage in excessive self-disclosure or more serious boundary transgressions. Continuing professional development, supervision and therapy can all help us discover healthier boundaries: ones that ensure we are not cutting off from others while still taking care of ourselves. I know for myself that my boundarying has become much cleaner and clearer over time; I've learned through mistakes.

When grappling with boundary issues, the overriding questions have to be: 'Is this in the client's interests and/or in the service of the relationship?' If we cannot answer a clear 'yes', then the boundarying is probably suspect, which may compromise the therapy.

I like Nick Totton's position:

> For a therapist to hold careful boundaries because they believe they must, or because they are afraid of the uncontrollability of closeness, cripples the potential for relatedness. But for a therapist to hold such boundaries as an honouring of the client's woundedness is itself relational. (Totton, 2010, p. 15)

Discussion questions

1. 'Boundarying is best done relationally rather than via rules'. Discuss.
2. Explain and evaluate how your online social media presence may impact on your clients.
3. Critically examine the point at which therapist self-disclosure becomes a problematic boundary transgression.

Summary

Therapeutic boundaries ensure an ethical, trustworthy frame to hold-contain testing psychotherapeutic processes. They guard the relationship and respect the rights of both client and therapist while setting limits to therapists' power and the potential intimacy of the therapy encounter. The answer to any boundary dilemma depends on the relational and practice context as well as personal values. Boundarying to contain the therapeutic process is a negotiated process, not a fixed line. The relational challenge is to work out each boundary question freshly, including when to transgress and when to hold firm.

7

Ethical 'Holding'

Box 7.1   A example of therapeutic holding

I have been a therapist for a long time. My problems; my issues had all been well explored in therapy. But I'd never really let myself go when expressing stuff.

That all changed in one session. I was giving my therapist a lot of knowing about my emotions. If you just read my words, you'd think: 'Oh, this is really meaty stuff'. But my therapist knew that I wasn't really connecting; I wasn't fully present. He listened to me and then said: 'Well, that's all really very interesting. But I am not feeling it.'

'What do you mean?' I asked

'Let go; open to me', he said.

'What are you talking about?'

The tension built and I cried out, 'Just what do you want me to do?!' Suddenly, something physically released in me. I became vulnerable; was no longer in control; my tears started to flow. In that very same moment as he grasped my hands.

'I've got you. I'm here.'

And I felt his 'holding'. I don't think we said much after that. But for me it was a huge moment of healing: Somebody was there for me; they would 'hold' me; they wouldn't let me fall.

This chapter examines the relational-ethical implications of the many ways of therapeutic holding – metaphorical and literal – from mindful holding to full-blown physical cradling. Metaphorically, therapists offer clients a supportive environment by being sensitively attuned, solidly present, protective and reliable. Inside therapy space we hold and contain clients' anxiety, anger, confusion, grief and pain. Less frequently, we may hold a client more literally, offering a hug, for example. The example in Box 7.1 combines the two. Probably, all therapists endorse the value of metaphorical holding, but actual physical contact is hotly contested and is sometimes seen as transgressing ethical boundaries.

The first two sections explore **metaphorical** and **physical holding** respectively, highlighting the relational-ethical implications. The third section offers an extended discussion about the loud debates (theoretical and ethical) around the **use of touch**.

Metaphorical holding

The concept of holding evokes a maternal metaphor: that of a baby held tenderly and protectively in a mother's arms (or held, before birth, in comfort in the womb). In therapy, this concept is extended to embrace the therapeutic environment and the creation of attentive spaces and regular routines that enable clients to feel secure, nourished and safe (Winnicott, 1953, 1971).

The therapeutic relationship in turn offers support which contains the expression and exploration of raw emotions. Holding involves the therapist listening, attuning and adapting to the client. With their needs and choices respected, clients learn to absorb the nurturing and get closer to their therapist. The key is for the client to feel held enough to 'recover, or to discover maybe for the first time, a capacity for managing life ... without continued avoidance or suppression' (Casement, 1985, p. 133). Over time, this emphasis on protection and safety yields ground and challenges are offered.

In practice, holding is enacted metaphorically and in different ways, such as the way therapists:

- hold a client's story in mind
- engage in analytic holding
- strive to hold a client's disintegrated parts
- offer virtual holding environments.

Holding a client's story in mind

> Genuinely holding someone in your mind spins delicate, transparent threads of intimacy across even the widest gaps, deepening confidence and trust. (Green, 2012b)

As therapists, we have a hugely important ethical role to play in both co-creating and holding a client's story. Our role may also include holding parts of the client's story which they are not yet ready to hold themselves (for example, anger) or of which they have lost sight (such as times when they had hope).

Perret (2015, pp. 60–61) provides the following example of how 'holding in mind' can contribute to the therapeutic relationship:

> She continued to completely forget the content of our previous sessions, especially the elements regarding the relationship between the two of us and the attachment. I find her with her frozen smile, telling me she does not know what to talk about as everything is going well for her. It is I who recalls for her where we were when we separated for the holidays. It is I who refreshes her memory, gently and with benevolence. It is I who maintains the permanence that she is not yet capable of ensuring.

As Yalom (2001, p. 158) advises, *'therapy works best if it approximates a continuous session* [italics in original]'. In this way, issues can be returned to, reworked and worked through. Clients can feel seen and cared for when we remember what they said, whether months ago or just last week. As one therapist recalls:

> I have one client who is deeply grateful for the way I remember the fine details of his life story. Three years on from when he first came to me, I can point out the transformation I see. He knows that I 'see' him and that I *want* to remember what he says because it – he – is important. This is what he is missing developmentally. His alcoholic mother was routinely unable to remember their conversations and often missed seeing him all together.

Frequency of contact is an important factor to consider. The key ethical question is: 'What needs to be held and for how long?' For some of my clients a fortnightly appointment involves far too long a gap. They lose the sense of being held by me or fear that I would too easily 'lose' them and their story. For others, a fortnight feels about right. Of those clients I see less regularly, some cannot afford weekly therapy and, reluctantly, we compromise. At other times, it's a conscious choice. One client I worked with over several years completed his therapy journey by reducing contact over time. Later he returned for monthly sessions to re-engage with his own story – something he found helpful while writing his autobiography.

When clients lack a sense of themselves or their own importance, it may make a difference to know that their therapist thinks about them *between* sessions. I might make a point of sending such a client an email or a receipt for a session several days after the session. While such between-session contact could be considered a boundary transgression, at times it offers clients helpful extra holding. It communicates: 'I am thinking of you' – a powerful challenge to a client with a 'do not exist' injunction. [This concept comes from *transactional analysis* theory, which identifies numerous 'can't'/'mustn't' injunctions which people have internalised and embedded in their life-scripts, including: Don't be (don't exist), Don't think, Don't feel, Don't cry, Don't grow up, Don't be important, Don't be close, etc.]

Analytic holding

Analytic interpretation can also be used as ways of holding charged emotion. This involves the use of words to convey to the client that the therapist knows, understands and empathises.

Psychoanalytic holding refers to the therapist's capacity to tolerate contact with the intensity of the patient's feelings, to contain emotions and make sense of them interpretatively. The process of analytic holding offers sufficient safety for the client to re-experience extremes of unsafety in the transference:

> ... what *can* be provided is a security within the analytic relationship that allows the patient to feel understood, sensitively responded to, and analytically 'held,' by an analyst who can tolerate what is yet to come in the course of the analysis, without collapse or retaliation. (Casement, 1990, p. 89)

Patrick Casement (1985) describes the case of Mrs F, who had become dependent on medication and desperately pleaded with him to talk to her doctor about raising her dosage. He offered her more therapy time instead, interpretatively responding that her need for soothing medication was a substitute for her need to be held by a person. It proved a significant intervention. Mrs F gained the insight that what she really needed was not a 'dummy' (the medication) but rather reassurance that her needs were not overwhelming and could be met. (As a small child, Mrs F had repeatedly experienced her mother taking away her dummy without responding to her emotional needs.)

Analytic holding is linked to attunement, while the therapist *holds on to* being a functioning, solid, analytical therapist:

> Patients have taught me that when I allow myself to feel (and even be invaded by) the patient's own unbearable feelings, and if I can experience this (paradoxically) as both unbearable and yet bearable, so that I am still able to find some way of going on, I can begin to 'defuse' the dread in a patient's most difficult feelings. (Casement, 1985, p. 154)

Holding disintegrated or disowned parts

In longer-term, integrative or relational psychotherapy, we are often called upon to hold parts of a client's self/emotions that they might disown (consciously or unconsciously) (Erskine, 2015). (And, of course, working relationally, it's possible the client also picks up our own disowned stuff!)

When working with severely traumatised, dissociated clients, we might focus therapy on holding (and containing) disparate parts of 'selves' that emerge during sessions. More specifically, in *gestalt* work, we might invite clients to put a feeling part of themselves that they don't want to acknowledge onto an empty chair and explicitly dialogue with it; and so perhaps enter into a more self-compassionate, accepting relationship with this aspect of themselves. Working *psychoanalytically*, we might receive a projective identification that we need to contain and offer back in an acceptable form.

Sometimes the holding can be **imaginal** (Erskine, 2015). The following therapy session began with the therapist drawing attention to 'Julie's' defensive processes. This led to the discovery of an abandoned and feared part of Julie that held intense anger and despair. In childhood, Julie had been profoundly abused by her mentally ill older brother, with neither parent intervening to keep her safe:

K: Is there any way that you and I might enter into communication with this angry part of you in a safe way, right now[?]...

J: There's a fence and something else holding back ... Like in *Silence of the Lambs*, where they're held and wrapped up so they can't move...

K: So that would feel safer to you if that part of you were contained like that?...

J: They're just trying to yell, crying, just so upset.

K: What might that part of you need to feel calmed, soothed and reassured...

J: (long pause). I feel like slowly going over and hugging myself, or that person, and slowly taking off the wraps... (eyes closed in spontaneous trance state, absorbed in inner drama) At first they're fighting me when I hug them. And I just keep hugging them and tell them that I love them. ... She's just crying, really hard crying, so much she can't talk.

K: ...What are those tears saying do you think?

J: They're so upset about what happened, and finally someone is listening. ... I let her out completely and she falls to the ground and I catch her ... I'm just holding her. (Lamagna and Gleiser, 2007, pp. 39–40)

In this excerpt, the client imaginally holds her own damaged 'part', but this is done in the context of the therapist's safe holding. Together, client and therapist facilitate the emergence of that distressed part into awareness.

Virtual holding environments

Therapy using distance technology and cybertherapy (e-therapy via virtual space) enable distinctive forms of holding and intimacy, ones which can both help and hinder the therapeutic process. **Virtual** holding environments include the use of telephone, texts, email, online forums, chat media, Skype/FaceTime-type therapy, video conferencing and avatar therapy. Therapy through these modes can be engaged together with, or instead of, face-to-face work. However, extra measures need to be taken to ensure confidentiality and security. Currently, at the time of writing, FaceTime is seen to be more 'secure' than Skype. In time, professional bodies may circumscribe some online forums as being insufficiently secure.

Referring to the use of sessions via mobile phone or **Skype/FaceTime**, Tosone (2013) argues that e-therapy offers intriguing possibilities for creative work, along with the possibility of holding clients who live in remote areas or find it difficult (psychologically or physically) to travel. It also makes it possible to continue a therapeutic relationship when one person is relocating.

However, working at a distance may curtail some visual and bodily cues about a client's mental state, making it harder for the therapist to attune. Extra care must be taken to safeguard appropriate ethical boundaries, including those relating to confidentiality and ensuring a safe physical space. The inevitable disruptions triggered by technical failures also need consideration.

Overall, my own experience of using Skype/FaceTime for both therapy and supervision has been positive: I've found it works surprisingly well. But poor internet connections often intrude, with disruptive, frustrating, and occasionally destructive, consequences. One client felt so averse to this ongoing disruption of contact that she abruptly terminated therapy. With those who persevere, I tend to work harder to be present and to hold the therapy space. In some cases, this has the paradoxical effect of benefiting our work together. Keeping a sense of *humour* is also helpful. For instance, one of my clients jokingly maintains that losses of contact on FaceTime occur whenever she experiences the work as too intense, when a part of her feels relieved to dissociate.

With specific reference to mobile phone use, Innocente (2015) discusses how clinician–client **texting** can be used relationally as an expansion of the holding therapy environment. Texting between sessions, she acknowledges, can violate and confuse therapy boundaries. However, in some circumstances, allowing inter-session communications may be the most healing intervention. She gives an example from her social work doctoral research where she decided to do therapy via texting:

> Although Matt was in his home experiencing an emotional crisis, his fear, anger, and abandonment did not remain contained inside him. He composed his text message on his phone and indiscriminately hit 'send'. His crisis travelled several miles through a mobile operating system until it found its way to my house, where it arrived as an uninvited visitor requiring my immediate attention. Whether I liked it or not, the clinical holding environment had expanded. ... By holding him, literally in the palm of my hand, and metaphorically with my willingness to be with him through his crisis and meet him where he was in a virtual holding environment – a powerful reparative relational experience occurred that had a significant therapeutic impact. (Innocente, 2015, pp. 83–84)

In the case of clients orientated towards technology or social media, e-therapy (using distance, online and/or virtual methods) might facilitate both their access and their openness to therapy (see Box 7.2). The National Institute for Clinical Excellence (NICE), for example, is currently trialling a new digital CBT program called 'deprexis' for the treatment of depression. Deprexis is a 10-module mobile App and online program using the principles of CBT. Early research is promising (NICE, 2018).

Box 7.2 Digital therapy?

A number of studies have evaluated the use of digital technology and demonstrated they can play a positive role for mental health:

1. **Berger et al. (2018)** conducted a randomised control trial in Germany (n=98) to study the effectiveness of the digital DBT program deprexis. The researchers compared deprexis as an adjunct to face-to-face psychotherapy with face-to-face psychotherapy alone. At 12 weeks, people who engaged

(Continued)

(Continued)

deprexis plus psychotherapy had statistically significantly greater improvements in their depression symptoms than people having psychotherapy alone. At six months, the deprexis group continued to have improved depression scores compared to psychotherapy alone.

2. In a systematic review of 15 randomised controlled trials of the effectiveness of self-help internet interventions, **Griffiths and Christensen (2006)** found most interventions were reported to be effective in reducing risk factors or improving symptoms.

3. **Boschen and Casey (2008)** surveyed the use of mobile phones for those suffering from specific phobias. A particular advantage of using mobile phones was that clients could contact their therapist from their current location and engage in homework tasks *in vivo*. Internet features on the phone also helped clients to access relevant websites, including images of their feared stimuli.

4. **Day and Schneider (2002)** compared face-to-face therapy with audio and video therapy over a five-week CBT approach. They found all programmes were equally effective.

5. **Ludman et al. (2007)** compared eight CBT sessions for depressed patients administered by phone with primary care pharmacological treatment and found both were effective.

6. **Khanna and Kendall (2010)** reported a small-scale, randomised controlled trial comparing individual, clinic-based CBT for 7–13-year-old anxious children with computer-assisted treatment. Both treatments were associated with significantly greater reductions in anxiety than a placebo control condition. Improvements for both continued over the three-month follow-up period, with no difference in outcome.

Physical holding

The practice of physically holding clients is of course highly dependent on the cultural and institutional context as well as the needs and preferences of those involved. Clinical and ethical complexities are at stake (Crawford, 2012). The type, frequency, quality and intention of physical holding also varies enormously. Work in a children's unit or hospice, for instance, may involve touch that is playful, along with soothing, loving hugs. In contrast, restraining-constraining protective holding might be used in mental health units where the aim is to contain violent, destructive behaviour.

Extensive use of physical holding occurs less often in one-to-one counselling or psychotherapy with adults. That said, situations arise which invite us to engage in some degree of holding. We also need to distinguish between touch that is initiated by the client (for example, a handshake or hug) and touch that is initiated by the therapist, which could be interpreted as a possible violation unless explicitly negotiated (for example, by a question such as 'Can I hold your hand?'). *The context and intention of the physical contact are crucial.*

While not advocating for, or normalising, touch as a clinical intervention, Crawford (2012) provides some examples of when she has initiated touch:

> I have willingly and appreciatively accepted hugs from clients that were clearly spontaneous expressions of gratitude, appreciation, or connection.
>
> I have covered clients in regressed states with the blanket in my office, and sat on my ottoman near to them.
>
> I have been known, on occasion, to hug a receptive client good bye after a long stretch of deep work, or to re-greet the same client with a hug hello after a lengthy absence.
>
> I have escorted terrified, suicidal or decompensated clients to the psychiatric emergency room holding their hand, or with my arm around their shoulder.
>
> I have encountered clients in medical crisis in and outside of the office and held or touched them to assist them in getting to medical treatment, or to keep them calm until help arrived.
>
> I have occasionally put an arm around clients, with their permission or at their request, when they have been in very significant crisis or after a sudden or shocking death, or following a life-threatening event.
>
> And sometimes contact has emerged as a spontaneous expression of joy after a miraculous surprise. One or two clients over the course of the past two decades may even be able to report that I danced a little jig, and engaged with them in a sort of silly mutual square-dance-like ring-around-a-rosy while squealing with glee like kids at the circus. (Crawford, 2012)

Beyond situations like these, direct bodily holding work can prove extremely powerful, particularly when the therapist has some specific training and experience in this way of working. Body psychotherapies and group therapy are two therapy fields which come to mind.

Somatic or *body-orientated* **therapists** will often explicitly engage physical holding and bodily movement or therapeutic massage. Calming forms of holding might also be used to still and contain emotions. Taylor (2014, p. 104) describes one such instance:

> A young client 'expressed' his extreme trauma in very poor concentration and abrupt disorganized movements. I did not find it easy to contain him. One time he was pacing the room anxiously and then lay down on the sofa. I quietly offered him a blanket and placed cushions all around him. I rested my arm gently across a cushion on his torso at which he quietened down considerably and began to put some words to his experience. I imagined that the extra weight gave him a clearer sense of his body. I could sense his capacity to think return.

Group therapists (including drama therapists) also engage in activities which involve direct physical holding, pushing or leaning. They might use 'trust exercises', including those involving a group lift or falling/catching or leading someone blindfolded, or they might initiate group hugs. These types of holding exercises are particularly useful in human development/encounter type groups and can be a fun way of working productively, particularly with young people.

At a less full-bodied but equally profound level, Yalom (2001) describes his experience of leading a support group for patients with cancer where they ended each meeting with a holding exercise of joining hands in a guided meditation:

> The meditation was calming and restorative but it was the touching of hands that particularly moved me. Artificial boundaries – patient and therapist, the sick and the well, the dying and the living – evaporated as we all felt joined to the others by a common humanity. (Yalom, 2001, p. 191)

Using touch ethically

Professional ethical codes tend to limit the use of touch in therapy unless it is used in specialist ways and/or is explicitly consented to. Where guidance is offered, most codes draw an explicit line before the point where therapeutic touch may be misinterpreted as being intimate or sexually invitational. Before using any touch as a component of therapy, explanations should probably be given and permission received.

Some guidelines include a more explicit 'touch/no touch' policy, for instance, the Northern Guild (UK) guidelines below, concerning the use of touch with children, emphasise the need for supervision to think through the benefits and costs of touch:

> Practitioners are aware that the use of touch with children is complex. It is acknowledged that there are benefits of therapeutic touch and there can be situations when the abstinence would be unkind and have the potential to cause psychological or neurobiological damage. However, touch can also be experienced as intrusive and unwanted, particularly for those who have been sexually or physically abused.
>
> Practitioners will therefore use supervision to think through their use of touch, including the possibility that the use of touch may satisfy their own needs rather than the clients.
>
> Practitioners consider carefully the use of 'safe holding' with children who are hurting themselves, others or damaging property and only use this if they have had specific training in this area and when no other action has been successful. (Northern Guild, 2015, p. 5)

In the following excerpt, Richard Erskine (2014) demonstrates holding-containing *integrative psychotherapy body work*. (I recommend reading the fuller account, which is freely available online, as he highlights body work without touch also.) The example comes from a five-day therapy marathon with therapists. This is important because the context was a holding-containing cohesive group. Erskine and 'Jennifer' also had an established supervisory relationship based on trust which would have helped to hold the work. As he notes: 'I want clients to feel protected so they can relax their physiological retroflections, to finally put into movement what was previously inhibited, and to have a chance to make the necessary physiological and affective expressions – expressions where the neurological system is transformed and healed' (Erskine, 2014, p. 29). (Retroflection refers to the holding in – 'bottling up' – of emotions).

> With the protective presence of the group, I invited her to go back to the physical and emotional experience of curling up and rocking. As she tightened into a fetal position, with eyes closed, she wiggled away from me and tried to hide under one of the many mattresses. I put my hand on her back, over her heart. She was extremely tense as though her back was an iron barrel. I began to massage the tight muscle of her upper back, at first lightly, and then with more strength. During the massage she squirmed and wanted to escape being touched. I had her look at me and reminded her that I would stop immediately if she said, 'Richard Stop'.

> She pushed on the cushions; I sensed that it wasn't me that she was pushing away. I encouraged her to make sounds, any sounds that reflected what she felt inside. As I did a deeper massage in the thoracic area of her back she clawed at the mattress, cried like a young child, and struggled to move away. For the next few minutes she repeatedly howled 'go away,' 'don't touch me,' 'don't feed me,' 'I don't want you,' while alternately squeezing and scratching a cushion.

> I could hear her sounds of helplessness and see that her full expressions of natural protest were still inhibited. If she was going to have a therapeutic closure that could alter the neurobiology of the original neglect and/or trauma, she needed to move her body in a grander way and to feel the sense of anger that she was still retroflecting. I had her roll onto her back. I sat behind her head and began to massage her tight trapezius muscles. In this supine position she was able to move her legs and slowly began to push with them. I asked the group members to surround her with mattresses and pillows. As I continued with a deeper massage she began to kick. I encouraged her to kick harder and faster and to say out loud anything that came to her. She kicked wildly, with such a great force that it took six people to hold the mattress. During the intense kicking she screamed in a strong and determined voice: 'I don't want your touch, Mother.' 'You have always hated me.' 'You squashed me, but now I know the truth.' 'It was never my fault.' 'You are the hateful one … not me.' 'I was a good child and you never saw who I was.' 'All my life I have blamed myself and kept myself hidden – no longer, mother. I am now free.' 'I don't want to carry your depression.' 'I am not going to hide who I am.'

> Throughout this therapy my body resonated with Jennifer's physiological and affective expressions. I experienced a series of alternating sensations: compassion, worry, anger, relief, as well as the ongoing processes of my own internal somatic and affect regulation. My shoulders, back, and legs tightened as I vicariously sensed the retroflections in Jennifer's body. I resonated with the inhibited, frightened, and disgusted little girl. Each of my internal sensations served to keep me attuned to Jennifer's changing affect and body reactions and provided me with a sense of direction in our psychotherapy…

> Then she relaxed into the caring touch of several group members who gathered around to hold her and express their support. (Erskine, 2014, pp. 30, 31)

This compelling account of holding and containing describes deep, cathartic work that took place in a particular (professional, relational and theoretical) specialised context. In other contexts, the boundaries crossed using cathartic touch would be hotly disputed on theoretical grounds and would perhaps also raise serious ethical questions. While holding-containing cathartic work is not uncommon in groupwork, relatively few therapists would have sufficient training and experience to use massage. But here, the therapist was experienced in this sort of work, and his client was well prepared, resourced and fully consenting. That Jennifer could control the level of physical touch by using the 'safe words' 'Richard Stop' helped to ensure a safe ethical boundary.

From the therapist's point of view, he stayed present while resonating with (and holding-containing) the expressed emotions. As Erskine notes, his relational attunement helped him empathise and intuit what was needed moment to moment. This is the art of practice – and the essence of our relational challenge.

Debating the use of touch in therapy

The use of touch in therapy lies at the centre of one of therapy's most contested and divisive debates. The controversy concerns whether touch might be experienced as violating, invasive and/or a step towards the 'slippery slope' of sexual relationship and impending lawsuit (McGuirk, 2012), rather than as something that is natural, nurturing and contact-fully healing.

While all professional ethical guidelines agree that sexual touch between therapist and client is unethical, counter-clinical, an abuse of power and professionally illegal, other kinds of touch are open to debate. Whether or not touch is appropriate depends on context as well as the type of touch involved. One suggested range is '(1) touch as comfort; (2) touch to explore contact...; (3) touch as amplification; (4) touch as provocation; (5) touch as skilled intervention' (Totton, 2003, p. 100). Because there is so much debate about this subject, all of us should perhaps think deeply and widely about it, bearing culture, context and our changing world in mind. As a practitioner, you need to determine your own position about the acceptability and unacceptability of different forms of touch.

Brafman (2006) highlights how the acceptability of touch depends on context. A *psychoanalyst* from Brazil, he gives an amusing account of his first analytic session as a client after moving to London. Meeting the analyst, he shook their hand, and then proceeded to take off his shoes before lying on the couch. There ensued some interpretations about this behaviour. He got the clear message that, in future, he should adopt the 'proper' behaviour of not touching the analyst and keeping his shoes firmly on! Even the seemingly simple act of shaking hands is open to interpretation: for some, it signifies politeness; for others, it constitutes problematic behaviour. It all depends on context and perspective.

In Brafman's example, both the cultural context and the theoretical one (psychoanalysis) are relevant. Whether non-erotic touch in therapy is, or is not, acceptable depends on social, relational and contextual factors and on our own personal values. The **meanings** communicated through touch are key. Therapists must recognise and respect the customs, practices and norms of the local community and of any relevant institution. Culture, ethnicity, religion, gender, age, sexuality, class, and issues of authority and power need to be appreciated before a therapist determines their attitude in any specific therapeutic encounter. These variables cannot all be debated here but I do want to emphasise our need to be socially aware and culturally sensitive – a point enshrined these days in most professional guidelines and ethical codes.

Box 7.3 describes two research studies on touch. The studies derive from different historical and cultural contexts and offer snapshots of the field. Tune's research indicates that touch may be used much more often than practitioners acknowledge (Tune, 2005). However, this reluctance may now be on the decline, with increasing numbers of therapists sharing touch experiences publicly in a more open and accepting environment.

The remainder of this section considers the layered theoretical debates concerning therapeutic touch. Broadly, the *psychoanalytical* school regards touch as unacceptable, while *humanistic* practitioners frequently embrace touch, which is understood as part of being human. In practice, the lines are not clear-cut, confusions arise, and debates occur within, as well as between, respective fields. Relational and integrative practitioners often choose their own way to straddle extreme perspectives. Ultimately, every therapist must develop their own perspective and their own way of dealing with, and justifying, variations within the specific context of their work.

Box 7.3 Research on touch in therapy

Pope, Tabachnick and Keith-Spiegel (1987) surveyed 456 members of Division 29 of the American Psychological Association (APA) in the US about their beliefs and practices concerning a range of behaviours with ethical implications. With regard to touch, they found that 44.5% of the therapists hugged their clients rarely and 41.7% more frequently. Just 4.6% considered the practice of hugging to be clearly unethical, although 41.2% believed it was ethical only under rare circumstances. About a quarter of respondents reported kissing their clients, either rarely (23.5%) or more often (5.0%). About half viewed kissing as unethical, while 36.6% believed it to be unethical in most circumstances.

Interestingly, therapists of differing theoretical orientations were found to have very different beliefs about the practice of touching clients and its likely effects. For example, 30% of humanistic therapists indicated that non-erotic hugging, kissing and affectionate touching might benefit clients in psychotherapy. In contrast, only 6% of psychodynamic therapists favoured this kind of touch. Psychodynamic therapists thought touch could be easily misunderstood, but humanistic therapists did not agree.

(Continued)

(Continued)

Tune (2005) reports his doctoral, grounded theory qualitative research on the dilemmas concerning the ethical use of touch in psychotherapy. On the basis of interviews with 23 UK-based therapists from a range of theoretical backgrounds, he found that many of them followed their intuitive feelings with regard to touch, and that engaging in touch was *not* confined to any particular theoretical orientation. All participants disclosed that they had used some form of touch (particularly that arising from social rituals such as handshakes). Only on 19 out of 89 occasions were these touch incidents discussed with the client or in supervision. Of the 89 incidents, 33 were mentioned in supervision. Roughly half of these incidents involved just three therapists. Importantly, many therapists hid the fact that they touched clients from their supervisor, fearing disapproval. Tune discusses the implications of recognising different types of touch and the value of processing any touch engaged.

Debates within psychoanalytic practice

The taboo concerning touch is firmly rooted in psychoanalytic therapy, with Kahr (2006, p. 2) going as far as to argue that most psychoanalysts 'cringe at the thought of any physical contact with the patient'. This taboo stems from Freud's emphasis on the need to protect both the client and the therapeutic relationship through a 'no touch rule', which ensures sexual urges are never indulged during therapy.

Contemporary psychoanalysts in object relations, Jungian and relational psychoanalytic fields tend to be more flexible and might well use touch judiciously. Even so, most are against engaging in physical contact except after careful thought and discussion in supervision concerning possible transferential processes. Extra care is clearly needed to manage the charged psychoanalytic atmosphere of erotic transference where the spectre of therapist abuse of power always lurks.

A subtler debate within the psychoanalytic field concerns those who caution against triggering unconscious memories of abuse or trauma *versus* those who might use touch to offer a 'corrective emotional experience'. Winnicott, for instance, is known to challenge the tenets of classical psychoanalysis in his use of touch (though the full extent of his use is not entirely clear). For example, in an often-cited account, Margaret Little describes her own psychoanalytic treatment with Winnicott, which involved some regression to infancy:

> Literally, through many long hours, he held my two hands clasped between his, almost like an umbilical cord, while I lay, often hidden beneath the blanket, silent, inert, withdrawn, in panic, rage, or tears, asleep and sometimes dreaming. (Little, 1985, p. 21)

A contrast is offered in a paper by Casement (1982) that has become something of a classic regarding the pressures on the analyst for physical contact during the re-living of an early trauma. Here, he describes the story of Mrs B, an analysand in her early thirties, who insisted on holding Casement's hand as she worked through an infantile trauma memory. When she was 11 months old, she had

poured boiling water over herself and had to undergo several painful skin sur-
geries. During one operation, performed under anaesthetic, her mother held her
hand but fainted. The girl remembers the trauma of her mother's hand slipping
away. This history helped explain Mrs B's need to hold Casement's hand.

After thinking deeply about whether to extend his hand symbolically,
Casement refrained. Several sessions followed where Mrs B was in a state of
heightened distress, anger, confusion and possible delusion. Together, therapist
and client explored her experience. Eventually they both saw that if Casement
had agreed to hold her physically, it would have been a way of soothing her and
shutting off what she was experiencing from them both. This might well have
confirmed her fear of neediness, of that terrible awareness that support (whether
in the form of Casement or her mother) might collapse or disappear:

> I had to continue to be the surviving analyst, and not become a collapsed analyst, in
> order that she could 'defuse' the earlier phantasy that it had been the intensity of her
> need for her mother that had caused her mother to faint. (Casement, 1985, p. 165)

Casement (1985) makes the point that it was important that he/they thought it
all through rather than giving in to (the projective identification) impulse to
hold her hand – or blindly following a 'no contact' rule.

Other psychoanalysts, working in more explicitly *relational* ways, insist on
touch as a therapeutic possibility and readily explore its meanings. Susie
Orbach (2003a), for example, advocates abandoning the taboo about talking
about physical touch and making a space for gentle, judicious, benign touch:

> In bringing our bodies into the room, we are going a step further in the democratiz-
> ing of the process. Two bodies, two minds, two souls, two subjectivities. Does touch,
> benign, thoughtful and tender, extend this democracy? (Orbach, 2003a, p. 25)

Throughout her writings, Orbach offers numerous case examples of the use of
touch (or not) and the importance of attending thoughtfully, and in a relational
way, to situations where touch becomes a possibility. She describes how a
male therapist struggled with his reluctance to give a hug to a female client
who had vaginismus. Her asking for a hug catalysed his awareness that he was
out of physical sympathy with her; he experienced a putrid smell in the room,
like that of a 'rotting mango'. Discussion in supervision allowed him to explore
how he might handle this olfactory counter-transference by seeing this smell
as an expression of her ripeness for the sexual intercourse she longed for:

> His wariness or discomfort about receiving or giving her a hug was made possible
> by her creativity in communicating to him via the countertransference just how
> ghastly she felt in her body, how turned off she was to entering into her own body,
> let alone letting another enter what felt so physically repulsive and unseemly to her.
> The hug was absolutely pivotal. In the therapist struggling with his countertransfer-
> ence so that he could authentically receive the 'putrid' body, Sara was able to
> reverse the corporeal hatred that had stemmed from the touch neglect of her par-
> ents for whom physicality was only medicalized. Her vaginismus dissolved. *Her
> body, not her symptom, now came to therapy.* (Orbach, 2003b, pp. 4–6)

Debates within the humanistic-integrative field

In the humanistic-integrative world, touch is arguably less contentious. However, practice varies widely, with some practitioners in the 'never use touch' camp and many still averse to speaking about their use of touch, a reluctance which suggests that traces of stigma, shame and taboo still loiter. In general, *body psychotherapists*, and *humanistic* practitioners, employ touch more readily. In contrast, *cognitive-behavioural* and *systemic* practitioners, and those engaged in brief therapy, tend to use touch less frequently, perhaps limiting the touch to social rituals like handshakes.

The debate centres on the acceptability of different types of touch. Forms usually seen as acceptable include ritualistic touch (handshakes), consolation touch (brief hand holding, a pat on the back) and playful or celebratory touch (congratulatory hugs). More controversial is touch as 'corrective emotional experience' (for instance, cradling a sobbing client). Some argue that use of any kind of touch with survivors of sexual abuse is contraindicated at all times; others point out how it might be received as safe, affirming and nurturing (Lawry, 1998).

Babette Rothschild, an integrative *trauma therapist*, prefers not to touch when working with clients who have been traumatised. She recommends enabling such clients to get their needs met outside the therapy:

> I don't say that the therapist should never touch a client. I also don't say that they should always touch clients. ... There can be a trap in having the client rely on touch within the therapeutic setting.
>
> I would much rather teach my clients how to get their needs for touch met outside the therapeutic setting, and to have them know what kind of touch they need, what their limits are, what their tastes are, how to set boundaries and to ask for what they want, and to equip them to go out into their lives and get those needs met there. I see problems when touch gets emphasized in the therapy relationship. It can overly weight the transference, both positively and negatively. It can make the therapy into something more special or dangerous than it should be. (Rothschild, 2002)

A different position is taken by *body psychotherapists* (for example, Reichian, bioenergetics or biodynamic psychotherapy), who are trained to use touch as a primary therapeutic tool. Here attention is paid to breathing, movement and posture; therapists actively intervene with techniques which vary from supportive holding to deep manipulation to free inhibited energy and release bodily blocks. With this orientation, trauma clients, for instance, might be viewed as having an over-bounded musculature, indicated by holding their bodies stiffly. One interpretation could be that they have developed a belief that they cannot rely on external support and must protect and manage themselves. The focus of the work with the body is to unlock the body armoury, help it yield and release the emotions trapped inside.

Body psychotherapists working in the trauma field who draw on *neuroscience* argue for the value of touch as human connection in that it triggers the release of oxytocin. This hormone (in interaction with others) is associated with love, bonding, attachment and feelings of safety in relationship, indicating a relevance for therapy. However, most would argue that the use of touch in therapy still needs to be engaged carefully, perhaps in a graded way, and with reflective exploration. Also, as Erskine (2014) explains, body psychotherapy does not need to be done via actual touch; other body-centred techniques can be used, for example, following the breath, use of fantasy, and through using non-verbal mediums such as art, music and dance/movement therapy. 'It all depends on what the client needs; not the theory or mood of the therapist' (Erskine, personal communication).

A more routine, everyday use of touch is advocated by *existential* therapist Yalom (2001), who argues for responding to clients in a loving, human way. He makes a point of touching each patient at least once in a session – a clasp on the shoulder, perhaps. If clients are in great despair and ask to hold his hand or be hugged, he would offer that holding too. But he would also try to encourage discussion about what that holding meant, including sharing his own feelings. Interestingly, he notes that if he has concerns that his actions might be interpreted as being sexual, he shares his concerns openly. He is clear that sexual impulses will never be acted upon as nothing is more important than ensuring patients feel safe in therapy.

McGuirk (2012) offers an impassioned argument for the use of touch. She argues that the duet of talk *and* touch may increase 'a sense of empathy, safety, calm and comfort, as well as enhancing a client's sense of being heard, seen, understood and acknowledged by their therapist':

When we touch an other, we are touched ourselves. … There are two people in the relationship, each impacted by the other. When there is contact of the skin, intimacy increases and intensifies, sharing is occurring, experiencing is deep. It is inevitable that nurturing and healing will flow both ways…

Crossing the boundary of the skin, the organ of embrace, when appropriate, can promote bonding and attachment, increasing depth of connection and trust between therapist and client. Touch can also increase client self-disclosure, provide containment, communicate empathy, increase the client's interpersonal risk taking, and enhance the therapeutic alliance – the best predictor of therapeutic outcome. … In fact, there are instances where touch is not simply a recommendation, it is essential – offering an opportunity for corrective experiencing and re-parenting.

The 'bodymind' speaks, it aches, screaming out to be heard, for its needs to be recognised – for healing to occur, for movement to flow. (McGuirk, 2012)

Box 7.4   Ethical-relational touch?

Across all therapy practices, irrespective of theoretical persuasion, some degree of consensus emerges: therapists need to be cautious about using touch carelessly or automatically and without due regard for context and consent. Whatever touch we use, it should be thought through, appropriately boundaried and therapeutic in intent (Ogden et al., 2006). Full-on contact (as in body therapists' use of therapeutic massage) demands extra training and

(Continued)

(Continued)

should only be deployed when working at relational depth. If touch is sexualised or seductive and feels like it needs to be kept a secret, then it is likely to be a boundary violation and perhaps sanctionable. More subtly, if contact feels shaming, charged, uncomfortable, and/or either therapist or client feels ambivalent about it, then this needs to be explored (in therapy and supervision). Who is feeling uncomfortable and why? Is there a potentially abusive, exploitative dynamic of power that needs attention?

Touch is a powerful tool if employed ethically – sensitively, carefully and thoughtfully – by an attuned therapist who has appropriate training/support and the client's permission. Touch may be appropriate if it is intended for the client's benefit and they have consented, the boundaries are clearly understood by both, and when the therapist feels comfortable with it and explores its use in supervision (Hunter and Struve, 1998). It's important to explore what the touch means (to *both* client and therapist) in supervision, particularly considering culture, gender and history. If the therapist is in doubt about using touch, then it is better to err on the side of caution and work symbolically, either by talking about touch or engaging touch imaginally. For these reasons, novice therapists might be best advised to beware and wary of touch.

We need to move beyond the simple question of whether or not to use touch and consider the **relational** dimensions more explicitly distinguishing between different types of touch (touch that is social contrasted with touch that is therapeutic; or touch that is healthy and healing versus touch that is problematic). A socially-mandated, ritual handshake is different from the therapeutic touch we engage in (whether as our primary mode of intervention or as something we employ responsively and selectively as part of working holistically). We need to note who is initiating the touch. And we should constantly interrogate and process our use of touch, both in therapy and supervision. Only then will we be able to employ touch ethically and reduce the shame, stigma and taboo concerning touch in therapy – and also perhaps re-evaluate the way all of us use our bodies in everyday life.

Concluding reflections

Therapeutic holding involves multi-layered relational and ethical challenges. It is a co-created process occurring in a relational context rather than something a therapist *does* to a client. The client invites the level of holding needed, their responses impact on the therapist, and so on. As therapists move to hold a client and whatever is emerging relationally in the process – or backs away from doing so – metaphorically they also hold themselves and are simultaneously held by a supervisor.

Holding involves attuning to what the client needs as well as to our own needs and the needs of the relationship (Hycner, 2017). Immersed in the relationship, we engage in an intricate dance, one that involves us being present to all three dimensions while also being curious, attentive and open, and able to step back and think. In the fluid moments between intimacy and distance, the nature of our holding shifts, as do our points of focus. In one moment, we might be deeply immersed in holding a client's story or literally holding them; in the next we're holding on to ourselves, struggling to anchor ourselves by stepping back reflectively to avoid getting caught up in a relational maelstrom.

For relational therapists, doing and being involves responding to the *relational* context. We can't just decide to 'hold' the client. The client needs to be receptive; they need to accept and take in that holding and *feel* held. What level of holding can the client tolerate? And, in turn, we need to be alert to when the client is accepting (or resisting) being held. How does that impact on us and how do we respond back to the client? We also need to factor in our own needs and readiness. If we are uncomfortable using touch yet still push ahead with it, this may have negative implications for the relationship (see Box 7.4).

Decisions as to when and how to hold involve exquisitely delicate processes of clinical reasoning and negotiation. Providing a holding environment appropriate for a particular client, and our relationship with them, requires us to think things through and engage in a process of creative negotiation.

If I find myself pulled to physically hold a client, I might ask myself 'why?' Am I intuiting the client's needs? Or does this feeling have something to do with my own needs? Could it be something that is emerging from the relationship? In whose interest is this holding?

When I'm clear that a client needs holding, the challenge is to do this artfully. What kind of holding would be beneficial? *Imagining* being held by a long-lost mother might be a more powerful and effective intervention than me actually doing the holding. Holding a client's distress by printing up and filing email communications could be more useful than simply hearing my witnessing words.

I would also consider the stage therapy has reached. In long-term developmental work, for example, I'd want to grade the holding by gradually *holding myself* back. The focus shifts over time to working *with* clients on how they might hold and regulate themselves. The type of grading is particularly figural in long-term psychotherapeutic work where the experience of holding and touch may need to be symbolically repeated before being internalised. And as I hold clients and their process, I too need to be held and supported.

With experience, many therapists develop intuition about when and how to hold clients. If something doesn't feel 'right' it probably isn't right. The goal is to try to attune to the individual's needs, sensing the moment when a client is open to receive our holding embrace, whether offered physically or in metaphorical form. None of us is perfect and we are certain to 'get it wrong' for our clients occasionally. But when it works, there is a poignancy and delicate power in holding and of feeling held. The sense of safety, care and nourishment given can be healing.

Discussion questions

1. Explain how therapists offer metaphorical holding.
2. E-therapy enables distinctive forms of holding which may both help and hinder therapeutic process. Discuss.
3. Critically examine the cultural, theoretical and relational elements which make the use of touch appropriate.

Summary

Therapeutic holding is a co-created process rather than something a therapist *does* to a client. Metaphorically, therapists hold clients' emotions and stories through being sensitively attuned, solidly present and trustworthy. Sometimes, we – literally – physically hold clients. While all therapists would probably endorse the value of holding in its metaphorical sense, the use of touch is hotly contested and may be seen as transgressing ethical boundaries. Relational ethics requires us to think carefully about the specific context and distinguish between social or therapeutic touch and insensitive, problematic forms of touch that may be unwelcome, even actively abusive.

8

Ethical Containing

Closely linked to therapeutic holding is the process of containing. Although the two processes are sometimes presented as interchangeable, there are important differences between them.

Containment is understood in a particular way in *psychoanalytic* work. Here it can be defined as the capacity to provide a safe, holding frame while handling the other's overwhelming, alarming and/or destructive feelings or behaviour, enabling such feelings or behaviour to be coped with better. The concept of containment is also used in therapeutic practice in the wider *mental health field*: for instance, when working with people whose violent behaviour needs containing or restraining. Those working with children, too, may use containment or containing activities. Understandings of containment therefore differ according to context and practitioners' theoretical perspective. It's only when we actively contain another in practice, or when we ourselves experience being contained, that we can more fully appreciate the power and subtlety of this process.

To distinguish between the diverse practices of containment, I begin this chapter by laying out the specialised **psychoanalytic** psychotherapy applications. I then consider **humanistic-integrative** versions that might be engaged in broader arenas of integrative psychotherapy and pluralistic counselling practice. The **ethics of containment** and the use of **supervision** (to contain the therapist) are then discussed.

Psychoanalytic containment

The concept of containment is rooted in, and a fundamental concept for, *psychoanalytic* theory (particularly in the UK). Psychoanalytic understandings focus on clients' projections, which are seen as 'neurotic' ways to cope with unbearable emotional life pains. The therapist receives and manages (that is, metabolises and detoxifies) the projections and then 'gives them back' to the client in the form of a contained-containable-containing insight-giving interpretation. Client and therapist, working together, create a way to re-experience and possibly re-enact problematic dynamics safely.

Wilfred Bion (1962) is probably best known for his ideas about containment, although he never clearly defined the concept. His notion of the 'alpha function' of the mother or caregiver is germane. In this process, the mother receives unwanted or overwhelming projections from an infant, processes them and then returns the experience to the infant in a modified, palatable form. According to Bion, infants may become overwhelmed by their experience because they lack sufficient internal controls. The mother or caregiver listens to, and empathically tunes into, the child's communications, and gives them meaning before returning them in a modified, more manageable form. Containment thus develops the infant's capacity for self-regulation and plays a part in giving meaning to experience. This occurs as the infant takes in (internalises) a sense of being contained and experiences the mother's emotional availability. Eventually the child develops their own capacity for containment.

Bion wrote around the theme of containment in different, sometimes rather mysterious ways. He pointed to the *container–contained* dynamic, highlighting how largely unconscious processes of the 'contained' [client] interact, in relationship, with the capacity for reverie, dreaming and thinking of the 'container' [therapist]. Bion's (1961) theorising also described social groups in terms of their maternal holding environment.

Applying these ideas to therapy, there is some discussion in the psychoanalytic field about what constitutes the client's projections. What is it that clients are projecting: parts of themselves or emotions? Contemporary writers mostly argue that it is the emotions that are projected or received as a *projective identification*. For example, the client may feel that the therapist despises them (a possible projection-repeating history of feeling despised by a key caregiver). Alternatively, the therapist may suddenly feel overwhelmed by feelings and experience an urge to 'wipe out' the client (via projective identification).

On receiving the projection or projective identification, the therapist-container takes in feelings and experiences from the client, reflects on them (in 'reverie'), and then represents them back to the client in a modified form to make them more understandable and less destructive. More specifically, it is the client's unwanted negative emotions which are expressed and projected onto the therapist, who then transforms them interpretatively until the client can become their own 'container', better able to own responsibility for their conflict and anguish (Gravell, 2010). (See the example in Box 8.1.)

Box 8.1   Analytic holding-containing

In the course of telling me about how he had been referred for therapy, he began to shout and to bang the arm of his chair with a barely contained violence … I could feel myself becoming increasingly anxious. I realized that I was on the receiving end of a powerful projective identification; … *I felt afraid…*

Therapist:	You are thinking and speaking for me, based on what you have experienced with other people. I would like to say for myself what I am thinking. You expect me to send you away; but I am not going to send you away. I am going to offer to take you into therapy. However, I make one condition. I know you have a lot of violent feelings, which you may need to bring into your therapy. You can bring as much violence here as you need to, as long as it is confined to words. If this becomes physical violence, I cannot promise that I will then be able to continue treating you.
Patient:	So you are afraid! (Pause)
Therapist:	Yes, you are able to make me afraid of your violence; but I believe it may be precisely that which you need me to be in touch with – without having to send you away. I think it is your own fear of your violent feelings that you are needing me to help you with.

[The patient] began to calm down. … He had not (quite) given up hope that his fear of his own violence might somewhere begin to be contained by another person and found to be manageable. (Casement, 1985, pp. 145–147)

Working in a *relational psychodynamic* way, Orbach (2003b) argues the case for attending carefully to our counter-transferential bodily nuances (bringing the bodies of both client and therapist into relationship) as a counterbalance to the 'cerebral turn' of psychoanalysis. She offers an illustrative case study of her own alarming response, which she understood as revealing her client's need to have her be a stable body who could safely receive and contain his desperate, destructive impulses:

Rob was a 48-year-old man. … He was in a loop about being anxious about being anxious. A barrister who was required to perform in front of juries and judges, he could only get himself going on a case if he found a love or sexual interest. … The sexual interest took the weight of his anxiety which became transformed into pursuit and sexual performance anxiety. … He frequented call-girls, picked up prostitutes for dangerous car rendezvous around a red-light district and engaged in consensual sex so close to the edge that it took a great deal on my part to be curious rather than frightened.…

I found myself one day in a perfectly ordinary session suddenly fearful that Rob would rape me. ... I became rigid, started to sweat, cursed myself for not having an alarm alert in my room before I could find a way to still my momentary psychosis. ... I was stunned at the level of brutality and the visual acuity of a scene of bodily fluids, teeth and fight coursing through my body...

I took the savagery I experienced as a clue to his terror and his search for another body, for a body that could respond, a body that didn't collapse, a body that could meet his body. ... In my body countertransference experience of imagining myself the victim of potential savage rape ... the patient needs to destroy the object and the analyst need to survive the destruction. What became acute for me was engaging with the notion that my body was required to receive Rob's hatred and aggression, that I must manage my alarm, to allow myself to be disturbed by him, but not to collapse under that disturbance. Instead I was required to take the challenge to my physical integrity, remain stable, rooted in my own body in order for there to be a body in the room for him. He could only put together a body for himself via a violent encounter with another and yet on-the-edge and dangerous sex failed for him because he had to hold the boundary. He couldn't go the full destructive route. (Orbach, 2003b, pp. 4–6)

The group as a 'container'

In a group therapy situation, the group might be viewed as a psychic container whose boundaries distinguish the people inside from those outside the group. Different members offer different perspectives (to help develop thinking rather than engage in acting out) while the group-as-a-whole holds the process. Alternatively, bad feelings can be got rid of by projecting them onto the 'out-group' or by scapegoating individual members of the in-group. Here the scape-goat would be viewed as providing a function: that of holding the bad feeling projections of the group. As conflict and/or anxiety within the group arises, the group's containing function becomes even more important (Hinshelwood, 1987). Conflict and anxiety may originate in one person but can be passed to others (consciously or unconsciously) as if by contagion. The group can then seem to act as a single entity engaged in defensive behaviour. Collusive 'intellectualism' is one such group defence; here group members cite academic research in a bid to demonstrate their 'superior' knowledge – and keep anxiety at bay:

A group of trainee counsellors met fortnightly with a supervisor as part of their course to discuss their work. This process of talking about how they worked often felt exposing and created considerable anxiety. One member frequently quoted from theoretical papers ... often it would seem that the aim was to impress the others with her knowledge and to catch the supervisor out. ... A competitive, point-scoring atmosphere quickly developed. The difficult emotions aroused by the work with clients, the uncertainties of the trainee role and fear of inadequacy were defended against by the group members through a combination of intellectualization and competition. When this was pointed out by the supervisor, the group at first became angry and sullen. Gradually, however, members began to talk about their anxieties and fears and were able to return to the task of the group. (Morgan and Thomas, 1996, pp. 79–80)

Clarkson, working in an *integrative* psychodynamic way, offers an illustration of containing a group member's anger through a gentle challenge. The patient had a history of somatising and feeling victimised; it was difficult for him to relate to others:

> In a psychotherapy group one member asks about how I got paralysed when I was fourteen. Pleased to have the opportunity to tell my story again, I commence with tears in my eyes. The psychotherapist intervenes by stopping this. I protest: 'I am only telling what happened.' The psychotherapist reiterates that I should not continue with this tale of drudgery and misery, which had been told many times before. I scream at the psychotherapist, 'I hate you!' glaring at her with all the rage I can muster. ... The psychotherapist says, 'What would your mother do now?' I reply, 'What a stupid question! My mother would hit me and then send me to my room. She would never let me speak to her like this.' The psychotherapist continues looking steadily at me with what I can only describe as compassionate concern. Then she reached out her hands to me, palms upwards, without touching me, and I dissolved into tears as I realized that I can show my anger at her without being punished or rejected.... (Clarkson, 2003, p. 135)

In this example, Clarkson points to the contrast between the transferential expectation and the way the therapist provides a developmentally-needed, replenishing relationship, enabling the client's regression to dissolve into adult understanding and appreciation. The provision of 'corrective emotional experiences' can occur in various ways (for example, through the provision of mirroring/nurturing or through control/challenge or through permission-giving). However, care needs to be taken not to infantilise, manipulate or unduly encourage dependency; therapists need to be ever ready to contain potential misuses of their own power.

Humanistic-integrative versions of containment

In *integrative* or *pluralistic* practice, containment is used in various ways that overlap with, but are different from, those seen in psychoanalytic work. Outside psychoanalytic work, the term 'containment' tends only to occur in pockets of practice, most commonly in groupwork and when working with people who have been traumatised or who have a history of violence. The point of similarity across fields is the aim of enabling the client's own 'container' (that is, ability to contain their emotions) to become bigger and stronger. The process may start by the therapist doing the containing, but the eventual aim is for the client to self-contain.

The need for containment arises if a client becomes flooded with emotions: for example, when anxiety turns into dissociation or terror, or when annoyance becomes rage and leaks out behaviourally in unhelpful ways. The aim is to help the individuals become more grounded and aware through being contained in the safety of the therapy relationship and therapeutic space (the room, the group, and so on). This relationship contains the client's vulnerabilities, emotional explosions and other unbearable experience, and then supports and helps them gain understanding of their process and needs. Work can also focus on *cognitive restructuring*: enabling clients to think about, and express, their challenging experiences in different ways.

Below I offer examples of three approaches to working explicitly with containment, drawn from the fields of psychodrama, somatic trauma therapy and art therapy.

Using 'doubles' in psychodrama

Containment occurs with psychodrama in response to the acting out of emotional expressions (catharsis), or in reference to the supportive 'group-as container', or through the use of 'doubles', where another person acts as an alter-ego and may speak for the client protagonist as a kind of self-supporting voice.

In an intriguing elaboration of psychodrama, Hudgins has developed the Therapeutic Spiral Model (TSM) (Hudgins, 2017; see also therapeuticspiralmodel. com). In TSM psychodrama, there is a specific clinical action intervention called the 'Containing Double' – a variation of the classical psychodrama double role where a double might stand behind the client and perhaps put their hands gently on the client's shoulder. They then try to put into words (in the first person) what the client is feeling while at the same time offering the client unconditional support, stability and holding. The aim is to help the client identify and contain their challenging internal experience. In TSM, the Containing Doubles' main purpose is to help clients experience the right balance of thinking and feeling so they are present in the moment, thereby creating containment.

The Containing Double has three tasks, which offer a structure to the clinical action intervention. First, it reflects what is happening, using the first person ('I'm feeling scared, like I'm three years old, and I want to hide'). Second, there is a statement to promote containment ('I know I am scared and I can be curious about why I am experiencing this at the moment. I have a choice about what to do with my fear'). Third, there is a final statement which contains the experience in the here-and-now ('I am focused on my breathing and I can feel my feet on the ground. I look around the group members and I know I'm an adult having a memory. I know that nothing bad will happen at this moment').

TSM has been elaborated to include another device for internal role containment: the 'Body Double'. This contains dissociation, flashbacks and body memories; in neurological terms, it is thought to soothe the overactivated amygdala. In contrast, the Containing Double is like the corpus collosum and provides a balance of thinking and feeling. Together, the two devices create two elements of the 'Seven Prescriptive Roles of Trauma Survivors' Internal Role Map, which helps to create a sense of resilience and containment (Hudgins and Toscani, 2013; Hudgins, 2017).

The following example shows the Body Double device in action. The scene is a psychodrama group where 'Andrea' is getting distressed:

Andrea:	I hate my body. It is disgusting and I never want to eat again!
Team Leader:	Let me help you with these feelings by putting in a body double as extra support for you, okay? The body double talks like part of you – in the first person. The body double helps you remember when you did feel ok about your body. Can you pick someone to take this role? ... You are going to speak in the first person and you are going to make statements to help Andrea stay in the present where she is safe. Andrea ... if what Susan says to you is true, then repeat it in your own words. If it is not, then please correct it.
Body Double:	Even when I feel like this, I can notice my breath, the breath of life. It's not really my body that is the problem, it is what happened to my body that hurts.
Andrea:	Yes, yes, I know it is about what happened, the rape. I used to love my body. Now I hate it.
Team Leader:	Listen to your body double and if she is right repeat the words even in if the experience seems like long ago.
Body Double:	I do feel like I hate my body now, and I also remember when I loved it ... before the rape. Maybe now I can just take one deep breath and feel the aliveness of my life force today. (Hudgins, 2002, p. 54)

The use of 'braking' in somatic trauma therapy

In somatic trauma therapy, several containing techniques can be employed, often associated with *cognitive-behavioural* work. The techniques might be used first in therapy and then practised outside as part of building emotional resources to contain overwhelming emotions or impulsive script-led behaviour.

One particular technique is 'braking', which is analogous to learning to brake in a car before one learns to drive off. 'Putting on the brakes' is a way of going slowly and adjusting/containing levels of arousal (keeping them low enough to facilitate hippocampal function). Through braking, the client learns to handle flashbacks or other trauma symptoms, enabling them to feel more in control and ensuring they are not re-traumatised by the therapy process. The use of 'safe place' positive imagery or finding 'oases' (which are activities that demand attention) are techniques that can give the client a break (brake) from the trauma. Such techniques may also help the client engage in relaxing or self-soothing or energy-releasing activities. The point is to be creative and to find the resources that suit the individual, enabling them to return to their 'here-and-now' body, away from the 'there-and-then' of their trauma.

The following example is from Rothschild's somatic trauma therapy, an integrated approach which draws on body psychotherapy, NLP (neuro-linguistic programming), cognitive-behaviourism, EMDR (eye movement desensitisation reprocessing), gestalt and psychodynamic theory. The excerpt shows a client learning to dip into their trauma experience and return to safe/neutral ground. This teaches them that they can learn to master their anxiety and distress. In this excerpt, 'Iris' has been traumatised by being laid off work. The therapist teaches Iris to use an 'anchor': a grounding, steadying, positive image.

Therapist: Before we look at what happened at work, I want to make sure there is something we can use to change the subject that feels good to talk about. What would work for you?

We were establishing an anchor that could be used to put on the brakes when she became hyperaroused

Iris: That could either be my garden or my granddaughter (*she smiles*)...

Therapist: Does your granddaughter ever visit you in your garden, or ever help you with your work there?

Iris: Why yes. When she was a child, she used to come and help me a lot in the summers. ... Since college though, she never has as much time. But she sometimes comes on the weekends and helps me. Then we chat over lunch or tea. I love those days.

Therapist: How would that be for a solution then? To take breaks talking about your granddaughter working in the garden with you?

Iris: I like that idea. That would be fine.

Therapist: So, are you ready to talk about work?...

Iris: Everything happened so fast. My new supervisor, Melinda, she just came up to me in the middle of the secretarial pool and said really loud, 'Gather your things, Iris, you'll be leaving us today'...

Iris began to cry, a panicked kind of crying with an emphasis on the inhale. This kind of crying increases hyperarousal. ... It is not a release – it actually creates more distress – so I always put on the brakes when it occurs.

Therapist: Hold on just a minute. I'm going to stop you from crying like that. Say some words, tell me what is happening inside.

Iris: (*slows down, catches her breath*) I was starting to panic, remembering how shocked I was. I didn't know what was going on. It all happened so fast.

Therapist: What is happening to your body?

Iris: I can feel I'm shaking and my hands are cold.

Therapist: So let's use your anchor. When is the last time your daughter came to visit you in your garden?

Iris: A couple of weeks ago. She came on Saturday morning and helped me plant a bed of herbs. She lives nearby...

Therapist: Did you have lunch that day?

Iris: Oh, yes. Let me see. I made her favorite, my special chicken salad. She likes it just like I do, with celery and green grapes.

Therapist: How are you feeling right now?

Iris: Much better ... my hands are warming up and I've stopped shaking.

Therapist: What happened to the panic?

Iris: Oh! You are right. That went away completely...

Therapist: How did *you* stop it?

I wanted Iris to know she now had tools to reduce her panic herself – that it was not just some type of magic that only I could do.

Iris: By slowing my crying and by talking about my granddaughter and garden. That really worked! (Rothschild, 2003, pp. 127–129).

Art therapy: Containing through creative media

Containment can sometimes be achieved through the use of other media and objects. Violent emotions can be projected or contained within the boundaries of artwork or a letter that is written but not sent. In gestalt work, emotional parts of self might be put onto an 'empty chair' and worked with in a contained way.

The following story, told by an art therapist (and integrative psychotherapist), is an example of containing artwork applied in a secure unit:

Reece came into secure forensic services at 21 after committing a violent crime. He grew up in a 'busy and unruly' family. He often talked about having to quieten parts of himself to fit in. Substance misuse was a familiar occurrence in his circle. He enjoyed this life style as it helped him to escape from the suffocating chaos around him.

Now aged 30 he is creative and quirky. He wants to express himself authentically. He wears colourful clothes and experiments with hair colour, earrings, nose rings and makeup. He dances, plays music, paints/draws and writes lyrics and poetry.

In art therapy sessions he enjoys expression through metaphor and, in his art work, uses symbolism to share himself with me. He has tussled with the bigger questions in life and considers the work of philosophers, writers, musicians and artists to debate and question his journey in life.

Figure 8.1   Expressing Self through symbolism

The work progressed quickly as he had a certain freedom with the art materials and an ease within the therapeutic relationship. He enjoyed the sessions and looked forward to being able to reach certain depths of creativity, metaphor and a shared understanding. He felt out of place in the institution and regularly reflected on the 'mental health patient' as being 'wombed by the asylum' a place of sanctuary and of safety but also a place of creative stagnation. He questioned whether the institution was too containing and stopping men growing up. Our sessions acted as a containing outlet, a human connection that allowed him to be himself but safely. Our work offered him a catalyst, in order for him to feel a certain freedom within the walls of the hospital and also within his own skin.

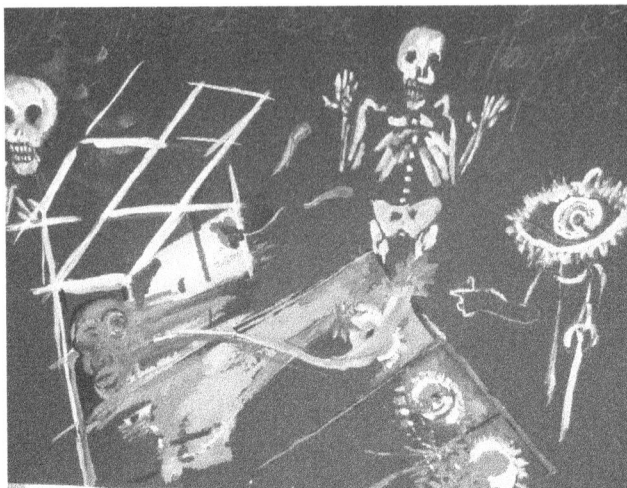

Figure 8.2 Exploring loss, violence and destruction

Providing the safe continuing relationship allowed us to explore his risk-taking behaviours, his creativity and his playfulness alongside his feelings of emotional suffocation. We recognised what led to his life-changing offence – something that shame pushed him to avoid previously. A theme that often rose symbolically in the artwork was learning to tolerate difficult feelings. We worked sensitively with his shame and vulnerability, recognising the little boy within who wanted to play and be accepted. Alongside, we recognised his power as a young man and put this in the context of his trauma, his mental health issues and his offence. Naming and owning his offence as 'murder' was an important part of our work and something that previously shame led him to avoid. The work explored and contained the loss of part of his life as it was, the forced change in his life path and quite brutally the destruction of another's. This all proved important for his healing. (Viki Jones, art therapist and integrative psychotherapist, personal communication)

The case illustrations above highlight the importance of the therapist (or group leader) being accepting and non-defensive when receiving what emerges as both an ethical and a therapeutic priority. The therapist holds a containing space by being solid and reliable. They first witness the client's experience, and then help them make sense of that experience and of what is happening in the process. The therapist then offers a different perspective geared to helping the client better understand their disturbing process. Importantly, work within sessions is just the start. The key growth comes when the client learns how to contain their own process outside the therapy room.

However, the process of containing emotional or behavioural excess itself is challenging. It raises ethical questions concerning how and why the containing is done, and in what circumstances.

The ethics of containment

When containing clients' emotions and/or behaviour, the first relational-ethical-therapeutic priority is to **attune** to the client and their world. The therapist invites, and respects, openness on the part of the client, even as they seek to contain potentially damaging, excessive explosions (which could make either party feel unsafe).

Then there is an ethical obligation to **understand** what may be happening in the process. In the psychoanalytical examples presented in the first section of this chapter, for example, all the therapists have clearly thought deeply about their counter-transferential reactions and impulses.

Finally, when practising ethically, we need to bracket and **boundary** our own internal processes in a healthy, non-defensive way. In other words, containing is a layered process, each layer of which has its associated ethical implications.

Relationally-speaking, therapists attend to the relationship and may even privilege a focus on the intersubjective experiencing over concerns with the client's internal world. The relationship becomes the vehicle for understanding the intrapsychic process, for instance, when therapists become aware of receiving unconscious negative transferences/projections which set them up as a 'bad object'. This is one of the hardest processes to face and contain. To extricate themselves from this enactment and stay in control of the process, therapists need to maintain a tight hold on their reflective capacity.

Mostly, therapists contain disturbing intrapsychic processes and deal with overt violent behaviour less often. But it is worth thinking about our rights and responsibilities across a range of situations related to therapists' power and subjectivity, including how to manage violence safely.

Containing therapist power

When therapists 'contain' clients, they are implicitly doing something to/with the client and, at some level, exerting some 'power-over' authority (Proctor, 2002). Is this being done with care? Is coercion involved (for instance, the use of physical restraints)? Does the client want to be contained? If they must be contained (for reasons of safety), who says so and why? Is it in the client's interest or that of the therapist? To what extent does the therapist have a right to superimpose their authority, overriding a client's autonomy?

This raises the question of violence, understood not simply in physical terms but also as abuse of power more generally. It's important to remember that expressions of anger from a client towards their therapist may not be a transference or projection but rather righteous anger in the here-and-now. It's in this sense that therapists can do violence: for example, by inadvertently failing to listen, or being overly challenging, or making an arrogant assumption.

Interpretation becomes a *consent* and *respect* issue when a therapist's interpretation is patronising or takes precedence over the client's view. In traditional *psychoanalysis*, for example, the analyst 'expert' has the power to make interpretative pronouncements. How respectfully are these offered and how are these received by the analysand? Therapists of relational persuasions would be more inclined to dialogue with the client about possible interpretations: the emphasis is on therapist and client going exploring together.

These questions highlight key debates between therapists coming from different theoretical perspectives. Some *humanistic* practitioners, for instance, would want to challenge the therapist's assumption of power and authority, favouring more 'unknowing' and dialogical ways of being. They'd deny engaging in containment themselves; their emphasis would be on interventions that foster a client's agency and ability to contain themselves. For such practitioners, the point is to encourage clients to explore their own meanings and engage in their own personal narrative-making.

In reply to therapists who deny they engage in containing processes, it could be argued that containing dynamics are still in play even if the therapists don't explicitly set out to contain behaviour. Therapists also will contain themselves. It's worth reflecting further on the nature of containment engaged.

Whatever position taken, the pivotal ethical requirements are **respect for the personhood** of the other and the obligation to be **reflexively mindful**. Here is an excerpt of the guidelines offered by the Australian Psychoanalytic Society (2012, p. 2), which recommends:

> ...a profound respect for the patient's individuality and separateness: the patient must not be thought the analyst's personal property; the analyst does not decide his fate for the patient; the analyst does not force his ideals upon the patient; it is not the analyst's job to re-mould the patient in accordance with any personal ideals; it is the analyst's job is to seek to arouse in the patient his own powers of initiative. Accordingly, the analyst is ethically obliged to be mindful of the forces in his own mind – his unconscious impulses and longings which seek to pull him away from his analytic obligations.

Containing therapist's subjectivity

As therapists, we hold our vulnerability in awareness. We also contain ourselves so as not to 'drown' our client. Such processes protect us from emotional harm. How alarming and unsafe would it be for the client if the therapist was unable to cope with their own feelings? How destructive, exploitative and unethical would it be for a therapist to use the client's therapy for their own support and healing? How are therapists to work on clients' deep trauma, avoidance and dissociation if they are cut-off themselves?

The issues of therapist **self-care** and **self-disclosure**, discussed in Chapters 3 and 6 respectively, are relevant here as it involves the therapist containing the leakage of their own subjectivity *in the interests of the client*. Careful, artful, intuitive judgement is needed to know when to show emotion and when to hold back; when to self-disclose and when not to.

Take the situation where a therapist is working with a young man, Benson, who is a full-time carer for his mother (who has a severe mental illness). As a carer, Benson is programmed to be alert to subtle emotional reactions in others; he constantly scans his environment. If his therapist were to show undue emotion, he would become overly concerned with the therapist's needs. In this situation, the therapist learns to hold back from revealing how impacted she is by his story. As therapy progresses, Benson learns that he does not need to take care of his therapist, enabling her to be more authentic.

As another example, consider the therapist who is currently caring for her sister, who is dying. Should she tell her clients about her own situation, given its likely impact on the work? The therapist consults her supervisor. Together they agree that the therapist would warn her clients she might suddenly have to go away for two or three weeks. However, instead of sharing details she would simply say that she is dealing with some 'family illness' and may be called away for 'business'. In this way her own grief and family stress are contained, enabling her work with clients to continue without undue contamination by her own issues.

Containing violence

In our work, the violence we face comes in different guises. Sometimes therapeutic interventions involve encouraging the free expression of emotion. Here, our role is to contain safely any releasing explosions and acting out. For example, when we invite a client to vent and do some emotional purging (such as angrily bashing a cushion), we need to make sure that all parties in the room are kept physically and emotionally safe. The therapist requires the competence and confidence to handle what might ensue. I would add that, prior to using a specialist technique, the ethical therapist will have some knowledge of its value and limitations, and of the debates surrounding its use. For example, the simple venting of anger has been found to be less useful than engaging deeper *catharsis*, which involves actively containing and processing it (Baron and Richardson, 2004). Lohr et al. (2007) even suggest the venting of anger increases the likelihood of anger expression and can do more harm in the long term. Instead, they recommend empirically-validated CBT techniques.

In their work on *mentalization* and Mentalization-Based Treatment (MBT), Peter Fonagy and colleagues provide a useful theoretical framework, along with numerous examples of how to contain and respond to violent people. Mentalization, in this theory, is the ability to understand self and others by inferring mental states that lie behind overt behaviour (something that is learned through attachment relationships). Loss of mentalizing in times of stress leads to impulsivity and destructive behaviour. Affect regulation requires mentalization where the person is helped to think rather than react.

Fonagy (2016) highlights how therapists' common response to a client's angry outburst is to reflect back, saying 'You seem very angry'. He points out that in work with violent people such a therapeutic intervention could have the unanticipated result of further enraging the person. He suggests that therapists instead take a step or two back in order to encourage greater mentalization and reflection. Paraphrasing Fonagy's words, a therapist might say: 'It's hard to think when you're shouting at me and you need me to think' or 'I think I've said something really wrong here. Can you help me understand?' Interventions like these bring the relationship to the fore but in a less threatening, confrontational way. A key message is to contain violence in a *relationally respectful* manner by helping the person understand that their thoughts and feelings matter.

In extreme cases, the ethical containment of violent behaviour (threats or abuse, whether physical or verbal) poses particular challenges. There isn't space here to examine the specialist work of how violence is managed in secure units or acute mental health services. We can just note that numerous practical, moral and ethical dilemmas arise, and that the management of violence takes an emotional toll on all who are involved.

From a relational-ethical perspective there are two competing **rights** at stake here: on the one hand, the right of the individual client to receive safe *care*/treatment which *respects* their needs, dignity and *confidentiality*, and, on the other, the right of the professional to be *safe* and do their job without abuse and danger. Any response to violence must be proportionate.

Professionals in the frontline must have specialist training in **risk assessment** and how to manage conflict (for example, through de-escalation or safe physical restraint techniques). We have a duty of care to try to calm the person and take steps to resolve the source of upset. As a last resort, staff members might be advised to leave the area. Consideration also needs to be given to deciding if the violent person is being given the most appropriate treatment and if they need to be referred on for further care.

In the UK, current clinical guidelines laid down by the NICE and the Department of Health, among others, advise that *physical restraint* to manage violent behaviour should be avoided whenever possible and only used as a last resort to protect the individual from harming themselves (or others) or in self-defence. Department of Health (2014) argues for the use of positive and *proactive care interventions* which reduce the need for restrictive interventions. On the assumption that compassion is incompatible with coercive, restrictive practices, such guidelines promote practice based on kindness and a thinking approach, while prohibiting inhumane or degrading treatment.

The kind of work we do as therapists is invariably challenging, all the more so in situations where we receive dark projections or more direct intimations of violence. At times our own physical or mental well-being is at stake. The ethical position is to prioritise the client's interests. But *we also have a right to ensure our own safety*.

Once, when I was working in an acute mental health facility, a client threatened to kill me, and I believed him. I couldn't see a way of 'talking him down', so I left the room. When this was discussed within the multi-disciplinary team and in supervision, it was agreed that the client would be temporarily restricted to the ward and that one-to-one counselling with me was not appropriate at this stage. In this case, what the client needed was a medical intervention: an increase in his anti-psychotic medication.

Supervision to contain the 'therapist-container'

There is … something gallant about the continued willingness of these labourers of the soul to put themselves in the firing line, to take on the task of subjecting themselves to the daily assaults of unconscious missiles day in day out. (Frosh, 2010, p. 14)

If we are to offer holding-containing boundaries to our clients, we ourselves need to be held-contained. As the quote above highlights, our work is incredibly challenging. Our therapy, supervision and continuing professional development (CPD), along with our books, theories and techniques, offer some of the resources. Supervision, both formal and informal (the latter offered by peers), is a key container and resource for our self-care (see also Chapter 3). It can help us express, think about, understand and manage processes that emerge in therapy. Crucially, it can help us to separate out what belongs to ourselves and what might have been received from the client but belongs to them. When we feel rage, anxiety or shame in relation to a client's work, whose is it?

The process of the therapist becoming a 'bad object' for the client to project onto can help support the client's expression of destructive impulses and malignant thoughts. But it is not easy to receive such projections and contain any acting out by maintaining one's thinking. Some self-protection is needed to maintain a continued solid, grounded, reliable frame that doesn't get destroyed. This is where supervision comes in – containing the 'container'.

To illustrate the challenge we can face as therapists, Little (2016) highlights the way he felt afraid, hopeless, useless and rageful in being a 'new bad object' for Barbara. He shows how one of the challenges of working countertransferentially as a bad object is that experiencing oneself as 'bad' can result in the therapist wanting to excise and wipe out that bit that has been evoked.

Apparently I had 'allowed' Barbara's friend to come and see me as a client. In doing so I had destroyed her sanctuary. I was flummoxed: I had no idea what, or who she was talking about. 'But what of me? This is my space,' she explained. I was being attacked, yet again. She began to bombard me with accusations.

I felt useless. I feared that this could go on for weeks, or months. I felt hopeless. She was threatening me again and had threatened me with ethics charges before. I felt frightened. … I wanted to be free of the torment of these feelings and phantasies. I wanted to wipe her out, obliterate her from my life. I felt the rage run through my body like an electric current. … Who was this that has emerged in me? (Little, 2016, p. 52)

In this type of situation, it would be vital to take these feelings to supervision (and possibly therapy). The supervisor will ideally help with disentangling what belongs to the client and what to the therapist, and then nudge the therapist's reactions in different directions if needed.

Beyond attempting to engage and transform clients' subjectivity, part of what the therapist holds and contains is their *own* subjectivity. Drawing on psychodynamic theory, Allan Schore (2001, p. 20) highlights how the mother/therapist needs to contain her own arousal before being able to contain the child/client. He points to the mother container acting as a 'regulator of the infants' arousal' but in order for this to happen, the mother 'must be able to regulate her own aroused state'.

In the following excerpt, a therapist explains her feelings of 'disgust' when with her client.

> I'm disgusted by Filip's adolescent body and thrusting needs. He talks in graphic terms about his urge to 'f***' as many women as he can and 'give it to them'. He's proud of his body and size of his penis and he wants people to know about it. But it's also the way he smells – both his body odour and the cheap cologne he wears. I feel repulsed but try to contain my disgust. Whose is this? Does it relate to his own shame and self-loathing underlying the narcissism? Is it his mother's? Is it my disgust of my own father?
>
> I take it to supervision and off-load. I see my supervisor's disgusted reaction in turn and feel some relief. It seems that my disgust is within the field. With her carrying some of the disgust, I am in a better place to then think with her about what Filip and I are enacting relationally. What do I need to do for Filip? Is it my acceptance he needs or witnessing his experience of his mother's disgust? I probe my own disgust and get in touch with some rage which comes from my own history. We wonder about Filip's rage and where it is being channelled... (Anonymous, personal communication)

In addition to using formal supervision opportunities, we need to use our own resources and find ways to employ our '**internal supervisor**' when we need support. Orbach (2003b) suggests a nice technique of imagining a protective shield around oneself while still feeling whatever is going on in the therapy. The art is to hold on to clients' emotions for long enough to make sense of them before being taken over by them. If the therapist cannot hold or contain and make sense of the emotions, or they linger long after the session, it may be necessary to give them back to the client. Or if the emotions need to be held, Orbach advises doing this with curiosity and compassion, and not being afraid.

In the following case illustration, the supervisor works to hold the therapist and contain her shame while drawing on his own internal supervisor.

> In a unit for children with extreme behavioural disorders, one child, Leo, presented a particular challenge to the staff. In his acting out, he found exactly the right buttons to push by testing every boundary that was set. Mostly the staff offered a consistent team response designed to contain Leo's behaviour. However, a new (client-centred) trainee on placement was unaware of the team strategy. When Leo started to kick her she tried to 'accept' his behaviour and show him unconditional support. However, he soon became uncontrollably violent. The supervising therapist then stepped in to intervene, gently but firmly holding Leo. The message, the student soon learned, was that Leo needed to feel safe and trust that he could be contained – something that had not happened in his early life.
>
> In a subsequent *supervision session*, the supervisor found himself actively holding and containing the trainee who was filled with shame at her 'ignorant mistake'. The

trainee now felt unsafe as she couldn't trust her decision-making and her shame was threatening to leak out into her other work in the unit. The supervisor suggested that it might be useful for the trainee to take her shame back into therapy. At the same time, he was soothingly supportive, noting that she had not known the team policy and that so-called mistakes were common in daily practice. He apologised for not intervening earlier before Leo's behaviour had escalated. (In the process, the supervisor used his internal supervisor to contain his own feelings of guilt and shame about his 'mistake'.) (Finlay, 2016a, p. 73)

The example above highlights how students, therapists and supervisors alike need to be held and contained, just as they hold and contain clients' processes. Professional knowledge, skills and techniques offer some scaffolding and a safe framework in which to practise and function under pressure. But probably the best, most effective holding-containing comes from having an attuned, affirming, supportive supervisor.

Concluding reflections

This chapter has explored the ways in which containment is understood and practised in different settings and across theoretical perspectives. While psychoanalytic practice emphasises *intrapsychic containment*, other therapists might focus more on *containing acting out* or disturbed behaviour through grounding and de-escalating techniques, and through encouraging mentalization and reflexivity. The relational-ethical imperative across the spectrum requires the containing of both clients and ourselves with care, respect and compassion, and in the clients' interest.

As therapists, we need sufficient robustness, emotional competence and containment to avoid loading the client with distress and disturbance accumulated from our own past experience. Heron (2001, p. 12) notes that we must ensure that our disturbance does not 'drive and distort' our interventions. Only when the therapist holds their own, neither 'rescuing' nor 'persecuting', neither being destroyed nor being made unduly anxious, can a place of safety and security for the client be sustained.

This does not mean the therapist always remains intact and unaffected. Nor should the therapist become a fortress. Recognising our imperfections, limitations and openness to damage grants us the humanity and humility that allows us to empathise with our clients and work in their service (Adams, 2014). Gibertoni (2013, p. 50) puts it well when she writes of having 'thought of myself as a container, sometimes with leaks, holes or cracks in need of repair, a pot with a cover that does not do its job very well'.

It's about using our vulnerabilities in the service of clients. From his phenomenological-contextualist *psychoanalytic* perspective, Stolorow (2014) urges us to draw on our own existential vulnerabilities:

If we are to be an understanding relational home for a traumatized person, we must tolerate, even draw upon, our own existential vulnerabilities so that we can dwell unflinchingly with his or her unbearable and recurring emotional pain. When we dwell with others' unendurable pain, their shattered emotional worlds are enabled to shine with a kind of sacredness that calls forth an understanding and caring engagement within which traumatized states can be gradually transformed into bearable and nameable painful feelings.

Given our human vulnerability, it is an ethical imperative to be reflexive about our processes and make active use of supportive opportunities (therapy, CPD, supervision, and the like) which offer precious moments to be held and contained ourselves. Sometimes we need to prioritise our self-care. This is both a professional 'duty' and being relational as it concerns our relationship *with ourselves*. If I lack the necessary support for the difficult work I do relationally, particularly when such work connects with unresolved issues of my own, there is a danger of my using therapy with a client out of awareness to act out (or get the client to act out for me). I need to give myself time to think and process. This is the containing safety net that should surround every therapist, helping us hold all that difficult, painful and disturbing material (Gilbert and Evans, 2000).

Discussion questions

1. Explain how containment is viewed differently across theoretical perspectives.
2. Is it possible to ensure an ethical use of power? Discuss in relation to the way therapists contain clients' behaviour/emotions.
3. To what extent should therapists contain their own subjectivity during therapy?

Summary

Containment is most commonly used in psychoanalytic contexts or in fields where emotional expression and behaviour needs to be contained, as when working with violent offenders. When containing, therapists manage clients' emotional-behavioural acting out and then offer reflections to help the clients' understanding and restore their capacity to think. The key growth comes when the client learns to contain their own process outside the therapy. The relational-ethical challenge of containing is to be sufficiently aware of what might be happening relationally, for instance, in the counter-transference, and to ensure an ethical, respectful use of 'power'. Then, we need to bracket and boundary our own internal processes in a healthy, non-defensive way.

9

Ethical Endings

Termination is a jolting reminder of the built-in cruelty of the psychotherapeutic process. (Yalom, 1985, p. 373)

The layered, sometimes painful, process of ending therapy can be challenging for both client *and* therapist. Without sufficient care, it can prove a messy or unduly hurried process. To ensure ending is done professionally, constructively and without the client experiencing it as an 'abandonment', the therapist needs to actively engage the client in a separating/ending process. The aim is to offer a positive, growth-fostering point of departure.

As with every other stage of therapy, ending requires the therapist to hold an ethical-professional boundary and to respect clients' choices. This chapter explores the relational ethics involved. The first two sections, on **ending dilemmas** and the **horizon of loss** (grief and avoidance), discuss some of the challenges of this phase. Then, the practice of **holding ending boundaries** is explored. The penultimate section focuses on **evaluation** and the ways both therapist and client can review – and celebrate – any progress made.

Ending dilemmas

Consider the dilemmas in Box 9.1. Beyond what is set out in professional codes, the answers, as always, depend on the context (cultural and relational) and your own values and policies. Reflect on your responses to each dilemma. Have you ever been in similar situations? Do you agree with my responses, which follow? If not, why not?

Box 9.1   'Ending' dilemmas

1. Cecile has been coming to you for therapy every week for the last three months. She has made some good progress but there is still important processing to do. Suddenly she announces that her insurance coverage is due to run out and she cannot afford to pay privately for your services. What do you do?
2. Bernie has been coming to therapy regularly for three years and is now in a good place. However, the thought of ending scares her. She admits she can't bear the thought of not seeing her therapist and asks if it would be possible for them to meet occasionally for coffee. The therapist brings this dilemma to you as her supervisor. It seems the therapist feels their sessions have outlived their usefulness other than offering Bernie some affirming relational contact. She believes the odd coffee meeting could be hugely beneficial for Bernie. Do you agree?
3. A very rich client wants to give you an antique vase as a parting gift to say thank you. You feel uncomfortable as the gift is quite expensive. How do you handle this situation?

My responses

1. Cecile – In **legal** terms, much depends on what the initial contract specified. If the client was clear they needed to pay for services, and now can't, then the therapist is entitled to end. Ideally, Cecile would be offered other options (for example, referral to another service).

    In **professional** terms, there is more at stake. That this situation has arisen apparently out of the blue is itself suggestive of a problem. Therapists have a *duty of care* to head off this kind of dilemma earlier. It probably should have been explored when the contract was first established with an eye to what would happen when the insurance ran out. The therapist needed to be on the case, keeping a strict eye on how many sessions were remaining so that regular reviews of progress could be made. Arguably, they should also have been monitoring any impeding financial hardship and regularly taking the pulse of the therapeutic alliance.

    In **relational terms**, I also wonder how honest and open the dialogue had been. Why this bolt from the blue? Why hadn't the client said something earlier? What does this lack of openness suggest about the effectiveness of the therapy? Is the client implicitly saying they'd like to end therapy? These are questions to explore in therapy and in supervision. The therapist could consider their own part in co-creating the silence.

Personally, I would not advise the therapist to 'rescue' by offering free or reduced rates at this stage (this might have been possible had everything been properly thought through and planned in advance). However, with Cecile's interest to the fore, I would want to honour the good work that had been done. I might pragmatically suggest at least one more session (perhaps at a cut-price rate) to try to effect a positive ending. I would also respect her choice if she wanted just to end.

2. **Bernie** – While there is some wriggle room, depending on the particular relational circumstances, **professional guidelines** would advise against 'coffee meetings', which run the risk of messing with client/friend *dual relationship* boundaries. To what extent would such meetings be truly mutual, given the asymmetrical relationship involved? It's likely the client, still carrying transferential feelings, would need something more than a casual friendship from the relationship. Would both client and therapist be able to handle this?

   Alerting us to the lurking power dimension, the Australian Counselling Association (ACA, 2015, p. 11) provides the following advice:

   > 3.9.(b) Counsellors remain accountable for relationships with former clients and must exercise caution over entering into friendships, business relationships, training, supervising and other relationships. Any changes in relationship must be discussed in counselling supervision. The decisions about any change(s) in relationship with former clients should take into account whether the issues and power dynamics presenting during the counselling relationship have been resolved.

   In **relational** terms, it would appear that work to do with grief and loss needs to be done by Bernie *and her therapist*. If clients aren't taking the opportunity to talk spontaneously about feelings around ending themselves, they might need encouragement, and this is something we would want to work on throughout any or all sessions. Three years of therapy probably deserve at least a few months of work on the ending process. But in Bernie's case that process seems to be just beginning. Bernie and her therapist are not yet ready to end. There is also still work to be done on enabling Bernie to develop more nourishing social networks and resources.

   In my role as supervisor, I would also want to be attentive to the therapist's process. Is there a possibility she is unduly holding on to Bernie out of her own unconscious needs? How could she be helped and supported to 'let go'?

3. **Present from a rich client** – The ethics of accepting gifts from a client depend on the circumstances and meanings – personal, relational, institutional and cultural (Welfel, 2013). Any rigid application of rules should probably be avoided. The American Counseling

Association *Code of Ethics* (2005) highlights that much depends on the particular context, the symbolic significance of the gift and what it means to both client and therapist:

Section A.10.e. Receiving gifts

Counselors understand the challenges of accepting gifts from clients, recognizing that in some cultures, small gifts are a token of respect and showing gratitude. When determining whether or not to accept a gift from clients, counselors take into account: the therapeutic relationship, the monetary value of the gift, a client's motivation for giving the gift, and the counselor's motivation for wanting or declining the gift.

It's understandable that clients might seek to express their gratitude and mark the end of therapy by giving a gift to their therapist. However, the motivation for the gift, along with its monetary value, also need to be taken into account.

Some institutions maintain a strict rule against accepting gifts. In **legal terms**, however, accepting a gift can be seen to be ethical if it promotes the client's welfare, is consistent with cultural norms and does not compromise the therapist's professional capacity (Welfel, 2013). Care needs to be taken to ensure boundaries are not crossed. While a gift of flowers might be acceptable in the professional context, a more personal gift, such as perfume and jewellery, would not be. In some contexts, perhaps the gift can be accepted on behalf of the team or clinic.

When gift-giving feels more personal, some therapists see it as transgressing a professional–personal boundary. If gift-giving is sought to be used as a form of manipulation or inducement, it certainly should be refused. At the very least, it's worth considering if there are any 'strings' of gratitude or intimacy that might still be felt if the client ever returned to therapy.

While some would recommend clarifying gift-giving boundaries at the point of contracting, this could feel heavy-handed: it could well burden the delicate contracting process with yet another 'rule'. Also, circumstances can spring surprises which lie beyond the realm of rules. If a child offers you a small drawing produced during a family therapy session, it would be absurd to apply a 'no gifts' rule.

Relationally speaking, gifts can generate tensions and confusions on the part of both giver and recipient. Suffering a bit of embarrassment might be the price a therapist has to pay for accepting a gift in order not to offend or hurt their client.

Existential psychotherapist Spinelli (2015) is clear that in his private practice he has no hesitation in accepting small gifts. Interestingly, in the case of longer-term clients, he may well offer a gift himself: perhaps a relevant CD or book or even a hug – any small token with some therapeutic significance can work well.

I know of a therapist who accepted a beautiful silk scarf from a client but found herself unable to wear it as she felt her client's presence wrapped around her throat. Exploring this in supervision the following week, she belatedly recognised how her client had had fantasies about strangling herself and others. The therapist realised her mistake and duly returned the gift with a kind thank-you note.

In my private practice, my own preference (should the issue arise) is to work relationally, even though this can feel uncomfortable, charged and tricky in the moment. It's grist for the therapy process. For example, it would be worth exploring how a client might be trying to make an emotional connection by repeatedly bringing in small gifts.

In the dilemma above, I would not feel comfortable about receiving the expensive vase and I would admit that. I might even say that it was professional policy that gifts are kept modest. (For example, some Local Authorities in the UK put a formal cap of £25 on the value of gifts received.) If the monetary value was insignificant to the client, their expensive gift perhaps could be accepted – but it *would stay in the therapy room.*

The horizon of loss (grief and avoidance)

The horizon of loss when ending can present a challenge for both client *and* therapist, particularly when it results in avoidance of the process. The ending of therapy (particularly long-term therapy) may trigger some re-experiencing of past loss, rejections, feelings of abandonment and unresolved grief (see Joyce et al., 2007, for a review). Therapists' understandings of the impact of clients' experiences of previous attachments and losses during the termination phase will help clients be more connected to feelings (of pride and loss), to the therapist and to outside relationships (Aafjes-Van Doorn and Wooldridge, 2018). The key role for the therapist in the ending phase is to enable a client to work through any arising pain, deal with 'unfinished business' and then, finally, to let go. *It is important that therapy doesn't add to the list of our client's experiences of unsatisfactory endings.*

The **grief** that may be evoked for clients associated with long-term therapy comes from recognising both something they have never had (an affirming, loving parent figure) and something they are losing (our healing, caring availability). It is natural to feel sadness when losing a special relationship. For clients who have attachment issues and a history of significant grief, the ending can be experienced as a crisis (Marx and Gelso, 1987). This needs particular attention. In general, there may be some resentment and anger felt towards a therapist who is perceived as abandoning and having stopped caring; and perhaps even envy of, or jealousy towards, clients who continue. For those with a problematic attachment history, the response might be detachment and dissociation (Marmarosh, 2017). There may also be associated despair and loss of hope. More than the loss of a valued relationship, the client must relinquish current hopes that their hurt will finally be gone. The final goodbye churns such feelings afresh.

Clarkson (1989) offers the following illustration of the challenges for both client and therapist:

> During the final (withdrawal) phase of the counselling process with Gary he went through a period of regressed neediness and doubt about his ability to manage in the 'real world' without my weekly presence. For instance, during one session he recycled some of the introjected messages that he was a bad person and spent several days in a rather depressed state feeling that he had accomplished nothing in his counselling. At other times he felt pleased and grateful for the many things he had learned....
>
> Gary was also genuinely sad that his relationship with me was ending, and I felt sad too. For a while he thought of coming into training with me. In following this through with the help of guided fantasy, for example, a day in the week of a counsellor, he became aware that this was more to do with his desire to hold on to me...
>
> This became the last enactment of his pathological confluence played out with me. Working through the fear of being abandoned by me, the wish to reject me before I abandoned him, as well as the remnants of feeling engulfed was the bulk of the slow, careful work with Gary in this phase. (Clarkson, 1989, pp. 158–159)

The process of working through this potential bereavement cocktail involves exploring complex layers of denial, anger, bargaining, depression, acceptance, fear and hope. In working with denial or acceptance, we might have to remind clients about the agreed contract and the nature of ending. We then have a role in accepting the expression and exploration of feelings of anger, depression or anxiety, while bringing into the client's awareness transferential elements suggestive of unfinished business. Attempts to bargain may be a part of this as the client seeks to hold on through other means ('Can't we just be friends?'). With the client's interests to the fore, we would work to help them understand the meanings underlying their experience of endings, identify ways of staying engaged while feeling the loss, and establish resources to cope with feelings (Marmarosh, 2017). Our role in holding the boundary thus becomes a thoroughly relational-ethical matter.

If a client isn't taking the opportunity to talk spontaneously about feelings around ending themselves, then they might need encouragement. This isn't merely something which occurs in the final session. Marmarosh (2017) presents the following dialogue, in which a therapist offers a compassionate challenge to a client with avoidant attachment issues:

Client: (looking away) So, the movers came and I am packed. I leave on Tuesday to head home. I have so much to do ... it is a lot (keeps talking about the process of moving until therapist interrupts).

Therapist: I notice we are not talking about this being our last session together.

Client: (The client is talking quickly without breathing and detached emotionally.) Well, I have a lot on my mind. I am sorry. The move is a lot and I have so many things to do. I have this list and have barely checked anything off of it. (She appears to be protecting herself from the ending by being busy and focused on the future.)

Therapist: (talking more slowly) You do have a lot to do, I noticed that as you were talking, I kept thinking this is our last session (pauses), and I had this feeling of sadness (gesturing to chest) that this will be the last time I see you. Next week, you will not be here, and I will miss you.

Client:	(tears up immediately)
Therapist:	(leaning forward and speaking softly) you're tearing up ...
Client:	(tears rolling down her face) I am a little surprised you said that (looks down which could indicate shame and movement away from feeling something good with the therapist).
Therapist:	(trying to regain eye contact) What part?
Client:	(she looks up) I do not know ... (pauses). I think, when you said you will miss me (more tears roll down her face and looks away again).
Therapist:	Hearing 'I will miss you.'
Client:	(looking at therapist) I never had anyone say that to me before. I know I will miss you too ... I have been saying goodbye a lot lately. I have a lot of friends but deep down inside, I never really think they care that much (crying) ... Like with college ending now and moving, we say we will keep in contact, but most of the time you know you will not...
Therapist:	There has been a lot of saying goodbye lately, and you wonder if they really care. Do you wonder if I care right now? (Moving back to engaging and addressing transference with therapist.)
Client:	(crying and looking down) I think that is why I am crying. I know you care (looks up). (Marmarosh, 2017, pp. 7–8)

Beyond sessions specifically devoted to endings, Moursund and Erskine (2004) recognise that the 'little endings' within each session can be helpful rehearsals, providing an opportunity to face up to fears and places which hurt. In this context, clients can sometimes struggle with ending sessions, as demonstrated by the way they try to take control prematurely by ending the session abruptly (perhaps fuelled by shame) or avoid the loss of ending by attempting to extend the time. This pattern of avoidance and contact disruption offers another form of opportunity for clients to learn to face the pain of endings and to repair some damage.

Holding ending boundaries

How we handle the ending varies according to the context and type of ending involved (see Box 9.2).

Box 9.2   Types of endings

- Endings may be built into **short-term therapy** contracts: for example, agreeing to meet a client for eight sessions. Knowing that horizon, we would work towards the ending from the first moment. However, even though the date is fixed, there is a still an ending process to go through, marking the boundary of being in or out of therapy. The most constructive focus is to acknowledge progress and discuss what resources will be useful in the future. In some

(Continued)

(Continued)

therapy contexts, outcome measures and formal evaluation of the experience are engaged.

- Making the decision to end **longer-term therapy** where there is nothing structured into the contract raises more thorny issues. The tricky bit is deciding if any decline in energy signals that clients are ready to move on or if there is still some useful work to be done.
- Abrupt **unilateral endings** leave both client and therapist with unfinished business and perhaps a lurking feeling of shame. Murdin (2000) suggests that when a client stops therapy unilaterally, they do so in one of three emotional states: with *anxiety*, with *aggression* or in *silence*. Each of these signals a possible resistance; the respective flight, fight or avoidance responses can be seen as serving important protective psychological functions.
- **Temporary endings** in the form of therapy breaks may be considered. Such breaks acknowledge there is still ending work to do. For example, financial, domestic or work constraints may necessitate the client suspending therapy for a period. Or a therapist might suggest that one-to-one therapy is suspended while the client goes to see another therapist for marital work. Some 'holding' could be maintained by asking the client to 'check in' periodically by email.
- **Forced endings** can happen if there are changes of life circumstances: perhaps one party has to move away from the area or becomes ill or dies. Funding or organisational changes may also precipitate an ending. Ideally, the ending process has a chance to be worked through to avoid a sense of unfinished business or even abandonment. If re-location is the trigger, would working on Skype/FaceTime offer a satisfactory compromise? In the case of the sudden illness or death of the therapist, hopefully relevant support systems can be activated via a 'therapeutic executor' (for example, see: www.goodtherapy.org/blog/psychpedia/professional-will).

It can help to build the ending horizon into the contracting process. For instance, we might specify the number of sessions, or what would happen if funding were to stop. Data protection information is also relevant, particularly in the case of forced endings, such as if a therapist were to retire or die, what happens to the client's therapy and notes?

The following dialogue demonstrates the *negotiated*, relational nature of the process – and its importance as a means of dealing with a client's unrealistic expectations:

Therapist: During our appointment today we have been discussing some of the problems that you have been experiencing for the past six years … ever since your wife died. I wonder, have you given any thought to how many sessions might be needed to work through these problems?

Client: Umm ... not much. Maybe four or five sessions.

Therapist: Um-hum. Thanks for sharing those thoughts. We definitely could see some improvements in four or five sessions and some clients do completely recover in that amount of time; however, it typically takes the average client somewhere between 15 to 20 sessions to fully get better. ... How do those numbers sound to you?

Client: Well ... like you said, it is a lot more than I was expecting. I guess I can give it a try.

Therapist: ...I really want to find a right balance for you, a plan that will meet your needs, and match as close as possible with what you are hoping for. Let's see ... you said you were originally expecting four to five sessions. Maybe what we can do is plan to have five sessions together and then check in with your goals, see if you feel like you are done at that point or see if you feel like we could do another five sessions or so. That way, if you are feeling better, then we can talk about ending, but at the same time we will keep in mind that it typically takes many more sessions so you will not get discouraged if we aren't all the way there yet. How does that sound?

Client: Yeah, I can do that plan.

Therapist: Okay, now let's talk about how we will know if you are done at that point or if you have reached all of your goals... (Goode et al., 2017, p. 11)

Beyond contracting, therapists differ substantially regarding the boundaries they apply to ending. Some may suggest gradually reducing contact over time, effectively 'weaning' the client off therapy. Some explicitly offer future contact, if and when extra support or a 'tune up' (Reimer, 2017) is needed; others would consider this as reinforcing client dependency, or as avoiding a 'proper' end, and would plump for more definitive and final boundary. Amis (2017) suggests that raising the possibility of future working can be reassuring for the client, but that it should be done in a progressive rather than dependency-seeking way. Here a client might value continuing with a therapist who already knows their story while care is taken around messages given to the client.

Sometimes therapists need to accept that endings may not be fully acknowledged, let alone worked through. It can help to leave the door open for the client to return when they are ready. I am reminded of one particularly messy process of ending with a client, an experience which taught me a lot about my avoidant attachment tendencies and my role in co-creating problematic endings. I spent many hours discussing the process of ending (and not) with my supervisor and eventually learned to develop stronger boundaries in relation to this crucial final stage of therapy.

We started with some short-term work focused on her conflicted relationship with her persecutory (grown up) daughter. Ellie soon recognized her part in the drama triangle and, feeling satisfied with her gains, Ellie sought to end therapy. But within the month she was back, in crisis and paralysed in her rescuer-victim position. She didn't want to come back to therapy – she saw it as a weakness. I soothed and supported (rescued?) her, and confluently responding to her need to 'be strong', I set her on her way again after a couple of sessions. And once more, she returned in crisis. When this pattern was repeated a second time, I was clearer that we were both avoiding the process of doing the deeper work needed and of ending.

Eventually we both agreed that longer-term, committed, in-depth relational work was required. Over the next couple of years, we found ourselves unravelling a story layered with profound grief, shame, abuse, abandonment and multiple trauma (including some inter-generational trauma).

It took two more years for Ellie to be ready to begin to consider ending therapy. This time the process involved a slow 'weaning-off' over many months. Ellie started to come fortnightly, then monthly. At last Ellie said she felt safe enough to consider coming in just six months' time for a 'check in rather than therapy'.

She made huge gains in terms of her awareness and many new resources. She was clear when she no longer needed therapy as she carried me with her instead. In times of stress she was able to get some comfort from imagining my eyes and remembering my 'holding'.

For my part, I miss her. I enjoyed being with her. Her courage and the depth of the work she did still impacts me profoundly. And I also celebrate her new-found freedom and independence. I believe she is currently enjoying her retirement and travelling the world, and I'm happy for her. (Finlay, 2016a, p. 142)

While there are no one-size-fits-all formulae for how to end therapy, some **general principles** are:

1. It helps to see ending as a process which takes place over time rather than as something that happens in the last session. It can also help to keep 'life-without-therapy' in mind. Put another way, it helps to focus on what happens in the other 167 hours a week and not just focus on intrapsychic processes that occur for the one therapy hour. Promoting the client's resources for coping 'out there' with work/home life seems fundamental.
2. Ensure you have space to give your clients – and yourself – time to work through the issues. Van Deurzen and Adams (2011) go as far as saying that at least *one-sixth* of therapy time should be spent considering endings. So with brief therapy, the last session would be devoted to ending well; long-term work could involve months of working through the process.
3. It can help to engage an explicit and mutual (i.e. relational) exploration around loss and hope, need and resources, autonomy and dependence, regrets and appreciation, and so on. I often spend the last couple of therapy sessions inviting clients to reminisce about key moments and to review their journey overall. 'How have you grown?' 'Do you have any *regrets* or bits of unfinished business for the future?' 'What will you miss and what do you *take away* with you?'
4. The shift away from clients' inner worlds towards the interpersonal-social life world of work and relationships helps prepare clients for life-without-therapy. It is important to think through what would be in the best interests of the client in terms of their needs for the future and

how they might handle future challenges. Spinelli (2015) offers the useful technique of thinking about the similarities and differences between what is happening in the therapy room and life 'outside'.

5. Be clear about (and perhaps formally contract) possibilities for future contact (or not). Some therapists would encourage ex-clients to check in periodically or come back if ever they need extra support. Others would work towards more final endings. If the client would benefit from seeing another therapist, options could be discussed.
6. We should respect client's decisions to leave therapy, honouring their own choices when it comes to boundary setting. Clearly, we should not seek to keep hold of reluctant or disengaged clients out of our own narcissistic needs (Moursund and Erskine, 2004).
7. Where possible, clients should be left richer for having had contact with us, even as we acknowledge unfinished business (normalising the idea that we're all work-in-progress). We might give them some affirming feedback about changes observed, including the new resources they have developed and the courageous way they have faced, and worked on, their issues. Highlighting how the client is not the person they were when they first entered therapy can promote self-confidence (Amis, 2017).

Evaluating progress and outcomes

A key component of ending involves reflecting on change and/or progress. *Most ethical frameworks recommend we systematically monitor our practice and outcomes using appropriate means and in the clients' interests.* Beyond informally reviewing progress regularly throughout therapy, at a formal level we can use many assessment tools and questionnaires to measure progress. The myriad **outcome measures** available form a continuum, from *objective* measures utilising set criteria and measurements of behavioural change at one end to *subjective* feedback focusing on emotional responses at the other. Some are completed by the therapist, others by clients.

Some measures aim for **objective** monitoring of symptoms. *The Patient Health Questionnaire* (PHQ-9) and *Generalised Anxiety Disorder* (GAD7) are commonly used as part of the UK 'Improving Access to Psychological Therapies' (IAPT) initiative. For example, the nine items on the PHQ-9 can be quickly filled out and are useful in monitoring changes in depression. Other measures designed to assess degrees of distress include the *Beck Depression Inventory* (measures depressive symptoms); the HAD scale (measures symptoms of depression and anxiety); the *Panic Disorder Severity Scale* (measure levels of panic); and *The Impact of Events Scale* (measures levels of post-traumatic stress disorder).

Therapists tend to prefer more holistic measures which consider functioning and not just symptoms. The **CORE** system is commonly employed here. This was developed in the UK but has found international favour. It assesses clients' subjective well-being, symptoms, interpersonal functioning and risk to self/others, and yields a global distress score. The measure has been well researched in routine services, and there is a lot of information about the profile of scores associated with users of particular services (for example, primary as opposed to secondary care settings). The different versions of CORE are easy to use and usefully track progress at different times over the course of therapy.

Other more qualitative and **subjective measures** which are widely used include: the *'Personal Questionnaire'*, where clients rate the problems they wish to work on; the *'Helpful Aspects of Therapy'* scale, where clients rate the aspects of therapy that they have found most useful; and the *Outcome Rating Scale* (ORS), which plots changes in how the client is feeling. Research surveys and interviews also tap this subjective element (see Box 9.3).

Of particular interest to relational therapists are measures which focus on evaluating the client–therapist relationship. These include the *Working Alliance Inventory* (WAI), the *Session Rating Scale* (SRS) and the *Relational Depth Inventory* (RDI–R2). These measures, along with others, can be used for **research** and **audit** purposes as well as for evaluating an individual client's progress. Based on preliminary research, it seems that RDI scores can predict post-therapy outcome scores and that an experience or moment of relational depth is a significant predictor of positive therapy outcomes (Wiggins, 2013). Similarly, research on the use of tools like WAI shows that establishing a working alliance early on in therapy (for example, between the third and fifth sessions) is predictive of positive outcomes (Hovarth and Bedi, 2002).

Evaluations of client's progress can be usefully supplemented by the use of formal outcome measures. However, these need to be applied ethically. The BACP, for instance, recommends that outcome measures should be used routinely *as part of therapy*, rather than as an adjunct to it. They stress that such measures should only be used if they are of benefit to the client and enrich the therapy. Thinking ethically, requires us to attend to how any assessments and measures are engaged and to choose the most appropriate, with due regard for therapist's level of training and both the relational and cultural context. Therapists need to take some care when introducing the measures, obtaining full, informed consent and ensuring there is time to complete them. A discussion evaluating the extent changes are down to therapy could then be fruitful.

Box 9.3 Research on endings

Norcross et al. (2017) identified core termination behaviours found in successful psychotherapy across theoretical orientations. Sixty-five 'experts' reported the frequency with which they engaged in 80 tasks. There was a positive consensus on 51 items, indicating much commonality of practice across the theoretical spectrum. However, there was no consensus regarding 27 tasks.

The termination behaviours and tasks that achieved the highest degree of consensus included: supporting the client's progress; promoting client growth post-termination; following the ethics code; consolidating gains made; and highlighting the patient's recognition of competence.

The research identified eight core ending interventions as contributing to effective therapy:

1. process feelings of the patient and therapist
2. discuss the patient's future functioning/coping
3. help patients to use new skills beyond therapy
4. frame personal development as invariably unfinished
5. anticipate post-therapy growth and generalisation
6. prepare explicitly for termination
7. reflect on the patient's gains and consolidation
8. express pride in the patient's progress and mutual relationship.

Jofen-Miller and Fiori (2017) focused on the role of training and experience in shaping post-termination contact. Using an anonymised survey of 144 licensed clinicians (25% outside the US), the researchers found post-termination contact to be ubiquitous: 90.3% of the sample endorsed having some form of contact – often brief, lasting under a month; 25% of these clinicians initiated the contact; 70% of clinicians reported post-termination contact with their own therapist and these people anticipated more positive consequences of such contact with their own patients. The results indicated that recently trained graduates had received more training on post-termination contact and that these clinicians more readily anticipated negative consequences. The researchers note the likely increase of post-termination contact as a result of growing social media use, and recommend more training so as to alert clinicians to the negative as well as positive consequences.

Researching practice in Argentina, **Olivera et al. (2017)** engaged in 73 semi-structured interviews to explore former clients' perspectives of therapy termination. Interviews were transcribed and analysed qualitatively using an adaptation of *Consensual Qualitative Research* (CQR). Quantitative analyses were also conducted to examine associations between variables. Client-initiated termination included situations where the therapist (49%) and client disagreed (51%) regarding ending. This contrasted with therapist-initiated terminations, where 95% were agreed mutually with clients. These involved better therapeutic bonds and higher overall satisfaction with treatments.

Concluding reflections

Therapists are responsible for ending therapy ethically. The artful bit is deciding when and how to engage the ending process. The **'when'** is easiest if it's contracted from the beginning, setting a horizon with a containing boundary.

For longer-term work, the process is best negotiated via regular reviews, always with the relationship to the fore.

The critical clinical judgement involves deciding when the client is getting to the point of not benefitting as much from therapy as they did in the past. Here the Australian Counselling Association (2015, p. 6) offers some useful advice:

(c) Breaks and Endings

  i. Counsellors work with clients to reach a recognised ending when clients have received the help they sought or when it is apparent that counselling is no longer helping or when clients wish to end.

  ii. External circumstances may lead to endings for other reasons which are not therapeutic. Counsellors must make arrangements for care to be taken of the immediate needs of clients in the event of any sudden and unforeseen endings by the counsellor or breaks to the counselling relationship.

  iii. Counsellors should take care to prepare their clients appropriately for any planned breaks from counselling...

I worry sometimes when outcome measures are handed out routinely to clients without proper care or the client's active consent. I mistrust a situation where a client's complex experience is sought to be reduced to a few ticks and numbers. From my supervision experience of therapists in private practice, I find they are reluctant to use official questionnaires and outcome measures, fearing this might interfere with the therapy relationship and process. However, research suggests that in many cases clients are happy to complete such measures, which they see as 'professional' and 'scientific' (see Box 7.1). That said, clients still like to understand the point of such questionnaires – and feel that their answers are respected.

I also worry when various tests, along with ending rituals, are used without sensitive attention to *cultural acceptability*. An 'ending hug' might be a common practice in training workshops but may be inappropriate in other environments. Most published evaluations have been developed in the Western world and tend to judge certain behaviours, values and life practices in ethnocentric ways. For example, the 'autonomy' and 'independence' values enshrined in many codes may not resonate for those who come from countries where family dependence is taken for granted and valued.

The **'how'** to end part of therapy is less easy to prescribe. Much depends on the relationship and on the attachment styles of both the client and therapist (Aafjes-Van Doorn and Wooldridge, 2018). The challenges of separation and loss that come with endings – particularly in the case of long-term therapy and/or forced endings – can lead us to avoid, resist and deflect from the experience. But if we (*client and therapist alike*) can enter that space and embrace it, we will then be more open to new beginnings and the possibility of transformation. The key is to face the reality of transition, welcoming both the pain of ending and the excitement of new journeys. Then, when our client is ready to be on their way, we need to respect their choices and let them go. It's important that the therapist doesn't undermine the process by communicating that they're feeling rejected, hurt or abandoned themselves.

Part of our role as therapists is to help clients face the pain of the goodbye as part of embracing life. And then we are obliged to let go with *grace*. The prize comes as clients celebrate their growth, as they carry the good experience (of both the therapy and the ending) forward into the rest of their lives. This sharing can be part of our own healing, too.

> Saying good-bye hurts. Grief hurts. But to be allowed to say good-bye with gratitude and love as well as with sadness and loss is a privilege. (DeYoung, 2003, p. 203)

Discussion questions

1. Avoiding the use of outcome measures is unethical and goes against professional guidelines. Discuss.
2. Explain why ending with some clients can be challenging for therapists and what steps can be taken to ease the process.
3. Discuss the pros and cons of post-therapy contact.

Summary

Ending therapy ethically involves layered processes. For a positive ending to be achieved, the client needs to be well prepared. Thoughtful celebration by the therapist of the progress made during therapy strengthens the client's resources and coping ability as they step into the future. The art of ending lies in judging correctly when to end and how to negotiate this relationally and thoughtfully. While outcome measures can offer a useful gauge, they need to be therapeutically applied. Beyond negotiating the practicalities of the contract, we need to sensitively acknowledge any associated loss and the horizon of grief for both client and therapist. Part of our role as therapists is to help clients face the pain of the goodbye as part of embracing life. And then we are obliged to let go with *grace*.

PART III

RELATIONAL ETHICS IN PRACTICE

Preamble

> If relational therapy is our mode of practice we know that when we show up for real in our relationships with our clients, our hearts are involved. ... A moment of meeting is as much a moment of mutual loving respect as it is a moment of understanding. (DeYoung, 2015a, p. 202)

In these final chapters, I present five case studies: constructed, fictionalised accounts loosely based on composites drawn both from my own work as a therapist and supervisor and from others. Demonstrating relational ethics in action, they speak to many of the topics and themes raised in the book. I've tried to span a range of practice, from more straightforward brief therapy and solution-focused interventions through to long-term, complicated relational-depth psychotherapeutic work.

While the stories show therapy that has been successful, I hope I've avoided making them appear contrived or overly rosy. They aim to show 'good enough', rather than 'perfect', therapy. The therapists in these stories make mistakes and misjudgements and have their own vulnerabilities to manage. While most of the stories show positive outcomes, one doesn't. But even with the problematic therapy, it is not about the therapist being 'right' or 'wrong' – it's about recognising the subtle, challenging relational judgements at stake. It's also a salutary reminder that clients (and our processes) are not always within our control.

Writing these stories of individuals' therapy encounters has proved interesting. I've enjoyed getting to know my 'characters' as they've emerged; just as the fictional therapists have become attached to their different clients, so have I.

I've shared successive drafts with others. Some readers have asked if the story is about them, or a client of theirs. And it never is! Any resemblance between my characters and any actual person is coincidental. While recognising that certain themes may resonate in a 'familiar-feeling' way, I want to stress that these are constructed stories. I do not want to threaten confidentiality and anonymity agreements, nor do I want anyone to feel somehow exposed or objectified by being written about. If you recognise elements of your own experience in the stories, I hope you will feel reassured that others have had similar experiences to your own.

I hope you enjoy reading these stories. Each chapter ends with some **concluding reflections**. These start with a box listing '*good practice indicators*' to highlight the strengths of the therapist's interventions and show respect for the difficult work we do. Then I selectively focus on various relational-ethical concerns. Perhaps you will spot other points of 'relational ethics'; maybe you will disagree with the therapist's (or my) position. Join the dialogue!

10

Karim: Brief Therapy and CBT

Karim is employed by an international airline as cabin crew but has recently become afraid of flying following a traumatic, terrorism-related airborne incident. His doctor diagnosed post-traumatic stress disorder (PTSD) and signed him off work for three months. Karim was prescribed anti-depressant medication and recommended to attend weekly counselling at the surgery.

On meeting his counsellor, Karim expressed his willingness to try **12 sessions of counselling**. He explained, 'It's vital this is sorted out, otherwise I'm out of a job'. After hearing a few details about his current difficulties and life circumstances, the therapist recommended a three-pronged strategy:

  i. *cognitive-behavioural exposure therapy using virtual reality technology*
 ii. *anxiety management strategies, such as mindfulness*
iii. *a more holistic exploration of his emotional world.*

While CBT is not this therapist's favoured approach, she had recently been on a relevant training course and felt competent to deliver a suitable package.

Karim, for his part, was keen to start. Therapist and client soon agreed their **contract**. The therapist assured Karim that while the content of their sessions would be confidential, she was required to write a brief report at the end of their work to go into his medical notes. He liked her suggestion that they write this together.

In their first proper session, Karim is invited to **describe his experience**, both of the terrorist incident and his subsequent anxiety. As he recalls the incident, his anxiety level visibly rises as well as his embarrassment about being so 'pathetic'. The therapist gently reminds him that it is a memory and that he is safe now. She teaches him some basic slow breathing and grounding techniques. He learns to use his senses to separate the here-and-now from the there-and-then.

Feeling calmer, he is able to recount the story of him tackling a 'crazy man' who was trying to break into the cockpit while holding an improvised device that appeared to be a bomb and shouting 'I'm going to blow-up this plane!'. Karim took the responsibility to talk him down and coax him back to his seat. A burly passenger helped; together they restrained him physically. Suddenly another passenger stood up, pointed at Karim's turban and shouted, 'Bloody Muslims – they're probably in cahoots with each other. Tie him up, too!' Karim quelled his own emotional responses and tried to respond reassuringly but a senior cabin crew ordered him to go to the galley and lie low. All eyes seemed to stare in accusation and judgement as he walked to the rear of the plane. The tension and violence of the incident, the unfair punishment of being 'banished' to the galley rather than being hailed a hero, and his 'walk of shame' all tumbled about in his mind. That Karim is a Sikh, not a Muslim, added fuel to his sense of unjust victimisation.

Karim discloses that since the incident he experiences regular nightmares and daytime flashbacks which result in palpitations and sometimes full-blown panic attacks. He feels vulnerable, with a diminished sense of manliness, and is anxious about his future job prospects. He has isolated himself at home, not wanting others to see the 'emotional wreck' he has become.

The therapist reassures him that his response is 'natural and normal' after intense trauma and that it will pass once he learns some coping strategies. Taking a **psychoeducational approach**, she explains the nature of traumatic stress and how stress hormones are continually released during every flashback. Karim learns the technique of 'anchoring' and the use of 'oases' to help him control the anxiety spiral. His therapist recommends that he download a 'mindfulness app' onto his phone so that he can draw on extra support at home.

When Karim feels more confident in handling his anxiety, he and his therapist begin a **systematic desensitisation** programme. His therapist explains that this is a well-researched and scientifically validated technique which combines relaxation exercises, visualisation of boarding a plane and then flying, all in progressive steps.

To obtain a baseline score to measure his anxiety levels, they use The Flight Anxiety Situations Questionnaire (FAS) and the Flight Anxiety Modality Questionnaire (FAM) (Van Gerwen et al., 1999). FAS is a 32-item self-report inventory with a five-point Likert-type scale assessing anxiety experienced related to flying in different situations. FAM is an 18-item questionnaire measuring the symptoms of anxiety in flight situations.

Karim slowly imagines the steps necessary to go to work, prepare for a flight, board the plane and engage in routine cabin crew tasks. When his anxiety increases, he is invited to engage his relaxation techniques until his arousal level is sufficiently reduced. Then they return to the visualisation.

Soon, Karim comfortably imagines his return to work. At this point they try a 'virtual reality' (VR) program of flying in an airplane (Price et al., 2008). Being technologically-minded, Karim is fascinated by (and enjoys) the VR experience. While he recognises it wasn't quite his real-life cabin crew experience, he is reassured that the associated imagery did not trigger anxiety. That his 'fear of flying' was now under much better control was confirmed by his scores on re-taking the FAS/FAM assessments (outcome measure).

Together, Karim and the therapist discuss his next step. They decide on **'homework'**: specifically, visiting the airport armed with his relaxation strategies. He agrees, and together they plan how he might choose to wander around an unfamiliar terminal to avoid meeting colleagues. Much to his surprise, he enjoys the experience and generally feels empowered.

The final three sessions are devoted to reviewing Karim's progress and **ending positively**. They examine the kinds of incidents that could feel threatening in the future. Karim's therapist encourages him to gain a fresh perspective on what happened. For instance, she asks whether it was possible that his manager had sent him to the galley for his own safety. Karim is surprised and remembers other occasions when his manager had been supportive. He realises his initial assumption that everyone was against him was probably wrong. He sees that what had been triggered for him were those traumatic times at school when he had been bullied for his *Joora* (a Punjabi word for the 'top knot' of long hair, which he is forbidden to cut as a Sikh). Subsequently, he had experienced some racism when going for job interviews (at some he had been asked if he could 'get rid of' his turban).

Karim expresses anger about the racism he had experienced in his life and how he had felt so offended by being labelled Muslim. He owns his own prejudices against the 'Muslim immigrant community who do not integrate', which the therapist does not challenge. She shares an intuition that what was most hurtful for Karim was not being 'seen' as a Sikh when this was such an important part of his identity. He also recognised that in his efforts to 'blend into the crowd', he had not explained his religion to his colleagues. He resolves to share more and perhaps offer cultural sensitivity training to his department.

The therapist recognised Karim's respect for her authority and that he probably would have accepted her writing the end report herself. However, they ended their sessions by jointly drafting it.

While the therapist was pleased with the outcomes of the therapy, she was left feeling distinctly uncomfortable about her silence in the face of Karim's anti-Muslim sentiments. Instead of challenging his racist comments, she had let them slide. Together with her supervisor, they explore the possibility that she might carry some racist beliefs herself. Did she respond appropriately in the circumstances? Could she handle such processes differently in future?

Concluding reflections

> ## Box 10.1 Good practice indicators
>
> - Careful assessment, monitoring processes, and measurement of outcomes
> - Competent, collaboratively negotiated and carefully paced interventions
> - Cultural sensitivity
> - Professional development opportunities embraced by therapist

Before you read my personal responses below, think about the relational ethics involved in Karim's supported journey back to health. Which ones stand out for you?

For me, four relevant issues concern the process of contracting, care, professional development and cultural diversity.

The care initially taken with engaging Karim in therapy and in the **contracting** phase was crucial. The therapist's assurances that Karim's issues could be worked on in a positive way, helped by 'scientifically validated procedures', gave Karim hope, along with confidence in therapy and his particular therapist. The therapist's ability to attune to Karim's respect for science and technology, adapting her approach and interventions accordingly, proved crucial. If another client presented as being less keen to engage in technology or clinical protocols, then the relational position would be to find another route.

This case history emphasises the importance of getting clients' 'informed consent' *at each point of the therapy.* In this case, this extended to jointly writing their report at the end. I respect the integrity of this therapist in keeping the agreement to do a joint report, an agreement which also implicitly acknowledges Karim's legal right to see his notes.

The therapist demonstrated her **care** at many points. Most important was the careful timing of interventions so as not to re-traumatise Karim and to build his confidence. While CBT may not be her favourite approach, she used her clinical judgement about what would offer the best outcomes given the limited number of sessions allocated. Her relational *caring-with* commitment was additionally shown in the way she promoted their collaboration and also kept the therapy focused on his presenting issues (which was appropriate given the limited time they had) and didn't stray into exploring his wider life relationships. This focus is not always easy or appropriate and involves therapist judgement about when to open up issues or not. Therapists could be considered remiss for not at least checking out if there were other issues lurking.

Professional development comes in when we recognise that the therapist had received some extra training in the use of the standardised assessments and the specialist virtual reality program. The ethical obligation laid down in many professional codes is to undertake ongoing professional development

towards maintaining and enhancing competence. This includes engaging further professional training and keeping in touch with emerging practice issues,
theory, research and new technologies. For those therapists who do specialised
work with phobias, the use of virtual reality exposure therapy (VRET) could
be highly pertinent. While I personally have never seen VR treatments in
action, like the one in this story, I'm aware that their research-supported use
is increasing, and I think we need to keep up with trends. For instance, I have
heard of 'Spider World' to treat arachnophobia. (See https://appreal-vr.com/
blog/virtual-reality-therapy-potential/.)

Cultural diversity issues also figure prominently in this case history. The
therapist needed to be aware of the implications of the differences in beliefs
and practices between people of two different faiths (Sikhism and Islam) in
order to relate to Karim's concerns and his pride in his own ethnicity. It is not
easy here to acknowledge cultural differences without falling into stereotypical assumptions. It's important for this therapist to show some genuine curiosity about what was meaningful for Karim about the lived experience of his
ethnicity.

Issues around *anti-oppressive* practice might also be relevant, particularly as
the therapist recognised the potential for racist complicity. I respect the way
she owned her process. We can all become caught in unthinking behaviour
that subtly discriminates. Here, the relational-ethical stance is to question
ourselves, teasing out insidious beliefs while finding the balance between
challenge and respect for clients' views. But in the circumstances – with
Karim's own racism not being the focus of therapy – I sympathise with the
therapist. It sounds like she was responsive enough to encourage him to talk
about his ethnic identity. If she had called him out as a 'racist', it could well
have put their alliance in jeopardy. That said, perhaps she could have mentioned something in passing that acknowledged most ordinary Muslims battle
racism and are both peace-loving and against terrorism themselves. It takes
some finesse to be able to challenge clients' perspectives while remaining
accepting and authentically respectful.

11

Susan: Integrating Creatively?

Susan began her therapy by explaining she had had seven years of therapy previously and was returning to it after a 12-year break. She regretted that her old 'much loved' therapist was no longer practising but she felt 'OK' about a new start, as her previous therapy had ended well.

Pretty, neatly dressed and quietly spoken, she also presented as an 'experienced' client, apparently both open and emotionally contactful. She readily shared her history of childhood sexual abuse, first by her father and then later by her gymnastics coach. Her father had long since died, while her coach was in prison (Susan had been part of the group of women who had spoken out, resulting in a well-publicised court case that sent him there). Susan declared that all these issues had been 'well worked through' in previous therapy.

Her reason for seeking therapy now – aged 45 – was her recognition that she seemed 'unable' to find *and keep* a good relationship with a man. She had reached the stage where she wanted to settle down with 'the One'. Otherwise, she considered she had had a 'good life', including a nice home and garden (her 'safe, cosy nest'), lovely friends and rewarding work as a pharmacist.

The therapist, for her part, felt Susan might have disclosed this history a little too quickly and suspected the current picture Susan painted was too neat and positive. She felt Susan was 'covering over' more painful emotions but recognised they needed time to build a relationship. The therapist suspected the origin of Susan's current relational issues with men lay in her past, although Susan insisted she only wanted to work on future relationships.

As part of their initial **contracting**, the therapist agreed, for now, to go along with Susan's preferred focus. She kept her doubts to herself while indicating they could revisit this focus later. She felt secretly relieved that they would not have to legally follow-up the father's sexual abuse (possibly having to formally confront and report him). At the same time, she suspected the issues would remain live for her client. Susan's mother, who was still alive, had been seemingly complicit when she refused to accept eight-year-old Susan's accusations. While Susan had apparently 'worked through her anger with her mother' in her previous therapy, the therapist doubted this was settled as Susan and her mother still had an ambivalent ongoing relationship.

Both Susan and the therapist agreed that the first step was to build their **alliance** and trust. The therapist encouraged Susan to acknowledge how challenging it was to adapt to a different therapist when nursing a sense of loss for her previous one. Susan soon recognised sharp differences between her old (person-centred) therapist and her new (more relational analytic) one. The therapist was careful to be respectful of the good work that had taken place previously while privately she could not help being critical about what she saw as a more passive way of working. She wondered how Susan would handle her very different analytic approach, which, while providing room for greater interpretation and self-disclosure, was unlikely to offer 'unconditional positive regard'.

Once their alliance was in place, client and therapist faced Susan's **relationship problems** head on. At this point Susan confessed (with considerable embarrassment and self-disgust) that she had 'blown it' again. The previous weekend she had gone to a pub, got drunk, picked up a 'sleazy' man (one she would normally not have given the time of day to) and slept with him. Now it seemed he wouldn't leave her alone. She was torn between being 'nicely polite' and telling him brutally to stop harassing her and f*** off!

It turned out this was something of a pattern for Susan. The therapist was surprised. It was hard to imagine that the sweet-talking, home-loving Susan she had come to know would have drunken sex or tell someone to f*** off. Her instincts alerted, the therapist now wondered about the possibility of some DID (Dissociative Identity Disorder), given Susan's history of trauma and abuse. The therapist presented this idea to Susan and sought to probe the story of Susan's past sexual abuse. Susan froze and appeared angry. She rejected the idea of going back to the past, insisting she had 'done all that'. A mini-rupture and impasse seemed to come between them.

Taking this to **supervision**, the therapist realised she had become caught in Susan's past trauma story and possible linking diagnosis, losing a sense of Susan as a person. They wondered what was happening in the relational process that pulled this response. They also acknowledged her tendency to rush exploration instead of working initially with ensuring a proper grounding (for both client and therapist). The supervisor was supportive and respectful of the therapist's extensive experience of working with trauma and preparedness to own her limitations, which helped reduce the therapist's sense of shame.

In the next session, the therapist apologised to Susan and they processed their different perspectives, slowly re-building their relationship. Susan then admitted that the therapist might be right about the 'dissociation', which she described as 'like having an alien' take her over at times. A door opened, allowing new explorations to proceed.

The therapist tentatively suggested they explore this 'alien' part Susan sometimes experienced. Drawing on a psychodramatic/gestalt technique that she herself had gained a lot from as a client and had since used with many clients, she invited Susan to sit on an **empty chair** and speak from that place. Initially, Susan was reluctant and the therapist persuasively explained how it might work.

The chair-work proved an immediate epiphany. The 'alien' morphed into 'Susie' – a promiscuous, sexually provocative, extroverted 'party girl' who liked to pick up men for one-night stands. The therapist encouraged 'Susie' to express herself and talk about her relationship with Susan. 'Susie' obliged, saying she 'felt sorry' for Susan, 'locked away at home like some spinster', reading her 'trashy romantic novels', 'afraid to say boo to a goose'. 'Susie' saw herself as the strong one. She liked her own ability to have a 'good time' and worried about how lonely and alone Susan was.

Susan was then invited back to her original chair to give her response. Susan was a bit shaken. At first, she found it hard to speak, but they went slowly. She eventually admitted she found 'Susie' and her behaviour horrific. 'Susie' scared her, she said, as these men often turned violent or behaved in difficult ways. She declared she 'hated' 'Susie' and wanted nothing to do with her as she was ruining her life.

This began a stage of therapy where the outspoken 'Susie' joined the sessions regularly. It was clear that 'Susie' was not going to be silenced. The divide between Susan and 'Susie' was clarified. It showed up most markedly in the clothes that Susan imagined 'Susie' wearing: short skirts, tight, gaudy, revealing tops and thigh-high boots – all in stark contrast to Susan's more conservative, professional clothes. They diverged also in their responses to internet dating. Susan would go online looking for 'romance and commitment'; 'Susie' wanted 'hot sex'. While many relationships were begun, no man lasted long.

The therapist frequently felt that she was doing **couples work**, helping Susan-'Susie' communicate and connect with each other, and also explore their different needs. Therapist and client were able to identify Susan's yearning for safety and absence of relationship demands versus 'Susie's' craving for love and attention, which she could meet in the only way she knew: by pleasing men. Susan began to see how she disowned, and dissociated from, the 'Susie' part of her, which she eventually recognised as a direct product of her early sexualisation. Later Susan learned an important lesson: that 'Susie' was also a source of strength for her. Indeed, 'Susie' could at times be helpfully assertive – she just needed some 'controlling'.

The therapist invited Susan to begin to make choices about who she wanted to be in the future. Could she and 'Susie' come to a compromise arrangement and help each other? A new persona – 'Sue' – spontaneously appeared during one session when the therapist sensed Susan was somehow presenting differently; she was coming across with a different voice and manner. The therapist pointed out this subtly shifting new way of being, one that didn't seem to represent either Susan or 'Susie'. Susan promptly responded: 'This is a new me. I'm calling myself Sue.' In transactional analytic terms, the therapist suggested that 'Sue' was a more 'Adult', less adapted version of Susan – one who would eventually be a positive, integrating force for all the different parts of herself.

Over **two more years** of therapy, Susan/Susie/Sue lurched between her 'selves' and a series of disastrous relationships. These left Susan feeling victimised and were a source of concern to the therapist (who, in her maternal counter-transference, felt protective and frustrated at the way Susan kept sabotaging herself). Both therapist and Susan found the therapy tough: the therapist for what she had to 'hold'; Susan for facing her trauma and shame.

The therapist found her supervision supportive for holding those bits of Susan's experience she couldn't hold herself. At the same time, the therapist needed to off-load her own anger and frustration about Susan's abuse history and her self-sabotage towards helping her hold back from trying to 'rescue' with advice-giving.

Susan eventually learned that her needy, shamed and shaming parts of herself would never disappear totally but could be managed better once she was aware of her needs. She became more mindful of her choices, learning to keep herself safe by putting a boundary between herself and those who were toxic to her, while opening to more nourishing contacts. She also came to rely on 'Sue' and her ability to take responsibility for containing 'Susie's' more risky excesses while ensuring Susan was cared for. Eventually, it was 'Sue' who finally met a man with whom she could/would have a healthy long-term relationship.

Eighteen months **after their therapy ended** (and ended well with mutual sadness), the therapist received a wedding invitation from Susan. The therapist would have truly loved to have gone to the wedding, but after consulting with her supervisor she compromised (reluctantly) by simply sending a special card with a heartfelt message.

Concluding reflections

Box 11.1 Good practice indicators

- Reflexive handling of diagnostic possibilities acknowledging the history of abuse/trauma
- Owning of mistakes
- Creative and flexible therapeutic approach demonstrating competence
- Ending of therapy well managed regarding handling sadness and any dependency
- Regular use of supervisor for support, holding and challenge

The striking relational-ethical issues arising for me concern diagnosis and formulation of 'multiple selves', respect for other professionals, the use of techniques, power and boundaries. You might find it interesting to compare your own thinking with mine...

I have immediate issues regarding the use of **diagnosis and formulation of 'multiple selves'**. While the therapist *may* have been right about the DID diagnosis, she was so beguiled by the possibility of it that she lost sense of how Susan might react to it. I wonder if receiving this diagnosis felt objectifying to Susan or threatened her sense of self as having successfully worked through her trauma. Might she have felt let down by the therapist probing her past when she had explicitly asked for a focus on the present? I think the therapist needed to contain her clinical excitement, hold her diagnostic understandings more lightly and tentatively, and work more slowly.

However, I appreciate the way the therapist apologised. Given such apologies were probably lacking in Susan's history of abuse, it might have offered a significant relational repair. That there had been a mini-rupture in the therapeutic alliance probably wasn't a disaster in itself. Seeing the therapist make and own mistakes might even have helped model something useful and promote authentic, mutual dialogue.

I also have some ethical questions regarding the extent to which the therapist may have imposed on Susan her *interpretative formulation* of 'multiple selves'. The relational-ethical position is to see our interpretations as provisional hypotheses that can be challenged but which may offer some new understanding. They are not 'fact'; we might be 'wrong'.

Was 'Susie' around before or was she created in the session through therapist suggestion? Did the therapist herself subtly invent 'Sue' with Susan duly picking up her cue? In all probability, Susan and her therapist had plenty of opportunity to discuss the nature and function of the 'selves', and how real they felt. In ethical-relational terms, it would have been important for the therapist to clarify that this formulation of 'selves' was a metaphorical device: something they were using (playing with?) as part of a creative exploration.

There is debate in the field about whether engaging with 'alternate selves' is therapeutic or not. The International Society for the Study of Trauma and Dissociation (ISSTD) guidelines advise engaging with all parts of a person's personality in a non-judgemental, affirming way. In this way, the therapists act as a 'relational bridge', which helps the client relate to dissociated parts of themselves and disowned memories. However, it is recommended that the therapist still holds in mind this is one client and not collude with the dissociation by encouraging unnecessary elaborations or strengthening the autonomy of 'alters' (Spring, 2010). With the therapist feeling like she was engaging 'couples work', I wonder if she was in danger of colluding with the dissociation and splitting.

That said, the metaphorical use of 'selves' to represent parts of self in therapy can be a useful way of 'containing' problematic aspects of clients (which may or may not be owned). In this case 'Susie' had a contained space to express herself while the disparate selves (Susan/Susie/Sue) were held by the therapist until the client was ready to take them on herself.

This way of working figures regularly in my own practice. It makes sense to me and helps me attune to the parts-of-self in others. I like the way it calls forth an integrating energy that gives voice to a person's ambivalent, dissociated, and fragmented self-experience while also highlighting the value of having an accepting, compassionate relationship with oneself (Finlay, 2016b). That one part may be vulnerable and in pain also allows the possibility of having some containing distance from it, something particularly useful when working with rage, disgust or shame. At the same time, I'm aware of the need to avoid over-using (imposing) this device and to attend more to the client's experiential reality. Also, I know that, in practice, it can get very challenging (for all concerned) to hold all the pieces!

I like DeYoung's (2015b) formulation, which highlights the role of respect and compassion when working with chronic shame and multiple parts of self:

> Bringing shame to light often illuminates a needy part of self who is despised by a tough, independent part of self. Listening respectfully to both parts and helping each to find compassion for what drives the other brings better balance and harmony to the whole self system. ... Parts of self can find space to speak the unspeakable about need, longing, and humiliation, and in their speaking and being heard, integration happens. Often a time of working with 'parts' comes and goes in therapy, and later clients look back with fond nostalgia on parts they once encountered as 'other' but that are not just everyday aspects of the self they know. (2015b, pp. 132–133)

This case study draws attention to the kind of work we sometimes have to do when following in the steps of another therapist. There can be a tricky line to tread here: that of showing **respect for other professionals** even when we are critical of what we hear of their actions or approach. Of course, we rarely have access to the full story. In this particular case, it's possible the two therapists might have had a professional disagreement over theoretical approaches. But it would be important not to undermine previous work by being competitive or encouraging splitting processes between therapy experiences, perhaps by positioning a previous therapist as 'bad' and oneself as 'good'. This also applies to our attitudes to clients' parents or significant others. It's too easy to become confluent with clients' negativity whereas a healthier position might be to re-engage with past significant relationships in more realistic, even compassionate ways which acknowledge the positive along with the negative. The relational ethic here is one of respect for self and others.

I am saddened by our competitive professional 'turf wars', which can lead to us disrespecting other practitioners or positioning them as somehow less effective. The differences between theoretical approaches should not blind us to the similarities. Aren't we all agreed on the need for an initial therapy aim to develop the therapeutic alliance? Don't we all try to be sensitive and empathetic? We might surmise that the therapist here – like her predecessor, was non-judgemental about Susie's excesses, which allowed Susan/Sue to better accept that side of herself. I'm interested in the way the current *zeitgeist* favouring 'relational' work brings our approaches together (Finlay, 2016a). For instance, it's likely that a relational psychoanalytic therapist has more in common with another relational therapist coming from a different modality than with a traditional psychoanalyst.

The **use of techniques** like chair-work raises interesting issues that apply more widely to other techniques (such as role-play, bodywork, standardised assessments, etc.). Research shows that clients may experience embarrassment and awkwardness in such interventions and that even though they find it meaningful, it can be deeply demanding. The relational-ethical position is to respect the client's choice if they find it *too* artificial or intense and to allow time for clients to process their work, for instance, realising how they are active agents in their internal critical dialogue. *Thoughtful care* needs to be given to how the technique is going to be received and special attention to the therapy alliance is needed before clients are invited to engage (Stiegler et al., 2018). In other words, it's not the technique under debate, it's *how* it is used which determines its ethical-ness. In this case, I have questions about how ethical the therapist was being if she had set out to 'persuade' Susan to engage chair-work, and if Susan had been compliant rather than choiceful.

The issue of **power** is implicated when considering who controls the agenda and choice of interventions. Ideally, therapy should be mutually nego- tiated. We don't generally impose our ideas of what would be best without the client's consent (except in extreme situations); likewise, we're not there to offer knee-jerk succour by complying with clients' every expressed need and demand. In this case, Susan initially didn't want to work with her past, whereas the therapist had other ideas. They needed to find a compromise position, and this involved working – slowly, respectfully and creatively – with Susan's 'resistance' (and scare?) to re-opening the door on her past. I like Richard Hycner's dialogic take here:

> The challenge to the therapist is to meet the client at that point of contact in a manner that encompasses that resistance, rather than threatens it. It is to genu- inely see the resistance as a point of contact *between* rather than as merely an oppositional force. (1991/1993, pp. 151–152)

Finally, the therapist was right, I believe, to hold the **boundary** and not go to the wedding or send a present, however tempted. What would you have done and why?

12

Gary: Working with Anger in Context

Gary is a firefighter in his late twenties. He is referred for six sessions of therapy via an employee assistance programme (EAP) – an employee benefit scheme where employers pay for counselling for their employees with personal or work-related issues impacting their job. The referring request is to work with Gary's 'anger issues'. The therapist chosen to deliver the counselling works cognitively and systemically and has previous experience of working with the firefighting service involved. It seems the employers value both his experience and his background of having been in the armed forces.

On first meeting Gary, the therapist explains that this is an opportunity to talk through any issues, problems or tensions that are impacting his work. The therapist outlines the EAP **contract**, which clarifies that while the content of counselling sessions will be confidential, the therapist will have to write a brief report at the end for the employers (who are paying for the service). This will record dates of attendance and include any recommendations Gary and the therapist decide upon. Gary will receive his own copy of this report.

The therapist also shares something of his experience of working with the fire service. He acknowledges that its work environment remains male-orientated, with the 'macho' atmosphere making it difficult for firefighters to talk openly and easily about their feelings. Gary expresses his relief that the therapist shows this understanding. Both men chuckle when they note how tensions at work tend to be released through workplace banter, which can degenerate into pranks and 'sledging'.

The therapist then asks Gary what prompted the *'anger issues'* referral. His way of posing this question suggests to the therapist that he has intuitively adapted to Gary by adopting a somewhat authoritative tone. Gary owns that he's been 'pretty uptight lately' and has 'wrongly let it spill out at work'. His 'short fuse', already familiar to his colleagues, has recently led to his being formally disciplined for a 'road rage' incident while he was driving to an emergency.

Gary's wife had left him three years earlier, taking with her their two-year-old son, after a violent argument which culminated in Gary striking her in a fit of jealousy. On the morning of the 'road rage' incident, Gary had been notified of the decree absolute, finally ending his four-year marriage.

The therapist acknowledges how difficult receiving that decree absolute must have been and notes how Gary 'expressed himself' through driving aggressively. Talking around the subject of Gary's 'short fuse', the therapist is satisfied that Gary's intentions are to be a kind, loving father and husband; he is ashamed of resorting to being violent with his wife, which he says happened only the once.

Asked about his life generally, Gary talks of how he loves his work in the fire service, where 'the blokes are my mates'. Work fills his life; he often volunteers for overtime, finding his life outside work 'boring'. Although he watches TV a bit and sometimes goes down to the pub, he has a limited social life. Shift patterns make it difficult for him to socialise with his work-mates, many of whom are busy with their own families.

In the second session, the therapist explores more of **Gary's past and background**. It turns out that he was the second of three boys brought up by his occasionally violent father, his mother having died when Gary was young. The boys were a somewhat unruly lot. Gary describes his childhood as a little chaotic and involving a lot of competitive fighting and pranks. He also remembers a succession of 'women' his father brought home. Many had offered the children extra love and care, which was otherwise in short supply. Gary remembers a couple of them particularly fondly. One of these women had recently sent him a Christmas card out of the blue, and Gary resolves to track her down (he believes she lives in a nearby town) and pay her a call.

The therapist muses aloud that Gary had learned to fight his corner, which had probably stood him in good stead as a child. Now, however, it might not be so necessary or helpful. The therapist also suggests that the roots of Gary's jealous streak may link back to feelings of competition with his brothers. When Gary seems to accept this, the therapist issues him a gentle challenge: 'Now that you are aware that some of your behaviour is habit from the weight of your history, you have more choices. Do you *want* to just behave like you've always done, on a 'short fuse'?'

'You mean carry on and be like my dad?' Gary asks perceptively and receives a nod from the therapist. 'I don't want to be him. I wish I didn't lose my s*** so easily.'

The therapist nods again. 'Then this is what we can focus on in the next few sessions: looking at ways of reacting when you're angry and how to cope with those feelings.'

In the next three sessions, Gary tries out and practises a **range of relaxation and grounding techniques**. Therapist and client also discuss what Gary might do the next time a rage descends upon him. They explore the positive effects of humour and the potential value of physical activity, such as going to the gym, to help Gary release any pent-up emotions. The therapist encourages Gary to be creative and to have a bit of fun thinking up whacky ideas, such as going to the toilet and pulling funny faces at himself. With all of these techniques, the therapist is aiming to find strategies to help Gary contain his anger and express some tensions in lighter ways before they spill over.

Mindful of the contemporary research on catharsis (for example, Lohr et al., 2007), which has raised questions about its value, the therapist chooses not to recommend the option of cathartic 'shouting and bashing of cushions'. Instead, he adopts a psychoeducational approach. He explains the difference between anger, aggression and assertion, and explores issues around 'warning signals' and 'triggers'. Using role-play, the two of them then practise a few scenes. Gary is due for an appraisal at work by a manager he doesn't get on with and is worried about 'losing it' if he feels criticised. They rehearse ways Gary might de-escalate the situation while still holding on to his self-respect.

In their **final session**, Gary reports back saying that his appraisal had gone surprisingly well and that he'd put his new learning into action. The therapist is pleased for Gary. He goes on to suggest that much of Gary's current frustration probably derives from not having a relaxing, meaningful outlet outside work. For the rest of the session they explore ways he could enrich his social life with new hobbies and activities.

It turns out that Gary is a big *Game of Thrones* fan. Coincidentally, the therapist (also a fan) knows of a 'live role-playing group' in the area which engages in medieval fantasy enactments. The group is also open to children as members. Perhaps Gary could go to the next event as a volunteer 'staff' to check it out? Gary, curious and interested, takes some details down.

As they say goodbye, the therapist recommends a couple of local therapists with whom he feels Gary would work well should he wish to consider longer-term one-to-one therapy. He also informs Gary about a men's group which offers ongoing support. Finally, he passes on the name of a therapist who practises family mediation for divorced families with young children.

Concluding reflections

Box 12.1   Good practice indicators

- Therapeutic alliance and rapport established quickly
- Clearly focused, evidence-based therapy interventions
- Provision of helpful sources/resources for future support

Several relational-ethical themes arise for me in this standard brief therapy intervention. These themes go beyond obvious matters relating to contracting and confidentiality and include: the selective nature of the therapy focus, the therapist's chosen approach, his awareness of Gary's work context and the way therapy was ended.

Therapists engaged in brief therapy are often painfully aware of huge areas that are left untouched. Gary's marriage, marital violence and jealousy issues, for instance, were glossed over in the six sessions. Given the time-limited nature of the work, the therapist *had* to be **selective in his focus**. It would have been *unethical* to open up 'cans of worms' and then not have the time to put them back. That the therapist homed in on anger management is entirely appropriate, given the referral by the fire service (which was paying for the therapy). The aim of helping Gary find a new, more satisfying work–life balance would seem another useful intervention, given the time constraints. That said, other therapists might have focused elsewhere.

Given the short-term nature of the contract, it was reasonable that the therapist took a directive, psychoeducational **approach**. I also appreciate this therapist's attention to keeping up with recent research. Many therapists could not claim to be so diligent.

What interests me about his approach is how he intuited Gary's need for him to be more authoritative and 'muscular', suggesting a thoughtful attunement. However, we can't say whether a more 'feminine', empathically caring-with approach (or indeed a female therapist) would have worked out equally well. We can only speculate here, while observing that other therapists are likely to have shepherded the therapy in different directions. A softer approach might have elicited more of Gary's grief and prompted a greater focus on his sense of shame and his failed marriage. A therapist with parenting at the forefront of their own life might have prompted Gary to explore his future role as part-time father.

The point is that, in- or out-of-our-awareness, we inevitably impact on our clients and how the therapy unfolds. The relational-ethical priority is to be aware of that impact and of how we 'use' ourselves as tools in the therapy. Alongside this we need to assess our strengths and limitations realistically. For example, we need to recognise the types of client we tend to work best with, and the issues that engage us the most.

I appreciate the therapist's ongoing awareness of Gary's **social-cultural world**, revealed through his attending to the 'macho' culture of Gary's workplace and his concern for Gary's social life. It's debatable whether this therapist could or should do anything to challenge any institutionalised bullying, intimidation, harassment and discrimination he hears about – either when working with Gary or other in contexts. However, the therapist's previous career in the military perhaps gives him an interesting perspective on all this.

The significant ethical question for me is the extent to which therapists should challenge any *taken-for-granted assumptions*, whether their own or those of their client. In this particular instance, might a 'macho' work culture be seen as inevitable and therefore as somehow 'OK'? Also, we don't hear the full story about Gary striking his wife in jealousy. It seems the therapist has (rightly) checked to confirm that this happened only once. But what assumptions are being made? Might there be a child protection issue that is missed through making assumptions that Gary could be trusted rather than doing a more thorough risk assessment? Did he subtly condone the 'striking' as somehow 'understandable' and acceptable if it doesn't happen regularly'?

When we are confronted with a case of habitual marital abuse, our ethical responsibility is more clear-cut where we might decide to intervene to protect a third party. In cases where circumstances are more blurred (as in this example) we confront the challenge of working out the balance between expressing our personal values and staying in relationship with the client. Might any implied critical judgement be damaging to the therapeutic relationship? Or might the therapist's authentic response contribute more to the relational dynamic? What are the circumstances where therapists might let problematic client comments and behaviours slide?

When therapy **ended**, Gary left armed with helpful information about possibilities for ongoing support and future therapy. The therapist could have invited Gary to return as a private client on a separately negotiated contract not linked to his work. However, in some organisations (and cultures) this would be against policy and would be seen as exploitative and self-serving.

I also thought the therapist was right to give the name of a family therapist rather than opting to do this work himself. I know some therapists might have offered the family work themselves, but it's important to consider the relational boundaries. I would tend to keep things separate. For example, if my initial work was with a couple, I might possibly agree to having some individual sessions (especially if one party was not able to attend that session). However, I'd make sure there was a clear 'no-secrets' policy in place.

13

Star: Containing and Boundarying?

Star, 39 years old, was referred to an inner-city Women's Counselling Service via the police as part of their 'Support for Victims of Crime' programme. She had been mugged and sexually assaulted. She was deemed 'vulnerable' as she has a history of suicide attempts (overdoses) or self-harm (cutting herself) and her psychiatric records indicate both in-patient and out-patient treatment for 'dual diagnosis' (including substance abuse, depression and borderline personality disorder).

When she arrived at the Centre to be **assessed** by her counsellor, Star was well made-up, fashionably dressed, attractive and articulate. In a shaky and tearful manner, she told of how the recent attack had triggered flashbacks of childhood trauma, leaving her feeling fearful and overwhelmed. Noting her long sleeves despite the warm weather, the counsellor assumed she was hiding scars.

Star spoke of growing up with two alcoholic parents, routinely witnessing violent arguments and being physically beaten herself. She had run away from home aged 15 and had had no contact with her family since. She'd had a few encounters with community mental health services and occasionally ended up living on the streets. However, by drawing on various support services she'd eventually managed to establish herself in the community. Significantly, she decided to re-invent herself by changing her name and moving to another city. Despite her somewhat volatile work history, at the age of 28 she found her feet in a high street fashion shop where she was eventually promoted to floor manager. Being successful in her job was important to her, enabling her to build a more stable sense of self-worth. The same could not be said about her private life, where several 'serious' relationships had ended badly, leaving a trail of emotional wreckage.

Filled with compassion, the therapist expressed how impressed she was by Star's story of survival, resilience and courage. She commended Star for having done so well, despite her traumatic early experiences. She then offered Star 20 sessions of weekly supportive (humanistically-orientated) counselling to help her through this current crisis – the maximum allowed by that particular service. In addition, she suggested that Star might benefit from the aromatherapy relaxation group offered at the Women's Centre. This Star gratefully accepted.

They began therapy by exploring how Star might **manage her distressing flashbacks**, focusing on stabilising techniques. She seemed to find relief from talking about her early trauma and having it witnessed by this empathetic, listening therapist. Her initial shakiness receded, and their alliance grew along with Star's sense of 'survivor pride'. The therapist, for her part, enjoyed Star's vibrant presence and insightful expression of emotion. In addition to their weekly meeting, Star turned to her therapist at points through the week via texting. When faced with stress, she would reach out and was soothed and re-grounded by their text exchanges. Star admitted that without this she would have used her self-cutting for emotional release and to get self-soothing.

After three months, the therapist took two weeks' holiday while Star planned her 40th birthday night out, clubbing with friends. The evening proved disastrous and ended with Star in Accident and Emergency after drunkenly cutting her wrists. One of her cuts proved so deep it severed a tendon, flagging up her attempt as a serious risk. The duty psychiatrist referred her for formal assessment by the local community mental health team, which then fast-tracked her for dialectical behaviour therapy (DBT) with its own specialist Personality Disorder Service.

The counsellor only learned of these events after Star missed their next appointment, nearly a month after their previous contact. She phoned Star to find out what had happened. Star was apologetic, but her excuses didn't ring true. Star missed a further session before returning with a still bandaged arm and a fuller story. The therapist was openly shocked and distressed for Star but contained the uneasiness building in her that their work together had been less successful than she'd previously thought. She also felt bad that she had gone on holiday without thinking through self-care plans with Star. With some relief, she welcomed the idea of DBT as another resource for Star.

A week later, Star returned to her counselling in tears. She told her therapist that she had been assessed by the DBT team and offered six months of outpatients treatment – but was required to stop their counselling sessions. 'I don't want to lose you!' she cried plaintively. 'Can't we just carry on? If it's got to be them or you, I think you can help me much more. I want us to carry on anyway, but I'll tell them I'm not seeing you no more.'

The therapist felt pulled towards the idea of continuing with Star. But was she perhaps being 'played'? Uncertain of the way forward, she resolved to take her dilemma to **supervision** and suggested to Star that they think about it over the coming week.

Her supervisor's immediate response was to issue a challenge. Suggesting that she was too confluent and enmeshed, and in danger of 'rescuing', he posed the key question: 'What's in Star's best interest?' They considered the benefits of an intensive specialist DBT intervention, along with the potential drawbacks of continuing counselling alongside this. One danger was that Star might 'split' her therapy by playing off her counsellor against her DBT therapist. They also explored why the counsellor might have become pulled in, even perhaps 'enabling' Star's continuing self-destructive behaviour. Recognising the influence of her own history of caring for an alcoholic parent, the counsellor ruefully admitted that 'rescuing is part of my process'. The supervisor encouraged the counsellor not to hold on to Star 'out of ego' and rescuing for her own self-esteem.

The counsellor understood what she must do. The following week, she gently, though reluctantly, told Star they had to **end**. She recommended DBT as 'best practice' for Star at the moment while owning that she did not have sufficient expertise. Perhaps they could plan one more session to try to find a more positive ending and Star could consider returning to therapy with her in the future? Star was having none of it. She stormed out, shouting 'I thought you were on my side! But you're just like all the others.'

The next evening the therapist received a text from Star saying she was back in A&E. She signed off her text with 'I hope you're happy!'

The therapist replied the next day, and (after consulting with her supervisor) simply offered the date/time for a final appointment. Then, when Star didn't show up, she sent a 'discharge letter' saying that she respected Star's decision to not attend and hoped she would make the most of the DBT opportunity. She signed off with 'Warmest best wishes', and never heard from Star again.

The therapist felt burned and shamed that she had become so enmeshed with Star and guilty that perhaps she had 'let Star down'. Perhaps in parallel process with Star, she owned a sense of confusion, helpless loss, failure, abandonment and rejection.

Concluding reflections

Box 13.1 Good practice indicators

- A caring concern to hold and support the client between sessions
- Use of supervision to contain challenging relational processes
- Awareness of the context of inter-agency working

As therapists, all of us face times when we misjudge situations or therapy ends badly or we get caught up in wider messiness to do with organisational/institutional-politics. The relational-ethical question concerns how well (appropriately) we manage these situations, contain and tolerate our emotions and use our supports. Can we learn from our mistakes and try to protect future clients from them? It's also about ensuring that the wider services on offer are appropriately 'joined up'.

This case study raises many contentious issues, among them the significance of keeping the bigger picture in mind, the importance of holding boundaries, the issue of mutual trust, the need to pursue the client's best interests and the need to resist the urge to 'rescue'.

Keeping the bigger picture in mind – It is a relational-ethical imperative to consider the client in their wider life context – *past–present–future*. In this story, Star came into counselling with a traumatic and complicated past along with a lengthy history of previous diagnoses and treatments. While being treated, she also engaged with other psychological services. All this needed to be factored in, particularly as the therapist became aware of Star's adeptness at drawing in multiple support services. And, there are questions around the ethics of accepting Star as a client in the first place while she was still so vulnerable – maybe she needed a team response to begin with?

In part, it's about keeping the person's history in mind towards seeing their current needs more accurately. In Star's case, her history of repeated relational themes and trauma needs serious attention. But there is a tricky balance to be struck here. While I would be reluctant to resort to labels such as 'borderline personality disorder' (or even 'complex post-traumatic stress disorder'), in cases such as Star's I might keep such *diagnoses* loosely in mind as a precautionary footnote. Linehan (1993) described individuals who meet the BPD criteria as 'emotional burn victims' in the way they experience the slightest touch as intensely painful. Applied to therapy, the slightest miscommunication or empathic 'error' can have problematic consequences. The therapist in this story might have been forewarned by a better understanding of the patterns manifested by individuals with this tendency: unstable relationships; intense, changeable moods; negative self-image; and impulsive behavioural/emotional dysregulation. This would have made her alert to the repetition of problematic dynamics, and perhaps taking this all to supervision earlier may have helped.

Holding boundaries – Building on Masterson's work with personality adaptations (Masterson, 1988), the gestaltist Yontef (1993) argues that therapists need to be consistently and energetically present when working with individuals with *borderline* ('character') disorders. In particular, they need to maintain strong boundaries (containing and limiting), in a non-judgemental rather than authoritarian way, to encourage individuals to take self-responsibility. It could be argued that the therapist in this story tacitly encouraged Star to be dependent on her by offering soothing texts rather than nurturing Star's coping skills. That the A&E crisis occurred while the therapist was on holiday may well be relevant. It is a matter of debate whether the therapist being away at that time was a trigger or not. Could she have done anything to prevent the incident?

Therapists are likely to differ over whether texting between sessions should be viewed as useful or damaging. Some would say the therapist should have considered a 'no texting' boundary between sessions to ensure both parties were properly present and held in the appropriate sessional frame. Others might go along with the texting intervention while arguing that the therapist should have gradually reduced her availability.

Beyond questions about texting, there is an issue about how well the therapist held the boundaries of the therapeutic frame in terms of preparing her clients for her absence. Some therapists would organise some 'emergency contact' cover or at least discuss the use of self-care and support systems. While we are not told how well the therapist prepared Star for her period of absence, we can assume the therapist would have held a no-communication boundary over the holiday period. That would be appropriate, not least as good modelling for the therapist to have time off (self-care boundary).

Mutual trust – The idea that clients must trust therapists within the therapeutic alliance is well accepted. What is less often recognised is that this trust needs to be *mutual*. If the alliance is going to be effective, therapists need to believe (at least mostly) in what clients say and have some trust in their integrity and sense of responsibility: that they will turn up and follow through contractual obligations. Clients, too, need to be able to place a strong degree of trust in us. For example, they might ask themselves: 'Can I trust this therapist to respect and not belittle me?' (Recognising the role played by negative transference, therapists tend to be more sanguine about being shamed.)

That said, all therapists can expect to be deceived at points. It would be naïve on our part to assume that clients always tell the truth. Mostly, we can expect clients to be honest in the sense that they tell us their truth as they currently understand it. The approach here is one of a 'hermeneutics of trust' rather than 'of suspicion', where the client is viewed as offering defensive distortions (DeYoung, 2015a). However, clients might also be guilty of trying to manipulate the system and engage in deceptions about suicide risk, or other defensive, diminishing deflections around admitting to problematic behaviours. Less often, clients may engage in sustained pathological lying. Our role is usually to wait to build the trust, subtly asking questions that may challenge any confused or conflicting accounts.

In this story, it's possible that Star had massaged the truth for her own instrumental purposes. Over time, this eroded the therapist's trust, both in Star and in herself. Had the therapist picked up on Star's process here and explicitly worked with it, the relational-ethical approach would be to examine any deceptions for what they might indicate about Star's history, her past and/or current stresses, and her transferential relationship with her therapist.

Pursuing the client's 'best interests' – Judging what is in the best interests of the client is never easy, although this should be the question on the tongue of every relational-ethical therapist. In Star's case, would texting be therapeutic, or would it result in dangerously loose boundaries? These are the kinds of questions which tax us frequently in practice. When should we intervene? When should we step back? In this case study, some might argue the therapist shifted unhelpfully from being therapeutically 'beside' Star to something resembling collusion, with the therapist maybe being 'too much on her side'.

Thinking about treatment, which is in the client's best interests? The current therapy or DBT? And how should therapy be terminated? I would be concerned about the consequences of ending with a client who was not ready for it, or actively against it, since they might justifiably experience this as 'being abandoned'. On the other hand, continuing therapy may not be the most effective route and questions need to be asked about what the client is doing by 'pulling' in competing services.

Sadly, the very services set up for clients can sometimes let them down. This is particularly the case when different statutory and voluntary agencies and those in private practice do not communicate effectively or coordinate their treatments. Sometimes this can be due to arrogant assumptions that one's own service is better; at other times, problems surface at an organisational level, resulting in professional boundary confusions and breaches of confidentiality. Much depends on the specific cultural context.

In this case, some therapists would question the process by which Star received a psychiatric referral to community mental health, which (after assessing her) then fast-tracked her for DBT. Arguably, the health professionals involved should have known that Star was already working with a therapist. After offering crisis intervention, they could usefully have referred Star back to the therapist, perhaps with a recommendation for DBT with the specialist unit as a possible route forward later.

Given what happened, maybe the therapist could have liaised with the community or DBT teams to affect a more considered therapeutic route rather than just withdrawing. Here, we might even question the supervisor's insistence on the therapist's withdrawal. Might it have been possible for Star to continue working with both therapists on condition there was a 'release of information' to ensure a joined-up approach or were there too many other problematic issues around? The supervisor assessed the 'problem' as being to do with the therapist's enmeshment whereas maybe it was more about institutionalised practices. That said, the supervisor did well to highlight the value of the specialist DBT service and the risks of 'splitting' services. And, certainly, it would have been ethically wrong, and probably damaging, for the therapist to have colluded with Star's request to continue therapy 'secretly' (not telling either the DBT service or the supervisor).

That the proposed DBT would have been part of the NHS free service might need to be factored in had Star been going to counselling privately. It's questionable how ethical some therapists are being if they offer expensive private care when good quality care is available free of charge. That said, the deterrent of long waiting lists for free care may tip the balance.

Avoiding being a 'rescuer' – The parallels between Star's story and elements of the counsellor's own background help explain why the counsellor found herself getting pulled in to 'rescue' and why she found it challenging to hold containing boundaries. While we might criticise this counsellor for not consulting her supervisor earlier, the fact that she did so and 'came clean' at that crucial end stage is important.

However, although the supervisor was consulted, further relational-ethical issues are raised within the supervisory relationship. What would have happened if supervisor and supervisee disagreed? Guidance from the supervisor is normally guidance and not instruction. It's important that therapists use their own clinical judgement. Had this therapist not, I might wonder if some parallel process was being enacted around being manipulative and secretive.

We don't hear what support the counsellor received for her crisis of confidence; perhaps her supervisor reassured her that she wasn't 'responsible' for Star's bad choices. We can only hope that she received the 'holding' she needed as she confronted her tendency to rescue.

14

Luke: Intergenerational Trauma work

Seventy-two-year-old Luke looked like a spent old man when he first arrived for therapy. His wife had died two years earlier and while he had family (son, daughter-in-law and two teenage grandchildren), they lived busy lives in a distant town. His old friends had either died or moved away. Describing himself as alone, lonely and running on empty, Luke confessed that life did not feel worth living.

Luke doubted therapy would help but his doctor had persuaded him to try it as an adjunct to his anti-depressant medication. He was embarrassed about 'needing' this extra support. The therapist described what she offered as a relational integrative psychotherapist (Erskine, 2015; Finlay, 2016a) and what he could expect from therapy. They agreed he would try six sessions to explore his experience, with the option of staying on further. She explained that helping him find more a more fulfilling, meaningful life may take longer than six sessions, but they could work with some of his depressive thoughts and feelings initially.

The therapist felt an immediate pull of compassion for this sad, gentle, well-spoken old man. She recognised clear indicators of his depression: low mood, poor appetite, disrupted sleep, and slower than usual thinking. Engaging in a **risk assessment**, she asked Luke if he had ever thought of ending his life. He admitted to having considered suicide many times but always knew he couldn't and wouldn't follow through – he didn't want to hurt his living family or betray his wife, Rose, who had loved life so much. Relieved to hear of these 'protective factors', the therapist suggested he keep a diary, making a point to note down any suicidal thoughts so that the two of them could understand the triggers and processes arising at those times. This intervention also had the potential benefit of 'normalising' his dark thoughts and encouraging him to express them instead of pushing them down.

The therapist herself was aware of an acute sense of alarm, which she knew stemmed from previously working with a client who had committed suicide. Despite Luke's clarity that he would not act on his suicidal urges, she suggested they implement a 'crisis safety plan' for times when he might feel overwhelmed. Luke found travel documentaries soothing and so they based his plan on TV travel shows, emergency contact with his therapist and, as a last resort, calling the Samaritans if it was the middle of the night.

The palpable sense of loss permeating Luke's world became the **focus of therapy**. Somewhat to his surprise, his weekly therapy soon became an important highlight in his otherwise empty week and he was content to continue his therapy indefinitely. Luke used his therapy well, exploring both his bereavement and his wider social needs. He valued the deep, compassionate, relational listening offered by the therapist. 'Rose was a good listener, too', he said at the end of one session.

Luke talked of dearly missing Rose, his 'life companion'. He and Rose had enjoyed travelling the world following his retirement from a successful legal career (he had been a 'Silk', a barrister of the Queen's Counsel). Since her death he hadn't travelled anywhere. Luke described how he felt most alive when he was in distant parts, but he wasn't sure he'd ever be able to travel again. The therapist reflected back all these major losses – of his work, his travel and his wife – and reassured him his depression was entirely understandable.

As client and therapist explored these losses over the next few weeks, Luke's depression began to lift. His self-care and sleep patterns improved, and he joined the local bridge club to reconnect with a favourite pastime and enjoy the social contact it brought with it.

A couple of weeks on he arrived at a session in a preoccupied state. He had woken in the night from a disturbing dream but all he could remember was the terror of being 'lost' and that he had been 'sobbing uncontrollably'. The therapist noted that in all these weeks Luke had never cried freely. Perhaps something in the dream had triggered this outpouring? Luke couldn't remember the details but had a vague awareness that the dream was located in Africa.

Her professional antennae alerted, the therapist asked about the significance of Africa. At first Luke couldn't speak but eventually he said, 'I grew up in South Africa'. This was the first time he had mentioned his **childhood**. The therapist invited him to tell her more about this seemingly hidden side of his life and being.

Luke told a sad story. He had grown up a privileged, upper-middle-class child living in a large, beautiful suburban house with servants. But he had been a lonely boy. Contact with his parents was infrequent and perfunctory; they were busy with work and their socialising lifestyle. His father was often away, either working in Johannesburg or on big game hunts. Luke had been brought up by his nanny, Precious – and he considered her his 'mother'; precious indeed. Tears filled his eyes as he shared how she taught him to 'love the real Africa that lives in the soul as rhythm and colour'.

At the age of eight Luke had been sent away to boarding school in England (his parents' native land). How he had hated it! Only the long school summer holidays, when he could return home to Precious, kept him going. In 1960, when he was aged 14, he arrived home to learn that she was 'gone'. Luke's jaw and fists were clenched as he recalled the moment. His parents had refused to tell him what had happened. Over that summer he heard whispers of the terrible slaughter at a protest in Sharpville, and about the subsequent imposition of the State of Emergency. Precious's family had been farmers and he guessed they may have been caught up in civil unrest protesting against the 'pass laws', or perhaps they had been forcibly evicted from their rich ancestral lands. The not knowing was hard.

The therapist's heart went out to the boy Luke had once been and to the terrible loss he had suffered. That this was tied up with the horror and brutality of that apartheid era added to the trauma. She herself teared up when Luke stated, 'I knew Precious would not have deserted me. If she still lived, she would have... I know... She would have found a way to contact me.'

This profound loss added new layers of complex trauma to the grief Luke was currently experiencing. With the floodgates open now, Luke spent several sessions talking about childhood experiences. His rage against his father was an ever-present horizon: 'I'm so ashamed of my father!' he shouted one day, before he explained more quietly, 'His treatment of our servants was more than racist; he was abusive. He actually actively supported white supremacy and apartheid laws. He was a Nazi! I hold my father responsible for Precious's death even if he didn't kill her by his own hand.'

Over that fateful summer holiday – his first without Precious – his relationship with his father grew ever more distant. But his mother was often in the house and he began to spend more time with her. When Luke told his mother he did not want to return to South Africa the following vacation, she decided to travel with him back to England, formally separating from her husband. Luke became a weekly boarder at his school, returning to his mother at weekends: his first taste of 'home' in England. The two then lived together for the next 20 years, until his mother's death. While they never became close, they offered each other support as they grieved for the loss of Africa in their different ways. Neither wanted to return there.

The therapist was hugely impacted by this story, particularly the evoked spectre of Nazism. When she heard the word 'Nazi', she experienced a jolt. Suddenly a door flew open in her mind, revealing nightmarish images and unspeakable horror and grief. She was Jewish, and acutely aware of how her own ancestors had perished in the concentration camps of the Second World War. Her throat ached for the native African people and their forced migration. Momentarily ungrounded and caught up in her own process, the therapist fought to 'close the door'. She reminded herself to stay present to and for Luke. Instead of seeing him in a family of white supremacists, she remembered her compassion for the kindly and knowledgeable man in front of her, the man she had come to know, like and respect. She said nothing about her own heritage but resolved to take her disturbed dislocation to supervision.

If Luke's rage and grief were evident, so too was his shame. Together with his therapist he processed what the two of them came to call his 'colonial guilt': the shame he carried for his parents and white South African ancestors. Their persecution of others was his pain, particularly so as he recognised his own arrogance: in his childhood he too had ordered the servants around without regard for their personhood. And now he couldn't even remember most of their names. He pondered his sense of guilt as a privileged oppressor. He also became aware of his sense of powerlessness as a child, remembering particularly those times when he witnessed horrible violence against black people and how the white adults around him never intervened.

The therapist recognised the profound work Luke had begun and pondered about how to engage with these intergenerational implications. She chose to do a '**Parent Interview**' (McNeel, 1976; Erskine, Moursund and Trautmann, 1999; Erskine and Trautmann, 2003; Erskine and Moursund, 2011; Zaletel et al., n.d.) as she had more experience with this. She believed it would help him reconnect more sympathetically with his childhood history. This unusual transactional analytic technique involves a client embodying their internalised version of a parent (or ancestor) to therapeutically explore issues that may be currently out of awareness. 'This technique is not "playacting"', the therapist explained, 'it's about trying to take on another's persona from the "inside". Often, it is a way of giving therapy to that part of yourself and it might help you get in touch with unremembered memories and forgotten perspectives about messages you have "soaked up" as a child.' She suggested that over the coming weeks, without feeling under any pressure, Luke should think about doing an interview with his father.

Despite her excellent intentions, the therapist had misjudged the impact her suggestion would have on Luke. She was taken aback by the strength of his negative reaction and his resistance to working on any aspect of his relationship with his father. The therapist consulted her supervisor, who gently pointed out that her desire to see Luke work with his father might be driven by her own history of not working through issues concerning her own father.

A couple of weeks later, Luke returned to therapy. He said he was now interested in trying out a Parent Interview. However, he did not want to 'let his father into the room'; for him, the therapy room was a safe space that he didn't want contaminated by his father's presence. Instead, could he perhaps do this exercise with Precious? Recognising the 'unfinished business' surrounding Precious's disappearance, the therapist agreed that this could be useful. She explained that they would need extra time (a double session) to do the Parent Interview justice, so they set a date for the following week.

To begin the 'Parent Interview', the therapist invited Luke to sit in a chair he had not used before and to close his eyes momentarily while trying to bring Precious into his mind. She asked him to sit in the same way that Precious would have sat and adopt a facial expression to reflect what Precious would be feeling.

After a pause, Luke's body softened subtly. The therapist then spoke directly to Precious and thanked 'her' for coming in. She explained that the point of the meeting was to help Luke by recalling how important Precious was in his life. Then came a gentle question: 'To start, can you tell me a little about your life, Precious, and how you came to live with Luke's family?'

A powerful, and distinctly surreal, dialogue followed. 'Precious' expressed her love for Luke and her sadness that she had been unable to prepare him for her absence and say 'goodbye'. She wanted him to know that part of her spirit would always be within him and that she was very proud of the 'great man' he had become. She spoke with deep love of her land and people. She had died, she said, in a civil war. She had sought to protect her own family's lands. It was the White people's way, she said, it was part of a particular time in history. He wasn't responsible.

As the Parent Interview drew to a close, the therapist thanked Precious for her words and asked if she might be prepared to return at a future point.

To help restore the focus to Luke himself, the therapist invited him to return to his familiar seat and begin processing his experience. He sobbed deeply, but these were 'clean' tears of healing as well as grief. It was impossible to fully understand what had just taken place but Luke, in some awe, said he was aware of feeling lighter and having a new sense of peace.

A **new phase of therapeutic exploration** followed, with Luke now able to recognise the impact his heritage had had on him. He understood that his parents came from a different generation, one which saw the world in a different way. He grasped that both, in their own particular way, had loved Africa. While he was not ready to forgive his father's racism, he found compassion, and even some love, for his mother.

Through this relational work, Luke was able to challenge his long-held, shame-ridden belief that his parents had neglected him because he was 'unlovable'. He began to understand that in fact both Precious and, in her own way, his mother had loved him. But he couldn't recognise his father as having loving feelings and wondered what in his father's upbringing had made him into such a violent, bigoted man.

Luke's profound grief at having lost his Precious 'mother' was something he had previously kept at bay. But now, confronting it directly, he realised he also carried with him many wonderful memories of Precious's nurturing and love. He became conscious of his gratitude for the way in which she had shaped his strong sense of justice and ethics – something that he leaned on throughout his life as a barrister.

Over time, Luke decided that he needed to return to South Africa – something he had avoided for more than half a century. With growing excitement, he set about planning an extended tour. He asked if it would be possible to get back in touch with his therapist once he returned and possibly re-engage therapy. While he didn't feel he necessarily needed weekly therapy any more, he wanted to keep a regular link, perhaps having two or three weeks between sessions.

It was not clear how their work would evolve but the therapist felt it was important to stay in contact and not end finally. They discussed the possibility of Skype/FaceTime contact while he was away but Luke didn't feel this was needed. Accepting this, the therapist suggested he keep a journal of his travels and perhaps even drop her the occasional email. She confirmed that she would acknowledge all his emails and keep them safe until they could explore them on his return.

Concluding reflections

Box 14.1 Good practice indicators

- Careful risk assessment and safety measures put in place
- Treating client with dignity and respect
- Holistic appreciation of a wider cultural and intergenerational context
- Use of interventions within the therapist's sphere of competence and experience
- Therapist's own intrapsychic process appropriately contained

---

While this story raises numerous relational-ethical issues, four stand out to me: the suicide risk, cultural sensitivity, the specialist use of the 'Parent Interview', and the rather blurred 'non-ending'. As you reflect on these, you might tune into your own embodied/emotional responses and what these tell you.

The initial **suicide risk** assessment is significant. I think the therapist was right to prioritise this early in their work given the additional risk factors to do with Luke's depression, age, relatively recent bereavement and the fact that he lived alone. Facing the possibility of suicide head-on seems helpful. The ethics here concern taking appropriate action immediately to maximise the safety of a client known to be at high risk. It would also be important for the therapist, when contracting, to obtain *informed consent* regarding the limits of confidentiality and the possibility of her contacting Luke's doctor, if she found herself particularly concerned, with a view to activating more extensive support systems.

Therapeutic intervention around the suicide risk began (appropriately, in my view) in the first session, where Luke and the therapist discussed risk and coping. Given Luke's adamant view that he would not commit suicide, some therapists might find the therapist's approach unduly cautious and directive. There are relational-ethical implications concerning the *theoretical values* implicated here. Research by Moerman (2012) suggests that many person-centred counsellors, for example, shy away from directly questioning suicidal intent. They feel a conflict between their non-judgemental approach focused on client autonomy and the public health perspective of focused and directive risk assessment. However, Moerman argues that not carrying out a risk assessment is ethically unsound.

Suicide may or may not be a basic human right or choice. Different therapists will adopt their own moral position on this ethical question. Beyond personal values, I believe we have a professional responsibility to search out those layers of ambivalence usually involved when life-affirming impulses are juxtaposed with hopelessness or self-destructive thoughts. It was important here for the therapist to be able to monitor Luke's thinking carefully over time; inviting him to keep a record seems a helpful strategy here.

That Luke's mental state improved as he engaged with therapy was a hopeful sign. That he started to expand his social life was also important. This reminds us how we have an important relational role to play in focusing more *holistically* on a person's life situation and not just on work intra-psychically.

We don't hear much about how the therapist herself experienced the process of holding this potentially suicidal client. Assessing, and working with, the possibility of suicide is invariably stressful and distressing. Moerman's research shows how working with suicidal clients engenders feelings of responsibility, devastation, guilt, regret, a sense of failure and powerlessness, particularly if the therapist has had previous traumatic experience of a client's suicide. We can only hope that the therapist in this case study took her fears and concerns to *supervision* and allowed herself to be 'held'.

I greatly appreciate the **cultural sensitivity** shown by this therapist and her awareness of the value of embracing Luke's cultural-historical heritage. The intervention using a Parent Interview brought to the fore the intergenerational and intercultural layers of Luke's trauma, making this therapy special and compelling for me.

I also appreciate the therapist's decision to not *self-disclose* her own family history of Holocaust trauma. There was a danger of insufficiently bracketing her own process, which risked leaking out into the work and shifting the focus away from Luke's experience. In this instance, the therapist's Jewish background wasn't directly relevant to her client's own situation. And bringing in a Nazi link may have simply reinforced Luke's feelings of guilt. That said, it would be important for the therapist to take her unsettled-ness to supervision and perhaps therapy.

Being relational involves dancing between intimacy and reflective distance, the focus all the time shifting between self–other–relationship. When the therapist became ungrounded, she momentarily lost herself in her own process, moving away from both client and relationship. That she was mindfully and reflexively aware of what was happening was important. Here we need to acknowledge the relational-ethics of ensuring we have done the personal work necessary for ourselves before we can fully be present for others. In this case study, the therapist seems to have worked with her own intergenerational trauma, giving her sufficient groundedness to facilitate Luke's journey.

When it comes to choosing a specific specialist intervention, the ethical priority (as I see it) is to ensure that a therapist is sufficiently experienced and competent to use it; also, it needs to be culturally appropriate. In this case, **Parent Interview** is a potentially powerful imaginal technique but extra training (and ideally personal experience in one's own therapy) is needed. Then, it needs to be applied judiciously. As Hargaden and Sills (2002, p. 163) argue, 'a

Parent Interview with a Maori client would be viewed as at best weird and at worst deeply insulting'.

Of course, there are other ways to work with intergenerational trauma by attending to issues around attachment and culture. The systemic 'family con-stellations' approach which can map inter-generational processes or a psycho-dramatic enactment might have been equally valuable interventions. Choice of intervention is a relational-ethical issue because it rests both on our specific sphere of competence and on the context, including what suits our client's interests or capacity.

From my experience of Parent Interviews, I know it is important to allow plenty of time afterwards to process the experience. The interview itself can be distinctly disorientating and unsettling. While it can have a substantial long-term impact, time and space must be allowed for whatever might emerge. The therapist in the case study was respectful of these needs.

Many therapists would take issue with the somewhat 'messy' **non-ending of therapy** in this case. Should Luke and the therapist have had a proper ending, with the possibility of a return at some future time? Were they both avoiding yet another painful ending? Was the therapist finding it hard to let go? These are questions one hopes would have been explored in supervision.

Personally speaking, I'm content they mutually and creatively negotiated their plan. I'm also fine with the idea that Luke's therapy might take a differ-ent form on his return from his travels. While some might disagree, I think it's about responding to client's expressed needs and respecting their choices.

The therapist's idea to encourage Luke to communicate with her electroni-cally while he was away is interesting, isn't it? I can see the value of preserv-ing threads of attachment during a temporary break. I'm reassured that she was clear about holding his communications until his return, rather than promising to engage in correspondence. Doing the latter risked perhaps mov-ing towards becoming 'pen pals', involving problematic blurring of boundaries.

Epilogue

Thank you for joining me on this journey through the intricately layered terrain of ethics in practice. I hope you've found our travel interesting. Above all, I hope you've been inspired to debate and dialogue with colleagues, and that you've been challenged to examine your own clinical decision-making, and to think afresh.

I hope I've managed to convey something of my own enthusiasm for ethics, which has only been reinforced by writing this book. Perhaps now, like me, you see ethics as lively, challenging elements of everyday life, rather than as dry, philosophical principles imposed on us by professional bodies. Ethics dance and weave around us constantly; we negotiate and enact them in every relationship, whether in or out of our work as therapists. Practical ethics can only be understood and negotiated in the vibrant immediacy of the **relational context** concerned – a context that includes respecting the individuals involved (the values, needs, understandings of those concerned), their cultural backgrounds and the specific social circumstances of the encounter. And, if relational concerns should drive professional action, there also must be room for individual judgement, intuition and creativity.

As therapists, we strive to create safe therapeutic spaces of hospitality where the client can feel held, affirmed, supported, resourced, empathised with – and challenged to grow. Therapist integrity, duty of care and informed consent are key foundational relational-ethical principles, along with being open to dialogue that respects the other's difference. But the sheer messiness, uncertainty and complexity of practice defy easy answers; there are no clear-cut ethical recipes. As practitioners, we are left with trying to exercise our professional judgement as best we can, moment-to-moment, given our knowledge, ability and the context. If we do this sensitively, thoughtfully and with caring humane intention, that – for me – is being ethical.

References

Aafjes-Van Doorn K and Wooldridge T (2018) The complexity of loss during a forced termination: A case illustration. *British Journal of Psychotherapy* 34(2): 285–290.

Adams M (2014) *The Myth of the Untroubled Therapist: Private Life, Professional Practice.* Hove, Sussex: Routledge.

Adams M and Morgan J (2016) *An Evaluation of a Nature-based Intervention for People with Experiences of Psychological Distress.* Brighton: University of Brighton.

Afolabi OE (2015) Dual relationships and boundary crossing: A clinical issue in clinical psychology practice. *International Journal of Psychology and Counselling* 7(2): 29–39. Available at: www.researchgate.net/profile/Olusegun_Afolabi9/publication/301543374_Dual_Relationship_and_boundary_crossing_A_clinical_issue_in_clinical_psychology_practice/links/57daecde08aeea195932a1fb/Dual-Relationship-and-boundary-crossing-A-clinical-issue-in-clinical-psychology-practice.pdf (accessed September 2017).

Alleyne A (2011) Overcoming racism, discrimination and oppression in psychotherapy. In C Lago (ed.), *The Handbook of Transcultural Counselling and Psychotherapy.* Maidenhead: Open University Press/McGraw-Hill, pp. 117–129. Available at: www.aileenalleyne.com/wp-content/uploads/sites/6/2013/06/COLIN-LAGO-BOOK-CHAPTER-Final-edit.pdf (accessed March 2018).

American Counseling Association (2005). *ACA Code of ethics.* American Counseling Association. Available at: www.counseling.org/docs/default-source/library-archives/archived-code-of-ethics/codeethics05.pdf (accessed March 2018).

American Psychiatric Association (2013) *Diagnostic and Statistical Manual of Mental Disorders* (5th edition). DSM-5. Arlington, VA: American Psychiatric Association.

American Psychological Association (APA) (2017) *Ethical Principles of Psychologists and Code of Conduct.* Washington, DC: APA. Available at: www.apa.org/ethics/code/ (accessed March 2018).

Amis K (2017) *Boundaries, Power and Ethical Responsibility in Counselling and Psychotherapy.* London: Sage.

Audet CT and Everall RD (2010) Therapist self-disclosure and the therapeutic relationship: A phenomenological study from the client perspective. *British Journal of Guidance & Counselling* 38(3): 327–342.

Australia and New Zealand Association of Psychotherapy (2014) *Code of Ethics,* Revision 3. Sydney, Australia: ANZAP. Available at: www.anzap.com.au/images/ANZAP-download-documents/ANZAP_Code_of_Ethics_Rev_4_Nov_2014.pdf (accessed September 2018).

Australian Counselling Association (2015). *Code of Ethics and Practice: ...of the Association for Counsellors in Australia.* Version 13. Available at: www.theaca.net.au/documents/ACA%20Code%20of%20Ethics%20and%20Practice%20Ver%2013.pdf (accessed March 2018).

Australian Psychoanalytic Society (2012) *Code of Ethics.* Australian Psychoanalytic Society. Available at: https://static1.squarespace.com/static/5ae69554da02bc2c123b7693/t/5b988cb0c2241bdafc1edef5/1536724149063/apas-code-of-ethics.pdf (accessed March 2018).

Barnett, JE (2014) Distress, burnout, self-care, and the promotion of wellness for psychotherapists and trainees: Issues, implications, and recommendations. *Society for the Advancement of Psychotherapy* (newsletter). Available at: www.societyforpsychotherapy.org/distress-therapist-burnout-self-care-promotion-wellness-psychotherapists-trainees-issues-implications-recommendations (accessed March 2018).

Baron RA and Richardson DR (2004) *Human Aggression*. Boston, MA: Springer.

Berger T, Krieger T, Sude K, Meyer B and Maercker A (2018) Evaluating an e-mental health program ('deprexis') as adjunctive treatment tool in psychotherapy for depression: Results of a pragmatic randomized controlled trial. *Journal of Affective Disorders 227*: 455–462. https://doi.org/10.1016/j.jad.2017.11.021.

Berry MD (2014) Existential psychotherapy and sexual attraction: Meaning and authenticity in the therapeutic encounter (pp. 38–52). In M Luca (ed.), *Sexual Attraction in Therapy: Clinical Perspectives on Moving beyond the Taboo. A Guide for Training and Practice*. Chichester, West Sussex: Wiley.

Bion WR (1961) *Experiences in Groups and Other Papers*. London: Tavistock Publications.

Bion WR (1962) *Learning from Experience*. London: Heinemann.

Bolton L (2017) The ethical issues which must be addressed in online counselling. *Australian Counselling Research Journal 11*(1): 1–15.

Bond T and Mitchels B (2015) *Confidentiality and Record Keeping in Counselling and Psychotherapy*. London: Sage.

Bordin ES (1979) The generalizability of the psychoanalytic concept of the working alliance. *Psychotherapy: Theory, Research, Practice, Training 16*(3): 207–221.

Boschen MJ and Casey LM (2008) The use of mobile telephones as adjuncts to cognitive behavioral psychotherapy. *Professional Psychology: Research and Practice 39*: 546–552.

Brafman AH (2006) Touching and affective closeness. In G Galton (ed.), *Touch Papers: Dialogues on Touch in the Psychoanalytic Space*. London: Karnac. pp. 15–28.

British Association for Counselling and Psychotherapy (BACP) (2016) *Good Practice in Action 039: Commonly Asked Questions. Resource for the Counselling Professions: Making the Contract within the Counselling Professions*. Lutterworth, Leicestershire: BACP.

British Association for Counselling and Psychotherapy (2018a) *Ethical Framework for the Counselling Professions*. Lutterworth, Leicestershire: BACP. Available at: www.bacp.co.uk/media/3103/bacp-ethical-framework-for-the-counselling-professions-2018.pdf (accessed April 2018).

British Association for Counselling and Psychotherapy (2018b) *Core Competences for Work with Children and Young People*. Lutterworth, Leicestershire: BACP. Available at: www.bacp.co.uk/media/2335/bacp-competences-map-for-working-with-young-people.pdf (accessed March 2018).

British Psychological Society (BPS) (2012) *e-Professionalism: Guidance on the Use of Social Media by Clinical Psychologists*. London: BPS. Available at: www1.bps.org.uk/system/files/Public%20files/DCP/cat-1096.pdf (accessed September 2017).

British Psychological Society (2016) *Guidance Document on the Management of Disclosures of Non-recent (Historic) Child Sexual Abuse*. London: BPS. Available at: www1.bps.org.uk/system/files/Public%20files/guidance_non_recent_abuse.pdf (accessed December 2017).

British Psychological Society (2018) *Code of Ethics and Conduct – February 2018*. London: BPS. Available at: www.bps.org.uk/sites/bps.org.uk/files/Policy%20%20Files/Code%20of%20Ethics%20and%20Conduct%20(2018).pdf (accessed April 2018).

Brown S (2017) Ten reasons to feel good about being a counsellor today. *Therapy Today* 28(8). Available at: www.bacp.co.uk/bacp-journals/therapy-today/2017/october-2017/ten-reasons-to-feel-good-about-being-a-counsellor-today/ (accessed October 2017).

Canadian Counselling and Psychotherapy Association (2007). *Code of ethics: Canadian Counselling and Psychotherapy Association*. Ottawa, Ontario: Canada.

Casement P (1982) Some pressures on the analyst for physical contact during the reliving of an early trauma. *International Review of Psycho-Analysis 9*: 279–286.

Casement P (1985) *On Learning from the Patient*. London: Routledge.

Casement P (1990) *Further Learning from the Patient: The Analytic Space and Process*. Hove, East Sussex: Routledge.

Casemore R (2009) Ethics as a way of being. In L Gabriel and R Casemore (eds), *Relational Ethics in Practice: Narratives from Counselling and Psychotherapy*. London: Routledge.

Charura D and Paul S (2014) *The Therapeutic Relationship Handbook: Theory and Practice*. Maidenhead, Berkshire: Open University Press, McGraw-Hill.

Charura D and Paul S (2015) *Love and Therapy: In Relationship*. London: Karnac.

Chung RC-Y, Bemak F, Talleyrand RM and Williams JM (2018) Challenges in promoting race dialogues in psychology training: Race and gender perspectives. *The Counseling Psychologist 46*(2): 213–240.

Clarkson P (1989) *Gestalt Counselling in Action*. London: Sage.

Clarkson P (1999) *Gestalt Counselling in Action* (2nd edition). London: Sage.

Clarkson P (2003) *The Therapeutic Relationship* (2nd edition). London: Whurr Publishers.

Cooper M (2008) *Essential Research Findings in Counselling and Psychotherapy: The Facts are Friendly*. Los Angeles, CA: Sage.

Crawford M (2012) Holding and touch in psychotherapy. *What a Shrink Thinks: A Psychotherapist's Journal* 28 October. Available at: www.whatashrinkthinks.com/tag/holding-and-touch-in-psychotherapy/ (accessed 27 June 2018).

Day, SX and Schneider PL (2002) Psychotherapy using distance technology: A comparison of face-to-face, video, and audio treatment. *Journal of Counseling Psychology 49*(4): 499–503.

Department of Health (2014) *Positive and Proactive Care*. London: DH.

DeYoung PA (2003) *Relational Psychotherapy: A Primer*. New York: Brunner-Routledge.

DeYoung PA (2015a) *Relational Psychotherapy: A Primer* (2nd edition). New York: Routledge.

DeYoung PA (2015b) *Understanding and Treating Chronic Shame: A Relational/Neurobiological Approach*. New York: Routledge.

Dryden W (1985) *Therapist's Dilemmas*. London: Sage.

Egan G (2013) *The Skilled Helper: A Problem-management and Opportunity-development Approach to Helping*. San Francisco, CA: Cengage Learning.

Ellis C (2007) Telling secrets, revealing lives: Relational ethics in research with intimate others. *Qualitative Inquiry 3*: 13–29.

Erskine RG (2014) Nonverbal stories: The body in psychotherapy. *International Journal of Integrative Psychotherapy 5*(1): 21–33.

Erskine RG (2015) *Relational Patterns, Therapeutic Presence: Concepts and Practice of Integrative Psychotherapy*. London: Karnac.

Erskine RG and Moursund JP (2011) *Integrative Psychotherapy in Action*. London: Karnac.

Erskine RG, Moursund JP and Trautmann RL (1999) *Beyond Empathy: A Therapy of Contact-in-Relationship*. London: Taylor & Francis.

Erskine RG and Trautmann RL (2003) Resolving intrapsychic conflict: Psychotherapy of parent ego states. In C Sills and H Hargaden (eds), *Ego States: Key Concepts in Transactional Analysis, Contemporary Views*. London: Worth Publishing. pp. 109–134.

Etherington K (2007) Ethical research in reflexive relationships. *Qualitative Inquiry* *13*(5): 599–616.

Evans KR and Gilbert MC (2005) *An Introduction to Integrative Psychotherapy*. London: Palgrave Macmillan.

Fang L, Tarshis S, McInroy L and Mishna F (2017) Undergraduate student experiences with text-based online counselling. *The British Journal of Social Work 48*(6): 1774–1790.

Faris A and van Ooijen E (2012) *Integrative Counselling and Psychotherapy: A Relational Approach*. London: Sage.

Finlay L (2004) Feeling powerless: Therapists battle for control. In S Barrett, C Komaromy, M Robb and A Rogers (eds), *Communication, Care and Relationships: A Reader*. K205 Communication and Relationships in Health and Social Care. London: Routledge.

Finlay L (2012) Five lenses for the reflexive interviewer. In J Gubrium, J Holstein, A Marvasti and J Marvasti (eds), *Handbook of Interview Research*. Thousand Oaks, CA: Sage.

Finlay L (2016a) *Relational Integrative Psychotherapy: Engaging Process and Theory in Practice*. Chichester: Wiley-Blackwell.

Finlay L (2016b) Clarifying the adult ego state: Toward an integrating–integrated 'adult'. *International Journal of Integrative Psychotherapy 7*: 60–84.

Finlay L (2017) Championing 'reflexivities'. Editorial. *Qualitative Psychology* (Special Issue on Reflexivity) *4*(2): 120–125.

Finlay L and Evans K (2009) *Relational-centred Research for Psychotherapists: Exploring Meanings and Experience*. Chichester: Wiley-Blackwell.

Finn J and Barack A (2010) A descriptive study of e-counsellor attitudes, ethics, and practice. *Counselling and Psychotherapy Research 10*(4): 268–277.

Fonagy P (2016) Therapy for violent men. Available at: www.youtube.com/watch?v = nN-8NOiMbvWg (accessed March 2018).

Frosh S (2010). *Psychoanalysis Outside the Clinic: Interventions in Psychosocial Studies*. Basingstoke: Palgrave Macmillan.

Gabriel L (2005) *Speaking the Unspeakable: The Ethics of Dual Relationships in Counselling and Psychotherapy*. London: Brunner-Routledge.

Gabriel L and Casemore R (eds) (2009) *Relational Ethics in Practice: Narratives from Counselling and Psychotherapy*. London: Routledge.

Gale J (2015) *Creative Spaces: Inside 25 Counselling & Psychotherapy Rooms*. Available at: http://jodiegale.com/creative-spaces-inside-25-counselling-psychotherapy-rooms/ (accessed December 2017).

Gasseau M, Langley G and Teszáry J (n.d.) *Code of Ethics and Practice*. The Federation of European Psychodrama Training Organisations (FEPTO). Available at: www.fepto.com/about-fepto/constitution/code-of-ethics-and-practice (accessed April 2018).

Gibertoni C de S (2013) An occupational therapy perspective on Freud, Klein and Bion. In L Nicholls, JC Piergrossi, C de S Gibertoni and MA Daniel (eds), *Psychoanalytic Thinking in Occupational Therapy: Symbolic, Relational and Transformative*. Chichester: Wiley.

Gilbert M and Evans K (2000) *Psychotherapy Supervision: An Integrative Relational Approach*. Maidenhead: Open University Press.

Gilbert M and Orlans V (2011) *Integrative Therapy: 100 Key Points and Techniques*. London: Routledge.

Goode J, Park J, Parkin S, Tompkins KA and Swift JK (2017) A collaborative approach to psychotherapy termination. *Psychotherapy 54*(1): 10–14.

Gravell L (2010) The counselling psychologist as therapeutic 'container'. *Counselling Psychology Review 25*(2): 28–33.

Green R (2012a) Me and my shadow. In *Write to Be You*. Available at: www.writetobe you.com/ (accessed May 2018).

Green R (2012b) Hold me now. In *Write to Be You*. Available at: www.writetobeyou. com/tag/overwhelmed/ (accessed August 2017).

Griffiths KM and Christensen H (2006) Review of randomised controlled trials of inter- net interventions for mental disorders and related conditions. *Clinical Psychologist, 10*(1): 16–29.

Gutheil TG and Gabbard GO (1993) The concept of boundaries in clinical practice: Theoretical and risk-management dimensions. *American Journal of Psychiatry 150*: 188–196.

Hargaden H and Sills C (2002) *Transactional Analysis: A Relational Approach*. Hove: Brunner-Routledge.

Heesacker M (2018) Presidential Address: Counseling Psychology in the Trump Era. *The Counseling Psychologist 46*(1): 77–86.

Heron J (2001) *Helping the Client: A Creative Practical Guide* (5th edition). London: Sage.

Hinshelwood RD (1987) *What Happens in Groups*. London: Free Association Books.

Hobman P (2018) The meaning and impact of supervision for experienced counsellors: A relational narrative. Unpublished PhD thesis, University of Leeds, UK.

Horvath A and Bedi RP (2002) The alliance. In JC Norcross (ed.), *Psychotherapy Relationships that Work: Therapist Contributions and Responsiveness to Patients*. New York: Oxford University Press. pp. 37–69.

Hudgins MK (2002) *Experiential Treatment for PTSD: The Therapeutic Spiral Model*. New York: Springer.

Hudgins MK (2017) PTSD unites the world: Prevention, intervention, and training with the Therapeutic Spiral Model. In CE Stout (ed.), *Why Global Health Matters: How to (Actually) Make the World a Better Place*. ebook, pp. 294–325.

Hudgins, MK and Toscani F (eds) (2013) Healing World Trauma with the Therapeutic Spiral Model: Stories from the Frontlines. London: Jessica Kingsley.

Hunter M and Struve J (1998) *The Ethical Use of Touch in Psychotherapy*. Thousand Oaks, CA: Sage.

Hycner R (1991/1993) *Between Person and Person: Toward a Dialogical Psychotherapy*. Highland, NY: The Gestalt Journal Press.

Hycner R (2017) *What does it mean to be a relational psychotherapist?* Lecture given at the Scarborough Counselling and Psychotherapy Institute, UK, September 8, 2017.

Innocente GM (2015) Client–clinician texting: An expansion of the Clinical Holding Environment. Doctoral Thesis (DSW), University of Pennsylvania, PA. Available at: https://repository.upenn.edu/cgi/viewcontent.cgi?article = 1074andcontext = edisser tations_sp2 (accessed November 2017).

International Integrative Psychotherapy Association (IIPA) (2018) *Code of Ethics*. IIPA. Available at: https://integrativeassociation.com/the-association/code-of-ethics/ (accessed November 2017).

Jenkins P (2015) What is wrong with the *Ethical Framework*? Available at: www. contemporarypsychotherapy.org/volume-7-no-2-winter-2015/what-is-wrong-with- the-ethical-framework/ (accessed December 2017).

Jofen-Miller S and Fiori KL (2017) The impact of psychotherapist training and experi- ence on posttermination contact. *Psychotherapy 54*(1): 114–122.

Johannes CK and Erwin PG (2004) Developing multicultural competence: Perspectives on theory and practice. *Counselling Psychology Quarterly 17*(3): 329–338.

Joyce AS, Piper WE, Ogrodniczuk JS and Klein RH (2007) *Termination in Psychotherapy: A Psychodynamic Model of Processes and Outcomes*. Washington, DC: American Psychological Association.

Kahr B (2006) Winnicott's experiments with physical contact: creative innovation or chaotic impingement? In G Galton (ed.), *Touch Papers, Dialogues on Touch in the Psychoanalytic Space* (pp. 1–14). London: Karnac.

Kamitsis LI and Simmonds J (2017) Using resources of nature in the counselling room: Qualitative research into ecotherapy practice. *International Journal for the Advancement of Counselling 39*: 229–248.

Kapitan L (2003) *Re-enchanting Art Therapy: Transformational Practices for Restoring Creative Vitality*. Springfield, IL: Charles C Thomas.

Khanna MS and Kendall PC (2010) Computer-assisted cognitive behavioral therapy for child anxiety: Results of a randomized clinical trial. *Journal of Consulting and Clinical Psychology 78*(5): 735–745, doi: 10.1037/a0019739.

Kousteni ID (2018) Toward an extended view of evidence-based psychotherapy: Diversity and social factors. *Journal of Humanistic Psychology* [published online March 9]. doi/10.1177/0022167818762651.

Kramen-Kahn B (2002) Do you 'walk your talk'? *The Maryland Psychologist 44*(3): 12.

Krüger A (2007) An introduction to the ethics of gestalt research with informants. *European Journal for Qualitative Research in Psychotherapy 2*: 17–22.

Lac V (2016) Amy's story: An existential-integrative equine-facilitated psychotherapy approach to anorexia nervosa. *The Journal of Humanistic Psychology 57*(3): 301–312.

Lago C (2011) Introduction to Part 1: Towards enhancing professional competence – from training to research to practice. In C Lago (ed.), *The Handbook of Transcultural Counselling and Psychotherapy*. Maidenhead: Open University Press/McGraw-Hill. pp. 3–16.

Lamagna J and Gleiser K (2007) Building a secure internal attachment: An intra-relational approach to ego strengthening and emotional processing with chronically traumatized clients. *Journal of Trauma and Dissociation 8*(1): 25–52.

Lamprecht L (2013) *Therapeutic letter writing as relationally responsive practice: Experiences of clients receiving letters during therapy*. In Paper/Workshop Presentation at the International Conference: The Challenge of Establishing a Research Tradition for Gestalt Therapy. Cape Cod, MA, April 17–20, pp. 39–53.

Larner G (1999) Derrida and the deconstruction of power as content and topic in therapy. In I Parker (ed.), *Deconstructing Psychotherapy*. London: Sage.

Lawry SS (1998) Touch and clients who have been sexually abused. In EWL Smith, PR Clance and S Imes (eds), *Touch in Psychotherapy: Theory, Research and Practice*. New York: Guilford Press.

Lehavot K, Barnett JE and Powers D (2010) Psychotherapy, professional relationship, and ethical considerations in the Myspace generation. *Professional Psychology: Research and Practice 41*(2): 160–166.

Levin J (2010) Gestalt therapy: Now and for tomorrow. *Gestalt Review 14*(2): 147–170.

Levitt HM, Pomerville A and Surace FI (2016) A qualitative meta-analysis examining clients' experiences of psychotherapy: A new agenda. *Psychological Bulletin 142*(8): 801–830.

Linehan MM (1993) *Cognitive-behavioural Treatment of Borderline Personality Disorder*. New York and London: Guilford Press.

Little MI (1985) Winnicott working in areas where psychotic anxieties predominate: A personal record. *Free Associations, 1*(3): 9–42.

Little R (2016) Transference – countertransference focused transactional analysis. In RG Erskine (ed.), *Transactional Analysis in Contemporary Psychotherapy*. London: Karnac.

Lohr J, Olatunji B, Baumeister RF and Bushman BJ (2007) The psychology of anger venting and empirically supported alternatives that do no harm. *The Scientific Review of Mental Health Practice 5*(1): 53–64.

Lott DA (1999) Drawing boundaries. *Psychology Today*. Available at: www.psychology-today.com/articles/199905/drawing-boundaries (accessed September 2017).

Luca M (ed.) (2014) *Sexual Attraction in Therapy: Clinical Perspectives on Moving beyond the Taboo. A Guide for Training and Practice*. Chichester, West Sussex: Wiley.

Ludman EJ, Simon GE, Tutty S and Von Korff M (2007) A randomized trial of telephone psychotherapy and pharmacotherapy for depression: Continuation and durability of effects. *Journal of Consultation and Clinical Psychology 75*(2): 257–266.

Mair M (1989) *Between Psychology and Psychotherapy: A Poetics of Experience*. Florence, KY: Taylor & Frances/Routledge.

Mandi M (2016) A psychotherapist's lived experience of care: A hermeneutic-phenomenological study. Unpublished PhD Dissertation, Regent's School of Psychotherapy and Psychology, Regent's University, London.

Mann D (1997) *Psychotherapy: An erotic relationship – Transference and Countertransference Passions*. London: Routledge.

Mann D (2010) *Gestalt Therapy: 100 Key Points and Techniques*. London: Routledge.

Mann D (2015) 'Turning a blind eye' on sexual abuse, boundary violations and therapeutic practice. *Psychodynamic Practice: Individuals, Groups and Organisations 21*(2): 126–146.

Masterson JF (1988) *The Search for the Real Self: Unmasking the Personality Disorders of Our Age*. New York: The Free Press.

Marcos LR (1979) Effects of interpreters on the evaluation of psychopathology in non-English-speaking patients. *American Journal of Psychiatry 136*(2): 171–174.

Marmarosh CL (2017) Fostering engagement during termination: Applying attachment theory and research. *Psychotherapy 54*(1): 4–9.

Marx JA and Gelso CJ (1987) Termination of individual counseling in a university counseling center. *Journal of Counseling Psychology 34*: 3–9.

McConville M (2005) The gift. In T Levine Bar-Yoseph (ed.), *The Bridge: Dialogues across Cultures*. Metairie, LA: Gestalt Institute Press. Available at: www.icpla.edu/wp-content/uploads/2013/08/McConville-M-The-Gift.pdf (accessed April 2018).

McGrath L, Griffin V and Mundy E (n.d.) *The Psychological Impact of Austerity: A Briefing Paper*. Available at: https://psychagainstausterity.files.wordpress.com/2015/03/paa-briefing-paper.pdf (accessed February 2018).

McGuirk J (2012) The place of touch in counselling and psychotherapy and the potential for healing within the therapeutic relationship. *Inside Out*. Available at: https://iahip.org/inside-out/issue-68-autumn-2012/the-place-of-touch-in-counselling-and-psychotherapy-and-the-potential-for-healing-within-the-therapeutic-relationship (accessed November 2017).

McNeel JR (1976) The parent interview. *Transactional Analysis Journal 6*(1): 61–68.

Melnick J and Nevis EC (2009) *Mending the World: Social Healing Interventions by Gestalt Practitioners Worldwide*. South Wellfleet, MA: Gestalt International Study Centre.

Meyer E (2014) *The Culture Map: Breaking through the Invisible Boundaries of Global Business*. New York: PublicAffairs.

Miller SD and Duncan BL (2000) *The Outcome Rating Scale*. Chicago, IL: Authors.

Miller SD, Duncan BL and Hubble MA (2005) Outcome-informed clinical work. In JC Norcross and MR Goldfried (eds), *Handbook of Psychotherapy Integration* (2nd edition). Oxford: Oxford University Press.

Miller SD, Duncan BL and Johnson L (2000) *The Session Rating Scale*. Chicago, IL: Authors.

Ministry of Justice, Home Office and Office for National Statistics (2013) *An Overview of Sexual Offending in England and Wales*. London: Office for National Statistics.

Mitchels B and Bond T (2010) *Essential Law for Counselling and Psychotherapy*. London: Sage.

Moerman M (2012) Working with suicidal clients: The person-centred counsellor's experience and understanding of risk assessment. *Counselling and Psychotherapy Research 12*(3): 214–223.

Morgan H and Thomas K (1996) A psychodynamic perspective on group processes. In M Wetherell (ed.), *Identities, Groups and Social Issues*. London: Sage.

Morina N, Ijntema H, Meyerbröker K and Emmelkamp PMG (2015) Can virtual reality exposure therapy gains be generalized to real life? A meta-analysis of studies applying behavioral assessments. *Behaviour Research and Therapy 74*: 18–24.

Moursund JP and Erskine RG (2004) *Integrative Psychotherapy: The Art and Science of Relationship*. Victoria, Australia: Thomson/Brooks-Cole.

Murdin L (2000) *How much is Enough? Endings in Psychotherapy and Counselling*. London: Routledge.

Nanda J and Bayat G (2013) Working with cultural or racial diversity in relationships. In E Van Deurzen and S Iacovou (eds), *Existential Perspectives on Relationship Therapy*. Basingstoke: Palgrave Macmillan.

National Institute for Clinical Excellence (2018) Digital psychological therapy briefing Deprexis for adults with depression. London: NICE. Available at: www.nice.org.uk/Media/Default/About/what-we-do/NICE-advice/IAPT/iab-deprexis-for-publication.pdf (accessed September 2018)

Noddings N (2013) *Caring: A Relational Approach to Ethics and Moral Education* (2nd edition). Berkeley, CA: University of California Press.

Norcross JC, Zimmerman BE, Greenberg RP and Swift JK (2017) Do all therapists do that when saying goodbye? A study of commonalities in termination behaviors. *Psychotherapy 54*(1): 66–75.

Northern Guild Psychotherapy and Counselling (2015) *Code of Practice and Professional Conduct for Psychotherapeutic Counselling and Psychotherapy with Children*. Available at: www.northernguild.org/wp-content/uploads/2016/12/Child-Codes-of-Ethics-and-Practice-2015.pdf?x48662 (accessed November 2017).

O'Brien M and Houston G (2007) *Integrative Therapy: A Practitioner's Guide* (2nd edition). Los Angeles, CA: Sage.

Ogden P, Minton K and Pain C (2006) *Trauma and the Body: A Sensorimotor Approach to Psychotherapy*. New York: Norton.

Olivera J, Challú L, Penedo JMG and Roussos A (2017) Client–therapist agreement in the termination process and its association with therapeutic relationship. *Psychotherapy 54*(1): 88–101.

Orbach S (2003a) Part II: Touch. *British Journal of Psychotherapy 20*(1): 17–26.

Orbach S (2003b) Part I: There is no such thing as a body. *British Journal of Psychotherapy 20*(1): 3–15.

Page S (1999) *The Shadow and the Counsellor: Working with the Darker Aspects of the Person, the Role and the Profession*. Hove: Routledge.

Perret V (2015) Constantly present: A therapy for Julie. *International Journal of Integrative Psychotherapy 69*: 54–62.

Pettifor JL and Sawchuk TR (2006) Psychologists' perceptions of ethically troubling incidents across international borders. *International Journal of Psychology 41*(3): 216–225.

Pope KS and Keith-Spiegel P (2008) A practical approach to boundaries in psychotherapy: Making decisions, bypassing blunders, and mending fences. *Journal of Clinical Psychology 64*(5): 638–652.

Pope KS, Tabachnick, BG and Keith-Spiegel P (1987) Ethics of practice. The beliefs and behaviors of psychologists as therapists. *American Psychologist 24*(1): 993–1006.

Price M, Anderson P and Rothbaum BO (2008) Virtual reality as treatment for fear of flying: A review of recent research. *International Journal of Behavioral Consultation & Therapy* 4(4): 340–347.

Proctor G (2002) *The Dynamics of Power in Counselling and Psychotherapy: Ethics, Politics and Practice*. Ross-on-Wye: PCCS Books.

Proctor G (2018) Responding to injustice: Working with angry and violent clients in a person-centred way. Available at: www.researchgate.net/publication/265541156_Responding_to_injustice_working_with_angry_and_violent_clients_in_a_person-_centred_way (accessed June 2018).

Proctor G, Cooper M, Sanders P and Malcom B (2006) *Politicizing the Person-Centred Approach: An Agenda for Social Change*. Ross-on-Wye: PCCS Books.

Psychotherapy and Counselling Federation of Australia (2017) *PACFA Code of Ethics*. Melbourne: PACFA.

Read S (2014) The therapeutic relationship in the helping professions. In D Charura and S Paul (eds), *The Therapeutic Relationship Handbook: Theory and Practice*. Maidenhead: Open University Press. pp. 185–195.

Reimer EC (2017) Leaving the door open for 'tune ups': Challenging notions of ending working relationships in family work. *Child and Family Social Work* 22(4): 1357–1364.

Rogers A (2013) *Ethical complaints. Towards a best practice for psychotherapy and counselling organisations*. Unpublished doctoral thesis in Psychotherapy by Professional Studies, Middlesex University and Metanoia Institute, London.

Rogers CR (1980) *A Way of Being*. New York: Houghton Mifflin Company.

Rothschild B (2002) The body remembers: An interview with Babette Rothschild. *Psychotherapy in Australia* 8(2). Available at: www.somatictraumatherapy.com/the-body-remembers-an-interview-with-babette-rothschild/ (accessed November 2017).

Rothschild B (2003) *The Body Remembers Casebook: Unifying Methods and Models in the Treatment of Trauma and PTSD*. New York: Norton.

Rowe D (1989) Foreward. In J Masson (ed.), *Against Therapy*. London: Fontana.

Schore AN (2001) Effects of a secure attachment relationship on right brain development, affect regulation and infant mental health. *Journal of Infant Mental Health* 22: 7–66.

Shahar G (2018) The nature of the beast: Commentary on 'Can There be a Recovery-Oriented Diagnosis Practice?' *Journal of Humanistic Psychology* [online first], pp.1–10, https://doi.org/10.1177/0022167818777653.

Somers P and Stephenson K (2013) (eds) *A World Book of Values*. Antwerp: Van Halewyck.

Spinelli E (1994) *Demystifying Therapy*. London: Constable.

Spinelli E (2015) *Practising Existential Therapy: The Relational World* (2nd Edition). London: Sage.

Spring C (2010) *A Brief Guide to Working with Dissociative Identity Disorder*. Available at: www.carolynspring.co.uk/a-brief-guide-to-working-with-dissociativeidentity-disorder (accessed April 2018).

Starhawk (1987) *Truth or Dare: Encounters with Power, Authority, and Mystery*. San Francisco: Harper & Row.

Stern DN and the Boston Change Process Study Group (2003) On the other side of the moon: the import of implicit knowledge for gestalt therapy. In M Spagnuolo Lobb and N Amendt-Lyon (eds), *Creative Licensing: The Art of Gestalt Therapy*. New York: Springer-Verlag Wien.

Stiegler JR, Binder PE, Hjeltnes A, Stige SH and Schanche E (2018) 'It's heavy, intense, horrendous and nice': Clients' experiences in two-chair dialogues. *Person-Centered and Experiential Psychotherapies* [online first], DOI: 10.1080/14779757.2018.1472138.

Stolorow RD (2014) A non-pathologizing approach to emotional trauma. *Psychology Today*. Available at: www.psychologytoday.com/gb/blog/feeling-relating-existing/201412/non-pathologizing-approach-emotional-trauma (accessed November 2018).

Taylor L, McMinn MR, Bufford RK and Chang KBT (2010) Psychologists' attitudes and ethical concerns regarding the use of social networking web sites. *Professional Psychology: Research and Practice 41*(2): 153–159.

Taylor M (2014) *Trauma Therapy and Clinical Practice: Neuroscience, Gestalt and the Body*. Maidenhead: Open University Press.

Tosone C (2013) Virtual intimacy in the therapeutic space: Help or hindrance. In E Ruderman and C Tosone (eds), *Contemporary Clinical Practice: The Holding Environment under Assault*. New York: Springer. pp. 41–49.

Totton N (2003) *Body Psychotherapy*. Maidenhead, Berkshire: Open University Press.

Totton N (2010) Boundaries and boundlessness. *Therapy Today 21*(8): 10–15. Available at: www.therapytoday.net/article/show/2120/print/ (accessed August 2014).

Totton N (2011) *Wild Therapy: Undomesticating Inner and Outer Worlds*. Monmouth: PCCS Books.

Trautmann RL (2003) Psychotherapy and Spirituality. Available at: www.integrativetherapy.com/en/articles.php?id=42 (accessed May 2018). [Originally published in *Transactional Analysis Journal 33*(1): 32–36, January 2003.]

Tune D (2005) Dilemmas concerning the ethical use of touch in psychotherapy. In N Totton (ed.), *New Dimensions in Body Psychotherapy*. Maidenhead, Berkshire: Open University Press. pp. 70–81.

United Kingdom Council for Psychotherapy (UKCP) (2009) *Ethical Principles and Code of Professional Conduct*. London: UKCP. Available at: www.psychotherapy.org.uk/wp-content/uploads/2016/08/UKCP-Ethical-Principles-and-Code-of-Professional-Conduct.pdf (accessed November 2017).

UKCP (2018a) *UKCP Draft Code of Ethics*. London: UKCP. Available at: www.psycho-therapy.org.uk/wp-content/uploads/2018/05/UKCP-Code-of-Ethics-v1-revision-4.4.pdf (accessed June 2018).

UKCP (2018b) *International Women's Day*. London: UKCP. Available at: www.psycho-therapy.org.uk/news/international-womens-day-2018/ (accessed April 2018).

Van Deurzen E and Adams M (2011) *Skills in Existential Counselling and Psychotherapy*. Los Angeles, CA: Sage.

Van Gerwen LJ, Spinhoven Ph, Van Dyck R and Diekstra RFW (1999) Construction and psychometric characteristics of two self-reported questionnaires for the assessment of fear of flying. *Psychological Assessment 11*(2): 146–158.

Victoria Transcultural Mental Health (2017) *Working with Interpreters: A Resource for Service Providers Engaging with Interpreters in Transcultural Situations*. Fairfax, VA: Victoria Transcultural Mental Health. Available at: www.vtmh-workingwithinterpreters.online/ (accessed April 2018).

Welfel ER (2013) *Ethics in Counseling and Psychotherapy: Standards, Research and Emerging Issues* (5th edition). Pacific Grove, CA/Boston, MA: Brooks-Cole/Cengage.

Wiggins S (2013) Assessing relational depth: Developing the Relational Depth Inventory. In R Knox, D Murphy, S Wiggins and M Cooper (eds), *Relational Depth: New Perspectives and developments*. Basingstoke: Palgrave Macmillan.

Wilkinson K (2018) *Psychotherapy Training and Practice: A Journey into the Shadow Side*. London: Routledge. (First published 2008 by Karnac).

Winnicott DW (1953) Transitional objects and transitional phenomena: A study of the first not-me possession. *International Journal of Psychoanalysis 34*(2): 89–97.

Winnicott DW (1971) *Playing and Reality*. New York: Basic Books.

World Health Organisation (2018) *International Classification of Diseases*, 11th Revision. Geneva: WHO. Available at: www.who.int/classifications/icd/en/ (accessed March 2018).

Yalom ID (1985) *The Theory and Practice of Group Psychotherapy*. New York: Basic Books.

Yalom ID (2001) *The Gift of Therapy: An Open Letter to a New Generation of Therapists and their Patients* (revised and updated edition). London: Piatkus.

Yontef GM (1988) Assimilating diagnostic and psychoanalytic perspectives into Gestalt therapy. *Gestalt Journal 11*(1): 5–32.

Yontef GM (1993) *Awareness, Dialogue, and Process: Essays in Gestalt Therapy*. Highland, NY: Gestalt Journal Press.

Zaletel M, Poto nik J and Jalen A (n.d.) *Psychotherapy with the Parent Ego State: Integrative Psychotherapy Articles*. Available at: www.integrativetherapy.com/en/articles.php?id = 69 (accessed April 2018).

Zigmond AS and Snaith RP (1983) The hospital anxiety and depression scale. *Acta Psychiatrica Scandinavica 67*(6): 361–370.

Zur O (2009) Power in psychotherapy and counseling: Exploring the 'inherent power differential' and related myths about therapists' omnipotence and clients' vulnerability. *Independent Practitioner 29*(3): 160–164. Available at: www.zurinstitute.com/power_in_therapy_counseling.pdf (accessed January 2018).

Index

www.ingramcontent.com/pod-product-compliance
Lightning Source LLC
Chambersburg PA
CBHW080557030426
42336CB00019B/3221